The Politics of Race
in Latino Communities

Routledge Series on Identity Politics

SERIES EDITOR: ALVIN B. TILLERY, *Jr.*, *Rutgers University*

Group identities have been an important part of political life in America since the founding of the republic. For most of this long history, the central challenge for activists, politicians, and scholars concerned with the quality of U.S. democracy was the struggle to bring the treatment of ethnic and racial minorities and women in line with the creedal values spelled out in the nation's charters of freedom. We are now several decades from the key moments of the twentieth century when social movements fractured America's system of ascriptive hierarchy. The gains from these movements have been substantial. Women now move freely in all realms of civil society, hold high elective offices, and constitute more than 50 percent of the workforce. Most African-Americans have now attained middle class status, work in integrated job sites, and live in suburbs. Finally, people of color from nations in Latin America, Asia, and the Caribbean now constitute the majority of America's immigration pool.

In the midst of all of these positive changes, however, glaring inequalities between groups persist. Indeed, ethnic and racial minorities remain far more likely to be undereducated, unemployed, and incarcerated than their counterparts who identify as white. Similarly, both violence and work place discrimination against women remain rampant in U.S. society. The Routledge series on identity politics features works that seek to understand the tension between the great strides our society has made in promoting equality between groups and the residual effects of the ascriptive hierarchies in which the old order was rooted.

Some of the core questions that the series will address are: how meaningful are the traditional ethnic, gender, racial, and sexual identities to our understanding of inequality in the present historical moment? Do these identities remain important bases for group mobilization in American politics? To what extent can we expect the state to continue to work for a more level playing field among groups?

1 **Black Politics Today**
   The Era of Socioeconomic
   Transition
   Theodore J. Davis Jr.

2 **Jim Crow Citizenship**
   How Southern Progressives
   Remade Race, Citizenship and
   Liberalism in America
   Marek Steedman

3 **The Politics of Race in Latino Communities**
   Walking the Color Line
   Atiya Kai Stokes-Brown

The Politics of Race in Latino Communities
Walking the Color Line

Atiya Kai Stokes-Brown

Routledge
Taylor & Francis Group
NEW YORK AND LONDON

First published 2012
by Routledge
711 Third Avenue, New York, NY 10017

Simultaneously published in the UK
by Routledge
2 Park Square, Milton Park, Abingdon, Oxfordshire OX14 4RN

First issued in paperback 2014

Routledge is an imprint of the Taylor & Francis Group, an informa business

© 2012 Taylor & Francis

The right of Atiya Kai Stokes-Brown to be identified as author of this work has been asserted by her in accordance with sections 77 and 78 of the Copyright, Designs and Patents Act 1988.

All rights reserved. No part of this book may be reprinted or reproduced or utilised in any form or by any electronic, mechanical, or other means, now known or hereafter invented, including photocopying and recording, or in any information storage or retrieval system, without permission in writing from the publishers.

Trademark Notice: Product or corporate names may be trademarks or registered trademarks, and are used only for identification and explanation without intent to infringe.

Library of Congress Cataloging-in-Publication Data
Stokes-Brown, Atiya Kai.
  The politics of race in Latino communities : walking the color line / Atiya Kai Stokes-Brown.
    p. cm. — (Routledge series on identity politics)
  "Simultaneously published in the UK"—T.p. verso.
  Includes bibliographical references and index.
  1. Hispanic Americans—Race identity. 2. Identity politics—United States. 3. Ethnicity—Political aspects—United States. 4. Hispanic Americans—Politics and government. 5. Political participation—United States. 6. Hispanic Americans—Social conditions. 7. Hispanic Americans—Interviews. 8. Social surveys—United States. 9. United States—Race relations—Political aspects. I. Title.
  E184.S75S77 2012
  973'.0468—dc23
                            2011048400

ISBN 13: 978-0-415-69906-8 (hbk)
ISBN 13: 978-1-138-84904-4 (pbk)

Typeset in Sabon
by IBT Global.

For my parents, Dess and Denise Stokes whom I wish to honor for their faithfulness, sacrifice, and love

Contents

List of Tables and Figures		ix
Acknowledgments		xi
1	Introduction	1
2	The Meaning and Measurement of Race	17
3	The Foundations of Latino Racial Identity	30
4	Explaining Latino Political Orientations: The Role of Racial Identity	50
5	Racial Identity and the Politics of Latino Partisanship	67
6	The Impact of Race on Latino Political Participation	83
7	Latino Racial Identity and the Dynamics of Public Opinion	100
8	Conclusion	119
	Appendix A: Select Variables from LNS Questionnaire	125
	Appendix B: Focus Group Questionnaire	131
	Notes	133
	Bibliography	137
	Index	155

Tables and Figures

TABLES

1.1	Focus Group Participants—Demographic Characteristics	12
2.1	Descriptive Results—Latino Racial Identity	26
3.1	Predictors of Latino Racial Identity	39
3.2	Predictors of Other Race Identity	43
3.3	Predictors of Other Race/White Identity by Nativity	46
4.1	Latino Racial Identity and Political Orientations	57
4.2	Other Race Identity and Political Orientations	62
4.3	Latino Racial Identity and Political Orientations among Immigrants	64
5.1	Predicting the Direction of Latino Political Partisanship	75
5.2	Political Partisanship and Other Race Identity	77
5.3	Predicting the Direction of Latino Political Partisanship among Immigrants	78
5.4	Predicting the Strength of Latino Political Partisanship	80
6.1	Latino Racial Identity and Political Participation	91
6.2	Other Race Identity and Political Participation	95
6.3	Latino Racial Identity and Political Participation among Immigrants	96
7.1	Latino Racial Identity and Public Opinion	108
7.2	Other Race Identity and Public Opinion	112
7.3	Latino Racial Identity and Public Opinion among Immigrants	115

FIGURES

1.1	Modeling the development and political consequences of Latino racial identity.	3
4.1	Predicted probability—trust government to do what is right.	59
4.2	Predicted probability—government is run by a few big interests.	60
6.1	Predicted probability—Latino voter registration and turnout.	93

Acknowledgments

This book would not have been possible without the guidance, encouragement, and prayers of colleagues, friends, and family who have been with me at every step. First and foremost, I give glory to my Lord and Savior Jesus Christ, who paid the ultimate price for me. When I look back over my life and see where I am in this moment, I am reminded of his promise in Jeremiah 29:11, where He says "I know the plans I have for you. They are plans for good and not for disaster, to give you a future and a hope." The Lord has truly worked all things in my life for my good and I praise him for His grace and mercy.

I am deeply indebted to two special people, who, at different points in my life, took me under their wing and encouraged me to pursue my goals: Robin Kolodny and Paul Herrnson. I first met Robin when I was master's student at Temple University. Despite my weaknesses, Robin saw something in me and pushed me to follow my dreams and think "big." She encouraged me to value my voice and was a constant source of support and feedback. I have no doubt that had it not been for Robin, I would not have found my way to the University of Maryland, where I met Paul. Paul, with his incredible work ethic and commitment to excellence, simply challenged me to be the best I could be. In Paul, I found an advocate, mentor, and friend. I remember with great fondness the years I spent working for him at the Center for American Politics and Citizenship, where I had the pleasure of working with valued colleagues.

At FSU I had the pleasure of working with Ray Block Jr. and Melissa Stewart. Ray Block Jr. and his fabulous wife Christina made my family feel at home in Florida and have been extremely supportive of my research. Melissa, who was a graduate student when we first met, has also been the source of tremendous support. It has been a pleasure to watch Melissa transform into a talented scholar and wonderful mommy, and I feel blessed to consider her a friend. My colleagues at Bucknell, in and outside of my home department, have also been extremely supportive of me personally and professionally. I offer special thanks to two women whom I admire tremendously, both for their intellectual contributions to my research and for their love of life. Within days of our arrival to Lewisburg, Nina Banks very graciously welcomed me to campus and into her life. Through Nina I met Leslie Patrick. Over the last few years you ladies have been a source of kindness and wisdom and you've made me laugh more than I ever thought possible! I am also thankful for the relationship I have developed with Sherri Foster, who has taught me so much about living life with peace and joy.

I had the great fortune of receiving financial support for this research. My sincerest appreciation is extended to the Lindback Foundation for a grant which provided the funds to conduct the focus group interviews discussed throughout the text. I also received support for this project from the Center for the Study of Race, Ethnicity, and Gender at (CSREG) Bucknell University. The views expressed in this book are my own and do not reflect the views of the Lindback Foundation or CSREG. These grants also made it possible for me to work with two amazing undergraduate research assistants–Timothy Bolte and Alicia Wheeler. It has truly a pleasure to get to know both of you inside and outside of the classroom.

Finally, this or any other project in my life would not be possible without my family. I offer special thanks to my mother and father in law, Gus and Elaine Brown, and my sister in laws, Faith Smith and Tyla Sherman, and their families. Thank you for sharing your lives with me. I wish to express my sincerest love and appreciation to my parents, Dess and Denise Stokes, to whom I dedicate this book. I'd like to think that raising me was a dream and that I have been the "perfect" child. But alas, I am painfully aware that I did not always make things easy and gave you two more than your fair share of worrisome nights. But no matter what, you have always been there for me—cheering me on when I needed a cheerleader, wiping my tears when I thought I couldn't go on, and commanding me to straighten up and fly right when my head got stuck in the clouds. I am everything I am because you poured your hearts and souls into me. You have given me a legacy of love and faithfulness that I am now so blessed to share with my precious little one.

Last but certainly not least—I wish thank with all that is in me my two 'boys', my home team: my husband Gus and my son Kai. A little more than seven years ago, I dedicated my dissertation to my then fiancé in appreciation of the dreams that he made come true. Since then you have exceeded my wildest hopes and dreams by being the most amazing husband and father. Seeing you now through our son's eyes reaffirms what I believed so long ago—you are the man the Lord created to be with me and head the family I so lovingly desired. My dear sweet son—always know that you are and will be one of the greatest loves of my life. Being your mother has given me such joy and has given my life meaning. You are my strength and you are my light. I pray that God gives us the wisdom and courage to help you become a godly young man and that you always know how much and how deeply Mommy and Daddy love you.

1 Introduction

The U.S. has become increasingly diverse, fueled in large part by increased immigration from Mexico and Latin America. Latinos[1] are currently the largest and fastest-growing population in the U.S., accounting for over half of the nation's growth since 2000, and by 2050 will represent more than a quarter of the country's population (Fry 2008; Passel and Cohn 2008). This growing population is extremely diverse, as it includes many subgroups, typically identified in terms of national origin. Although persons of Mexican origin form the largest Latino population group in the U.S., sizable segments of the population also trace their ancestry to a wide range of countries and territories, including Puerto Rico, Cuba, El Salvador, and the Dominican Republic (Pew Hispanic Center 2009). Furthermore, Latinos have begun to settle in "new settlement states," including Georgia and North Carolina, in addition to traditional states like Florida and New York, ultimately increasing their geographic diversity (e.g. Marrow 2005). This is particularly noteworthy because we know that settlement patterns in ethnic enclaves serve to sustain the preeminence of nationality for many immigrant groups (Portes and Rumbaut 1996).

Group identity is most simply defined as the recognition of membership in a given group and an affinity with other group members (Garcia 2003). Although Latinos often choose to identify themselves based on ties to their home country or place of ancestral origin (e.g. de la Garza et al. 1993), they also adopt other identities that have social and political meaning. One identity most commonly studied is panethnic identity, which is largely defined as a collective, distinct, and separate identity that ties together Latinos of different Spanish-speaking populations (e.g. Padilla 1982, 1984). Much of the recent literature on Latino panethnicity explores the conditions under which this identity forms (e.g. DeSipio 1996; Itzigsohn and Dore-Cabaral 2000; Padilla 1984, 1986; Garcia 2003; Masuoka 2008) and its potential impact on political opinion and behavior (e.g. Calvo and Rosenstone 1989; de la Garza and DeSipio 1992; de la Garza et al. 1992; Stokes 2003; Jones-Correa and Leal 1996; Garcia 2006). The steady rise of Latino panethnic identification has significant implications for American politics as it suggests that there is a cohesive, unified group with distinctive and common interests and political goals. Despite the diversity within the Latino community, Latino panethnicity can be an important mobilizing political force (e.g. Baretto 2007). As result, there has been a great deal of discussion about the political relevance and political behavior of Latinos.

In *The Politics of Race in Latino Communities: Walking the Color Line*, I address questions about the political relevance of Latinos, focusing on identity and placing an emphasis not on national origin or panethnic identity, but racial identity. The U.S. Constitution mandates that the population be classified and counted every ten years for the purpose of representation and taxation. Since 1790, the classification directed by Article I, Section 2 has distinguished groups by race. Over the years, the classification by race has expanded and contracted, reflecting changing societal and political attitudes about race and citizenship (Nobles 2000). For example, in response to a growing preoccupation with defining Whiteness, the category "Mexican" was added to the census in 1930. With the assistance of the Mexican government, Mexican Americans lobbied against the change and the category was subsequently removed (Cortes 1980; Nobles 2000). Largely in response to demands from the Latino community, the first major attempt to categorize the Hispanic population was in the 1970 Census with the inclusion of a separate Hispanic origin question (Rumbaut 2006). Whereas the inclusion of a Mexican category in 1930 was viewed mostly as an explicit effort to stigmatize Mexican Americans, the inclusion of a Hispanic origin question was welcomed in the post–civil rights era as a source of data that could be used to protect Latino rights (Perez and Hirschman 2009: 8). The U.S. federal government defines Latinos as a panethnic group that includes persons of "Mexican, Puerto Rican, Cuban, Central or South American or other Spanish culture or origin, regardless of race" (Office of Management and Budget 1997). Because Hispanic origin (ethnicity) and race are treated as distinct and separate concepts in the census, respondents who ethnically identify as Latino/Hispanic may also identify with any of the five minimum race categories determined by the U.S. Office of Management and Budget's 1997 *Revisions to the Standards for the Classification of Federal Data on Race and Ethnicity*: American Indian or Alaska Native; Asian; Black or African American; Native Hawaiian or other Pacific Islander; and White. Furthermore, respondents are also permitted to choose more than one racial category or select a sixth category added to the 2000 and 2010 Census questionnaires—some other race. When asked to identify themselves using these categories, Latinos make distinctive choices, most choosing to self-identify as White, other race, or Black (Ennis et al. 2011; Logan 2003; Grieco and Cassidy 2001). My interest is in exploring the diversity of racial identities in the Latino community and the social realities these identities create. Therefore, the purpose of this book is to reconceptualize the study of Latino politics by focusing on the development and political consequences of Latino racial identity.

Conceptually, this book rests on several theoretical frameworks that inform our understanding of Latino racial identity formation (see Figure 1.1). Scholars have long argued that racial identities are constantly negotiated among the individual and society (Cornell and Hartmann 1998; Nagel 1995). Race is a dynamic social construct (Omi and Winant 1994), and thus the manner in which Latinos racially self-identify is not only a product of individual preferences and choice but of the social and political construction of the concept of race and racial boundaries in the U.S. One theoretical approach highlights the role of the state and institutional practices in racial formation. By counting groups of people through the census, the state determines which groups are legitimate members of the body politic and which social categories are acceptable (Kertzer and Arel 2002). A boundary-centered framework suggests that institutional actors like the state play a role in creating racial categories to legislate inclusion or exclusion (Wimmer 2008b; see also Frank et al. 2010). In the case of Latinos, the decision by the government to treat race as distinct from ethnicity creates a context where Latinos, individually and collectively, struggle over "which categories are to be used, which meanings they should imply and what consequences they should entail" (Wimmer 2007: 11). Latinos, particularly those who are foreign born, are challenged to disregard the complexity of their own national experience and submit to the logic of the dominant racial hierarchy of White and Black (e.g. Torres-Saillant 1998). Consequently, decisions made by the government have far reaching implications for demography, including how Latinos will be described and the number and type of racial options they can select. Therefore, Latinos' racial choices are in reaction to existing categorical boundaries dictated by the state. Those choices include rejecting existing racial boundaries by refusing to respond to race questions; challenging established boundaries by self-identifying as "other"; or

Competing Theoretical Frameworks -State and Institutional practices -National Origin, Phenotype, and other Demographic Characteristics -Socioeconomic Status -Discrimination, Linked Fate, and Commonality -Acculturation/Assimilation	→	State-Sanctioned Racial Categories -White; Black; Some other race; More than one race -American Indian or Alaskan Native; Asian; Native Hawaiian or Pacific Islander	→	Political Attitudes and Behavior -Political Interest, Efficacy, and Trust -Partisanship (Direction and Strength) -Participation -Public Opinion
		Competing Theoretical Frameworks -National Origin, Phenotype, and other Demographic Characteristics -Socioeconomic Status -Discrimination, Linked Fate, and Commonality -Acculturation/Assimilation	↑	

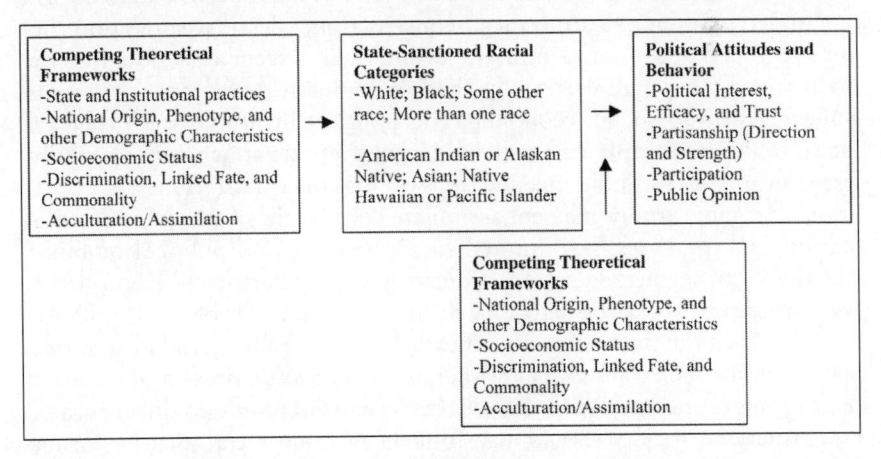

Figure 1.1 Modeling the development and political consequences of Latino racial identity.

accepting the boundaries by choosing standard racial categories (Wimmer 2008a; for further discussion see Frank et al. 2010).

Another framework focuses on the process of racial categorization and classification in Latin American countries to improve the understanding of Latino racial identification choices in the U.S. Approximately 40 percent of all Latinos are immigrants (Suro and Passel 2003) and bring with them an understanding of race vastly different from the one predominant in the U.S. Upon arriving, Latinos are immersed in a culture where the dominant racial paradigm is based on Black and White identity. In contrast, many Latin American and Caribbean countries have a ternary model of race relations that acknowledges intermediary populations of multiracial individuals (e.g. Daniel 1999). Coming from backgrounds where racial boundaries are loosely drawn and racial mixing is common, Latinos often see themselves deriving from more than one race (Rodriguez 1992, 2000), in part because race is largely defined by national origin, nationality, ethnicity, culture, skin color, or a combination of these (e.g. Kissam et al. 1993; Bates et al. 1994; Rodriguez and Cordero-Guzman 1992). Yet migrating to the U.S. is assumed to alter Latinos' racial identities (Itzigsohn et al. 2005), as they are often presumed by others to be either Black or White. Encountering a disparate racial classification system, Latino immigrants may change their racial identifications as they adapt to the U.S. racial classification system (see Golash-Boza and Darity 2008: 904). Latinos born in the U.S. may also re-categorize their racial identity as they navigate between the system of racial classification of their immigrant relatives and that of mainstream U.S. society (e.g. Marrow 2003; Bonilla-Silva 2003). This is clearly the case for many second- and third-generation Latinos, who are more familiar than their parents with the U.S. race classifications but are likely to be influenced by that of their parents and grandparents.

Theories of assimilation and acculturation have also been used to inform our understanding of Latino racial construction. Classic assimilation theory suggests that as Latino immigrants and their descendants move into the mainstream, they will eventually share a common American culture and achieve access to social, economic, and political institutions. As they are incorporated politically and socially, Latinos' ethnic attachment should be less relevant and less politicized. Critics of this conceptual framework often argue that some groups may not assimilate because they face severe discrimination and therefore have limited socioeconomic and political mobility. The theory of segmented assimilation advanced by Portes and Zhou (1993) posits three possible paths particularly for immigrants of color: assimilation into the White mainstream, identification with the Black underclass, or a new path in which immigrants deliberately retain the culture and values of their immigrant community. The degree to which Latinos are incorporated into American society should also influence Latino racial identity formation, so whereas social mobility into the mainstream may encourage some Latinos to racially self-identify as White, everyday social interactions that include experiences of discrimination based on perceived group membership may encourage some Latinos to choose other racial identities (Golash-Boza and Darity 2008; Landale and Oropesa 2002; see also Tienda and Mitchell 2006).

That life experiences and social interactions influence the way individuals view themselves racially suggests that shared experiences lay a foundation for group identification (e.g. Omi and Winant 1994; Portes and Rumbaut 2001; Rodriguez 2000; Waters 1999). A social identity framework focuses on the creation of group boundaries and holds that individuals align themselves and identify with members of social groups with which they feel commonalities (Tajfel and Turner 1986; Tajfel 1981). Similarly, believing that one's life chances are connected to the fate of a particular racial group and that the social and political problems experienced by that group are specifically associated with their race may also encourage some Latinos to adopt a particular racial identity (e.g. Dawson 1994). Adapting social identity theory and Dawson's notion of the "Black utility heuristic" to the Latino experience, it is likely that perceived commonality and a feeling of shared or linked fate with non-Hispanic Whites and Blacks and with Latinos from different national origin groups are also consequential to the understanding of Latino racial choices.

In summary, the structuring of Latino racial identity is a complex interaction between policies of the state and institutional practices, primordial ties, individual characteristics, and social interactions. Thus, the theoretical approach used in this book to explore the foundations of Latino racial identity includes socio-demographic factors (including national origin, phenotype, and socioeconomic status), individual perceptions of discrimination, linked fate and commonality with other racial groups, and measures of acculturation/assimilation. *However, understanding what factors influence the development of Latino racial identity is only part of the story.* Exploring the way in which Latinos construct their racial identity raises the question of whether racial group attachment among Latinos influences the formation of individual political attitudes, thereby creating substantial subgroup variations within the Latino population. Simply put, I contend that racial identity influences Latino politics, translating into politically meaningful behavior and attitudes at the individual level. Thus, we should expect to find variation in Latino political behavior. To be clear, extant research has found that many of the factors derived from the conceptual frameworks briefly outlined above explain this variation. Here I argue that variation in Latino politics can also be attributed, at least in part, to racial identity. Why might race be a predictor of Latino attitudes and behavior? Arguably, a number of social identities exist but are irrelevant to politics. What makes racial identity different? Why for Latinos might there be a connection between their racial identity and politics?

Social identity theory stresses that individuals' identification with overarching societal structures, such as groups and organizations, guide internal structures and processes. Social group identity is shared with a group of others who have (or are believed to have) some characteristics in common. Individuals align themselves with members of social groups with whom they feel commonalities, and over time develop part of their identity around such membership. Thus, group identity embodies strong social attachments and collective political evaluations and has come to be understood as a valuable political resource, playing a significant role in participation and attitude formation (Gurin et al. 1980). When an individual identifies solely with a particular group, there is a "self-awareness of one's objective membership in the group, as well as a psychological sense of attachment to the group" (Conover 1984: 761). At the most basic level, individuals can determine whether they are part of an in-group or out-group in reference to a target individual or group. It is this determination of group membership (and the status that comes with being part of that group) that provides reference points for political choices and behavior.

Race has long been used to classify groups of people in the U.S., creating a dividing "color line" (Omi and Winant 1994; Nagel 1994). Racial identities assigned to subordinate groups have created a lived context in which an individual's racial identity structures that individual's life chances. Thus, because race plays a significant role in determining the life chances and social position of groups, it is possible that racial self identification within the Latino community will influence individual political attitudes and behavior. Racial identities become salient and politically relevant when individuals define themselves as members of a group (Tajfel and Turner 1986) and realize that their life chances are connected to the fate of a particular racial group (Dawson 1994). Much of the early research on the political effects of group identity focused exclusively on African Americans and found that racial group attachment influences political attitudes and behavior. Despite economic and social cleavages in the African American community, African American political attitudes and behavior have been largely homogeneous because individual self-interest stems from group interests (Bobo et al. 2001; Dawson 1994; Kinder and Sanders 1996), creating a sense of commonality and political unity. Ethnic group identity functions in a similar fashion, shaping Latino attitudes and behavior (e.g. de la Garza et al. 1991; Calvo and Rosenstone 1989; de la Garza and DeSipio 1992).

Although ethnicity (particularly national origin) may be a primary (and the most preferred) identification for Latinos, the imposition of racial categories by the state signals the potential importance and relevance of race (and racial identities). Mainstream society typically classifies and treats most Latinos as non-White (Rodriguez 2000). Furthermore, numerous reports suggest that racial identity has real consequences for Latino life. Using 1970 and 1980 Census data, Massey and Denton (1992) find that White Latinos experience the greatest degree of spatial assimilation, living in closest proximity with non-Hispanic Whites, whereas Black Latinos remain highly segregated from non-Hispanic Whites. White and Black Latinos also live segregated from each other. The 2000 Census data shows that White Latinos have the lowest rates of poverty and higher incomes, followed by Latinos who racially self-identify as some other race, and Black Latinos. Despite having higher levels of education than other Latino racial groups, Black Latinos have the lowest incomes and highest rates of poverty (Logan 2003). If one takes a sociological view of the world, where life experiences and social interaction shape beliefs and actions, the reality that race is a fissure in Latino life increases the possibility that race could be a key component of Latino identity and is therefore *politically significant*. The social implications attached to a racial identity influence the individual's worldview, which then frames that individual's political perceptions. Because individuals perceive that their life chances are shaped by race, they may be more likely to rely on that identity to make political judgments (e.g. Dawson 1994). In this case, the socioeconomic advantage of White Latinos and socioeconomic vulnerability of non-White Latinos seems likely to have some degree of influence on their politics.

Connecting asserted racial identities to their effect on the political process has proven to be an overlooked yet notable aspect of Latino politics. The few studies that explore how racial identities affect Latino political choices all suggest that race has important implications for political behavior and policy. For example, Black Latinos are more supportive of government-sponsored health care and less supportive of the death penalty than are White Latinos. They also express a greater sense of commonality with African Americans, whereas White Latinos feel closer to non-Hispanic Whites (Nicholson et al. 2005). Race is also a significant predictor of Latino vote choice and political attitudes. When given the choice between a Latino candidate and a non-Latino candidate, Latinos who racially identify as Latino are more likely to choose the Latino candidate, whereas White Latinos and those who identify as other race are less likely to rely on ethnic cues and vote for the Latino candidate (Stokes-Brown 2006). Racial identity also impacts vote choice among naturalized Mexican Americans (Basler 2008). The data from in-depth interviews suggests that voting for George W. Bush in the 2004 presidential election and for California's Proposition 187 offered naturalized citizens a chance to align themselves with non-Hispanic Whites to obtain the social and political benefits inherent in Whiteness. Thus, Mexican Americans perceive and use their vote as a pathway into the "imagined community" of Americans—well off, well educated, and overwhelming White (Basler 2008: 125). In addition, research on Latino identity and political participation has found that Black Latinos are less likely to trust government than are other Latinos, whereas Latinos who self identify as some other race have lower levels of political efficacy and are less likely to participate in politics (Stokes-Brown 2009). Collectively, these studies suggest that we should pay close attention to the way in which racial identities influence Latino political life.

This book takes the perspective that as a consequence of diverse experiences that shape and are the result of perceived racial identity, members of different racial subgroups are likely to have varied political perspectives. In other words, different members of the broader Latino population will have distinct political attitudes and behaviors because of their racial identity. For some Latinos, the social reality of race may severely restrict political attitudes and behaviors that might otherwise be influenced by national origin, panethnic, or other ties (e.g. Waters 1994), thus making racial identity politically significant. Turning our attention away from the foundations of Latino racial identity and toward the implications of these identities for U.S. political life, I attempt to answer the call for more attention to socially meaningful consequences of race, focusing specifically on the realm of politics (see Bonilla-Silva 1996).

WHY RACIAL IDENTITY?

In many ways this book presents a somewhat unconventional view of Latino politics. Whereas much of the research on Latinos explores the ways in which Latinos develop a collective panethnic identity and the way in which that identity helps Latinos achieve political incorporation, this research highlights another layer of diversity. Unless we look explicitly at development and meanings of racial identification in the Latino community, we will never fully understand whether race is potentially a cross-cutting cleavage, fragmenting group interests and compromising efforts to promote unity and the opportunity to influence public policy. Just as there are contradictory interests among Latinos of different national origins, the growing racial divide among Latinos suggests that it may become necessary to address contradictory interests among Latinos who self-identify with various racial categories. Thus, this research attempts to address and ultimately raises questions about the salience of multiple identities in ethnic immigrant populations. This line of research also reevaluates and reinforces the importance of shared racial identity as an ascriptive tie that not only binds group members together but can serve as a resource for political incorporation.

The study of Latino racial identity also addresses important sociological debates over how Latino racial identity might affect future racial identification patterns. Race has long been conceptualized and understood in the U.S. as a binary hierarchy: Whites and non-Whites. Given the growth of the Latino population, one perspective predicts that the existing hierarchy of White/non-White will prevail, as Latinos will incorporate as racialized minorities who exist as part of a large community of "people of color" (e.g. Skrentny 2002). A second perspective suggests that a binary system will remain, yet our understanding of who is White will shift as this category expands to incorporate Latinos and Asian Americans (e.g. Warren and Twine 1997; Yancey 2003; Gans 1999; Lee and Bean 2007, 2004). Yet a third perspective suggests that Latino identity will eventually complicate the existing hierarchical structure between groups. The existing racial hierarchy of White/non-White will evolve into a three-tier model where lighter-skinned Latinos will occupy an intermediate and transitional category between Whites and Blacks and darker-skinned Latinos will fit into the collective Black category with African Americans (Forman et al. 2002; Duany 2005; Bonilla-Silva et al. 2003; Bonilla-Silva 2004; Tienda and Mitchell 2006).[2] Enhancing our knowledge about how members of the largest and fastest-growing group identify themselves provides additional insight into how the face of the country will look in the future. Thus, this research speaks to larger questions regarding the shifting nature of race identity and race relations, allowing scholars to make informed predictions about whether Latinos will over time self-identify as White or non-White, or become a third racial category in a new racial hierarchy.

Finally, the broader societal implications of Latino racial identity can also be observed when considering the propensity of Latinos to build electoral alliances with other groups, particularly African Americans. Many scholars have examined the viability of political coalitions between African Americans and Latinos, who despite their increasing numbers, need to build mass coalitions in order to wield substantial electoral clout.[3] The research presented here suggests that we might want to examine yet another dimension when considering the dynamics of interminority relations. Despite commonly held beliefs about the ideological similarity between these groups, most studies suggest that the development of long-lasting coalitions is unlikely (e.g. McClain 1993; McClain and Karnig 1990; Meier and Stewart 1991a; Kaufmann 2003, 2004) because of uncommon interests. Yet if racial identity can serve as the basis for coalitions, then identification with Blackness among African Americans and Afro-Latinos may serve a more cohesive and durable foundation, due in large part to perceptions of common or linked fate. Noting the degree of political homogeneity in the African American community (despite social and economic heterogeneity), Dawson (1994: 61) argues that "as long as African American life chances are powerfully shaped by race, it is efficient for individual African Americans to use the perceptions of the interests of African Americans as a group as a proxy for their own interests." Given the distinct social and economic realities between Black Latinos and other Latinos, it has been argued that "if it is necessary to combine [Black Latinos] with another group, there are now better reasons to classify Black Hispanics as Black than as Hispanic" (Logan, 2003: 10). To the extent that sociological experiences reinforce Blackness for Afro-Latinos, common or linked fate perceptions may increase the likelihood of the creation and maintenance of this specific interminority alliance.

RESEARCH AND DATA SOURCES

The research for this book is based on primary and secondary sources. I rely primarily on the 2006 Latino National Survey (LNS) and the

10 The Politics of Race in Latino Communities

2006 Latino National Survey—New England. The LNS is a large-scale, nationally representative survey of Latinos conducted from November 17, 2005 through August 4, 2006.[4] The survey contains 8,634 interviews of self-identified Latino residents from 15 states and the District of Columbia metropolitan area (including counties and municipalities in Virginia and Maryland). The universe of analysis contains approximately 87.5 percent of the U.S. Latino population. States were first selected based on the overall size of the Latino population and then added to capture the evolving nature of emerging populations in states without lengthy histories of large Latino populations. The Latino National Survey (LNS)—New England is the New England extension of the 2006 LNS.[5] It contains 1,200 interviews of self-identified Latino residents in three states: Massachusetts, Rhode Island, and Connecticut. The common survey instrument used for both the LNS and LNS—New England contains approximately 165 distinct items ranging from demographic descriptions to political attitudes and policy preferences, as well as a variety of demographic variables, social indicators, and experiences. The survey was administered by telephone using bilingual interviewers. All 9,834 respondents were greeted in both languages and immediately offered the opportunity to interview in either.

A Profile of the LNS Respondents

As in the general population, a majority of the LNS respondents are of Mexican descent (59.0%), followed by Puerto Ricans (13.9%), Dominicans (5.4%), Cubans (4.4%), and El Salvadorans (4.5%). Approximately 1 to 3 percent of respondents trace their ancestry to Guatemala (2.6%), Columbia (2.2%), Ecuador (1.3%), Spain (1.4%), Honduras (1.1%), and Peru (1.0%). The remaining participants trace their ancestral homes to Argentina, Bolivia, Chile, Costa Rica, Nicaragua, Panama, Paraguay, Uruguay, and Venezuela (all less than 1%). A majority of the respondents (65%) are foreign born. For this foreign-born population, the length of stay in the U.S. is on average 18 years, with about half living in the U.S. for at least 16 years. Less than one-fifth (16%) of the respondents are of the third generation or more.

The average respondent age is 42. Women slightly outnumber men, making up 55 percent of the sample. Half of the sample completed high school (primarily via GED), but very few (9.6%) have a four-year college degree and even fewer (6.7%) hold a graduate or professional degree. Although respondents earn on average between $35,000 and $44,999, the most common category of income reported by respondents is quite modest at $15,000–$24,999, followed by below $15,000. Approximately 11 percent of respondents reported earnings above $65,000. However, it should be noted that 2,128 respondents (22% of the total sample) did not provide this information.

Focus Groups

The quantitative findings from the LNS are supplemented by narratives from focus groups conducted in the summer of 2010. The focus group is a frequently used qualitative research method in the social sciences and is particularly useful for exploratory research where rather little is known about a topic of interest (Stewart and Shamdasani 1990). Typically, a moderator using a brief guide that contains a limited number of questions interacts with a small number of participants, between 5 and 10, to stimulate discussion and obtain information on the beliefs, attitudes, or motivations of participants on a specific topic (Patton 1990; Morgan 1997). Although there are numerous ways to use focus groups (e.g. Merton and Kendal 1946), they are often used to offer insight into statistical findings. Generally, although the information gathered cannot be generalized, the purpose of these groups is to garner a deeper understanding of how Latinos interpret and internalize racial categorizations using data that highlights the nuance and complexities of the relationship between Latino racial identities and politics.

New York and Chicago were chosen for the focus groups because they are home to some of the largest Latino communities in the U.S. and have varied populations (U.S. Census 2001).[6] The focus groups were planned and executed with the assistance of the firm Miriam Pollack and Associates, which moderated and recruited participants for the focus-group meetings. The first set of focus groups was held in Chicago on July 22, 2010. The New York focus groups were held in the borough of the Bronx on August 17–18, 2010. The participants were asked to provide their thoughts regarding race and racial identity, discussing among other things what their racial identity means to them and when it is socially and politically relevant (see Appendix B for focus group questions). The focus groups involved a total of 34 persons, of whom 22 (65%) were women and 12 (35%) were men. The average size of the groups was 7 persons: the largest group contained 9 and the smallest group contained 5. In most cases, each session lasted about two hours. Clearly, a set of five focus groups in two major cities cannot possibly capture all of the diversity within the Latino community. In terms of national origin and gender, the Chicago focus groups were largely comprised of Mexicans and women. The New York sample included slightly more men than the Chicago sample but was comprised mostly of women and Puerto Ricans. In both cities, the respondents were diverse in terms of age but Latinos with annual incomes of $50,000 or above were under-represented among the group participants. It is also worth noting that although participants were given the option to conduct the interviews in either English or Spanish, three out of the five sessions were conducted in English. The others were conducted completely in Spanish or in a combination of English and Spanish. A summary of the characteristics of focus group participants is provided in Table 1.1.

Table 1.1 Focus Group Participants—Demographic Characteristics

Chicago, IL—Group 1 (Spanish)

	Gender	Age	Education	Income	National Origin	Nativity
1	Female	46	Grad School	$50,000+	Puerto Rican	U.S.
2	Female	64	High School	$10,000–$20,000	Puerto Rican	U.S.
3	Female	65	8th Grade	<$10,000	Peruvian	Not U.S.
4	Female	69	<8th Grade	<$10,000	Mexican	Not U.S.
5	Female	55	<8th Grade	$20,000–$30,000	Mexican	Not U.S.

Chicago, IL—Group 2 (English)

	Gender	Age	Education	Income	National Origin	Nativity
1	Female	22	<8th Grade	$20,000–$30,000	Mexican	U.S.
2	Male	21	College	$20,000–$30,000	Ecuadorian	Not U.S.
3	Female	24	College	$30,000–$40,000	Mexican	U.S.
4	Female	—	High School	$10,000–$20,000	Mexican	Not U.S.
5	Female	40	College	$50,000+	Puerto Rican	U.S.

Chicago, IL—Group 3 (English)

	Gender	Age	Education	Income	National Origin	Nativity
1	Female	58	College	$20,000–$30,000	Mexican	Not U.S.
2	Female	35	High School	<$10,000	Mexican	Not U.S.
3	Male	44	College	<$10,000	Mexican	U.S.
4	Female	34	High School	$20,000–$30,000	Mexican	Not U.S.
5	Female	41	<8th Grade	<$10,000	Mexican	Not U.S.
6	Female	20	College	<$10,000	Mexican	U.S.
7	Male	64	High School	$10,000–$20,000	Mexican	Not U.S.

Introduction 13

New York, NY—Group 1 (English)

	Gender	Age	Education	Income	National Origin	Nativity
1	Female	19	High School	<$10,000	Puerto Rican	U.S.
2	Male	36	High School	$20,000–$30,000	Mixed Latino/(Puerto Rican & Cuban)	U.S.
3	Male	29	High School	$20,000–$30,000	Puerto Rican	U.S.
4	Female	28	College	$20,000–$30,000	Puerto Rican	U.S.
5	Female	27	College	$30,000–$40,000	Puerto Rican	U.S.
6	Male	53	College	$40,000–$50,000	Mixed Latino (Spain & Puerto Rican)	U.S.
7	Male	20	College	<$10,000	Honduran	Not U.S.
8	Female	75	Grad School	$20,000–$30,000	Puerto Rican	U.S.
9	Female	19	College	<$10,000	Mixed Latina/(Puerto Rican & Dominican)	U.S.

New York, NY—Group 2 (English/Spanish)

	Gender	Age	Education	Income	National Origin	Nativity
1	Female	53	College	$20,000–$30,000	Puerto Rican	U.S.
2	Male	71	Grad School	$10,000–$20,000	Dominican	Not U.S.
3	Male	21	High School	$10,000–$20,000	Puerto Rican	U.S.
4	Female	28	College	$20,000–$30,000	Puerto Rican	U.S.
5	Female	18	College	<$10,000	—	U.S.
6	Male	20	High School	$10,000–$20,000	Dominican	Not U.S.
7	Male	42	High School	Unemployed	Puerto Rican	U.S.
8	Male	20	College	$10,000–$20,000	Puerto Rican	U.S.

Note: "—" indicates information not provided by participant.

PLAN OF THE BOOK

Using an explicit racial frame, the book has three main goals. The first is to describe how Latinos identify themselves racially. I am interested in whether Latinos use standard racial categories found on surveys or other labels that contrast sharply with the historical White-Black racial hierarchy in the U.S. The second objective is to examine under what conditions Latinos choose their racial identity. The third objective is to determine the political relevance of Latino identity choices.

The book is divided into three sections. The first section describes race in theory and reality. Scholars have long explored the philosophical and sociological issues surrounding race. Chapter Two summarizes the literature on racial identity formation, highlighting in particular the role of the census in the construction and reconstruction of racial identities. In its ability to establish distinct group categories, to specify who belongs in which group, and to establish where each group's status is situated in terms of social hierarchy, the census plays a central role in shaping the racial order that "helps to guide the polity's and individual's choices about the distribution of goods and resources, and does a great deal to shape each person's life chances" (Hochschild and Powell 2008: 61). Although Latinos' conceptualization of race tends to differ from that most commonly expressed in the U.S., racial categories and classifications (how people are counted) perpetuates state-sanctioned notions about race and affect the way in which people view themselves and others. Thus, the rest of the chapter uses LNS and focus group data to explore how Latinos conceptualize their racial identity both within and outside the boundaries of the color line. Chapter Three examines the processes involved in the development of Latino racial identity. The profound diversity within the Latino community stipulates the use of a diverse theoretical model to determine the sources and contours of Latino racial identity. Thus, this chapter emphasizes and considers demographic factors and measures of socioeconomic status, perceived discrimination, commonality and linked fate, and acculturation/assimilation as key determinants of Latinos' racial choices.

The second section considers the political consequences of racial identity. Although I am limited to the topics included in the LNS, these chapters provide evidence on a wide range of political attitudes and behaviors that are critical for achieving political incorporation.[7] Given that the size of the Latino immigrant population has grown dramatically over the past several decades, each chapter also gives special attention to the role of racial identity in immigrant political attitudes and behavior. Chapter Four examines how racial self identification affects Latinos' orientations toward the political system (e.g. political interest, efficacy, and trust in government). These political orientations are pivotal resources for electoral participation and therefore have been widely explored within the voting and participation literature. The findings show that multiracial Latinos tend to be politically interested and efficacious, whereas Black Latinos have lower levels of internal and external efficacy and are less trusting of government. Other race identity is also negatively associated with some political orientations, as these Latinos have lower levels of external efficacy.

Chapter Five examines the link between Latino racial identity and partisanship. Although partisanship is one of the most influential determinants of political behavior predicting participation among the general population (e.g. Conway, 1991; Rosenstone and Hansen, 1993) and among racial and ethnic groups (e.g. Lien 1994; Uhlaner 1996; Kam and Ortiz 1998), one largely unexplored area in studies of the politics of Latinos in the U.S. is their relationship to political parties. Here, I find that multiracial Latinos are significantly more likely to identify as Republicans than as Democrats. This finding is particularly interesting considering that while most Latinos generally identify with the Democratic Party, Cubans are exception, in that they are more likely to prefer instead the Republican Party (Alvarez and García Bedolla 2003). Here we see that both national origin and racial identity can provide some insights into Republican Party attachments. I also find that among immigrants, other race identification negatively impacts the strength of identification with either of the two major parties.

Chapter Six examines nonelectoral and electoral participation. Although extant research suggests that other forms of Latino identity (national origin and panethnic identity) are strong determinants of Latino political behavior, few studies have examined whether Latino racial identity exhibits a similar effect. The findings in this chapter suggest that Latino political engagement is also shaped by racial identity. Although Latino citizens who self-identify as Black, multiracial, and other race are all more likely than White Latinos to register to vote, only multiracial and other race Latinos were more likely to vote in the 2004 presidential election. Black Latinos are more likely to engage in nonelectoral activities, using both formal and informal methods to address an issue or problem. I also find that among immigrants, multiracial identification is positively related to increased civic participation.

Chapter Seven examines the implications of Latino racial identity for public opinion. Here I find significant differences in opinion among Latino racial groups across a wide range of policy items, including Latino salient issues (immigration), implicitly racial issues (social welfare spending and government assistance), and more general policy issues (education reform, same-sex marriage, and abortion).

The book concludes by considering the broader implications of this research for the study of American politics more broadly and the prospects for Latino political incorporation. Here I also argue that variations in racial identification and the distinct relationship between racial identity and various measures of political attitudes and behaviors call for scholars to engage in new forms of research that continue to disaggregate the Latino population. To be clear—although the results highlight the political relevance of Latino racial identity, this research in no way invalidates or calls into question the development or relevance of national origin or panethnicity in Latino politics. Rather, the purpose of this book is to call attention to the heterogeneity of Latinos. More specifically, I seek to nurture a better understanding of race as a dynamic and influential social force that shapes identities within Latino communities and of the implications of those identities for political life. To borrow the phrase made famous by Cornell West's book (1994), race matters. It may be a secondary or even tertiary factor constituting identity for Latinos, but race and color are issues in the Latino community and racial categorization matters. Thus, understanding the experiences of Latinos requires us to acknowledge the complexity of Latino diversity, which includes diverse orientations toward racial identity.

Despite the development of panethnicity across all Latino national origin groups since the 1960s, numerous scholars have made great efforts to acknowledge Latino heterogeneity and explore the development of panethnicity and ethnic differences among Latino subgroups across a wide range of political attitudes and behaviors. This book follows in that tradition. Yet, by moving beyond standard demographic markers, I attempt to promote a new understanding of Latino politics, accounting for issues of race in Latino politics. Reflecting on the reality of Latino identity, I suggest that although the predominant U.S. racial constructs do not easily apply to this group, we must be careful not to trivialize race—rather we should open ourselves to explore the ways that race can enhance our understanding of Latino political attitudes and behavior.

2 The Meaning and Measurement of Race

The discourse on race has long focused on the racial identity formation: the placement of individuals into racial categories based on socially constructed, racially ascribed characteristics. The intellectual consensus is that racial identities are formed through a social process of both self-examination and external classification by others and it is the process of race-making that assigns individuals who are recognized as members of a given group to a specific position in the U.S. racial hierarchy (Bonilla-Silva 1997; Feagin 2006). According to the state, Latinos are an ethnic group and can therefore be any race. This has raised important sociological and political questions about how Latinos will navigate the existing racial hierarchy. Where do Latinos "fit" into America's White-Black dichotomy? And given the nation's established racial boundaries, how do Latinos define their racial identity? The process of racial formation is shaped by those in power and by those from below (Omi and Winant 1994); thus, a central challenge in exploring Latino racial identity is to observe how Latinos define themselves when confronted with a new system of racial categorization while recognizing that they are placing themselves in categories that do not adequately represent their self conceptions (see Hitlin et al. 2007; Brown et al. 2006, 2007). In many ways, Latino self identification is contingent on the alternatives available in various contexts and situations (Oboler 1995: 103). Research has shown that the categories included in race questions have significant implications for identification patterns, as Latinos are less likely to self-identify using standard OMB race categories (i.e. White, Black) when asked to identify their race using a question that includes standard race categories *and* a "Latino/Hispanic" category (Campbell and Rogalin 2006; see also Hirschman et al. 2000). Data from several nationally representative surveys also show that even when asked to identify their race using standard race categories only, some Latinos reject those choices, reporting their race to be Latino or Hispanic.[1] In my conversations about race with focus group participants in New York and Chicago, I have also found that when exploring questions of identify, context also matter. Most Latinos prefer and largely choose cultural and panethnic identifiers to identify themselves. Yet, when faced with the limitations of the existing racial hierarchy and with questions about race and ethnicity that reinforce that hierarchy, Latinos can and do make distinct racial choices that represent an authentic expression of their racial identity and lived social experience.

THE SOCIAL CONSTRUCTION OF RACE

Although race and ethnicity are often used as interchangeable concepts, here ethnic identity formation and racial identity formation are treated as separate processes. Whereas ethnic identity formation focuses on the categorization of individuals into groups based on a shared and similar history, culture, religion, language, or kinship, racial identify formation highlights categorization on the basis of perceived common physical characteristics, such as skin color or ancestry. Both race and ethnicity are socially constructed, meaning that ethnic and racial categories reflect shared social meanings and those shared social meanings reflect differences in power relations (Waters 2002: 25). The very idea of race assumes a hierarchy of racial groups (Bashi and McDaniel 1997: 671)—a hierarchy that is maintained by laws and policies that define the boundaries of racial identities and specify their relative disadvantages and privileges in the U.S. (Haney-Lopez 1996). Used to justify the exploitation of groups and preserve status differences, race has very real implications in shaping life chances and serves as an important basis of invidious treatment, limited economic opportunity, and social exclusion (Bonilla-Silva 1997: 469; see also Hacker 1992).

Given that race in the U.S. is largely defined by skin color, some reject the notion that Latinos identify with U.S. racial categories that can then act as a proxy for Latino political choices. In Latin America, race is organized along a continuum of categories that denote different degrees of mixture, representing a combination of Spanish, Asian, African, and indigenous heritages (Bonilla-Silva and Glover 2004; Menchaca 2001). Racial categories are defined by numerous factors, including skin color, socioeconomic status, and cultural elements, and are used to distinguish between Whites, mixed raced persons, Blacks, and indigenous populations. Because Latinos come from countries with distinct and different systems of social stratification, it is presumed that they do not fit easily into the U.S. racial structure and therefore racial choices constrained by that structure have little social meaning and few political effects. However, it is through the inescapable process of racial (re)classification that immigrant populations learn and then choose to ignore, resist, or accept state-defined categories and societal attitudes concerning race (Rodriguez 2000). Forced to live within the racial boundaries created by the state (through the creation of official categories), Latinos engage the existing racial hierarchy and are largely marginalized because of it. It is this reality that suggests that Latinos' self expression of race has social meaning and can influence political choices. If race is constituted by the state and expressed through racial classification standards (e.g.

Haney-Lopez 1996; Crenshaw 1998; Delgado 1995), then exploring the construction of race through the census is central to begin to comprehend how Latinos define themselves when confronted with this system and how that identity shapes the politics of Latino communities.

IDENTITY AND THE CENSUS: HOW RACE IS MEASURED

How has the state measured race? What role does the census play in the process of racial (re)organization in the U.S.? As several scholars have noted in their studies of racial classifications, definitions of race have been variable and fluid, changing over time in response to political events and societal perspectives (e.g. Haney Lopez 1996; Nobles 2000; Rodriguez 2000). The history of the census has been thoroughly analyzed, yet such analysis has only recently focused on the effects of census policy for Latinos (e.g. Rodriguez 2000; Rodriguez 1992; Hochschild and Powell 2008).

In 1787 the U.S. Constitution broadly established guidelines for how to count the nation's people. As Rodriguez (2000) notes, the Apportionment Rule, found in Article 1, Section 1, clause 3 specifies that the population was to be counted every ten years. A reference to race is largely absent; however, the clause makes a distinction between "free persons" and "other persons" who were slaves of African descent. Subsequently, this language was interpreted and applied in such a way that Whites were separated from "all other free persons" and slaves in the 1790 Census and racial classification was built into the population counts (Hochschild and Powell 2008; Rodriguez 2000). Although a bipolar structure of White and non-White was taking shape, mulattoes were counted in the 1850 Census. As Hochschild and Powell (2008: 68) note:

> "Mulatto" arrived on the census as the stalking horse for polygenist racial science, as a way for opponents of slavery to learn more about blacks, as one piece of the statisticians' omnivorous quest for knowledge, as the lesser of many evils to southern politicians, as an acknowledgement of increasing racial mixture and the distinctive economic and social position of many mulattoes, as a chip in the battle over Congressional control of executive agencies, and as an element of partisan contestation.

In subsequent decades, the census would expand again to include the categories Indian and Chinese (1870) and Japanese (1880) (Nobles 2000; Rodriguez 2000).

Despite the long history of Latinos in the U.S., the first systematic effort to count this population, specifically Mexicans, was introduced in the 1930 Census. Until this point, Mexicans were not considered to be formally distinct from Whites, but the category was added in response to political pressure by nativists who feared the massive Mexican immigration that took place in the 1920s (Nobles 2000: 73; see also Hochschild and Powell 2008: 80). Arguing that the category itself suggested discriminatory intent, Mexican Americans successfully lobbied to have the category removed. Protesting the group's exclusion from Whiteness, the 1940 Census reversed the 1930 policy and Mexicans (along with other Hispanic groups in the U.S.) were once again counted as White (Rodriguez 2000; Nobles 2000; Hochschild and Powell 2008).

The next effort to count the Latino population appeared in the 1970 Census. Facing pressure from the Hispanic community for a category that would facilitate their enumeration, the census included a separate question for Hispanic origin and a small subset of the population was asked to choose whether their origin or descent was Mexican, Puerto Rican, Cuban, Central or South American, or other Spanish.[2] In an effort to standardize its data collection on race and ethnicity and enable compliance with civil rights legislation, the Office of Management and Budget (OMB) issued federal directive #15 in May 1977 designating a total of five reporting categories: American Indian or Alaska Native, Asian or Pacific Islander, Black, and White (Nobles 2000). The fifth category, Hispanic, was defined as an ethnic category, allowing Latinos to place themselves in a racial classification other than White (Denton and Massey 1989).

For the first time in the history of the U.S. census, the 1980 Census asked all respondents to indicate their race and whether they were of Hispanic or Spanish origin (Rodriguez 2000). The Hispanic origin question read: Is this person of Spanish/Hispanic origin or descent?" The possible responses were: "No (not Spanish/Hispanic); Yes, Mexican, Mexican-Amer., Chicano; Yes, Puerto Rican; Yes, Cuban; Yes, other Spanish/Hispanic."[3] Almost identical to the item in the 1980 Census, the Hispanic origin question in the 1990 Census also included a write-in line to specify a group for "other Spanish/Hispanic" origins.

Measuring Race in the 2000 and 2010 Census

In October 1997, OMB announced revisions to the federal directive that provides standards for collecting and reporting data on race and ethnicity. In light of the discussion from hearings centered around proposals to amend the race item on the census, the Asian or Pacific Islander category found in the 1990 Census was separated into two new racial categories: Asian and Native Hawaiian or Other Pacific Islander. For the first time, respondents were also permitted to select more than one of the racial categories specified on the census to identify their mixed racial heritage (Humes et al. 2011).

Two additional proposals, including the proposal to include "Hispanic" as a race category, were not adopted.[4] Instead, the language of the Hispanic origin item was changed to read "Hispanic/Latino." There were also significant changes in the instructions given to respondents and changes in the placement of the Hispanic origin question. Rather than follow the race question as it had done in the 1990 Census, the Hispanic origin question was placed ahead of the race question and respondents were instructed to answer both questions (Grieco and Cassidy 2001). These changes represented a concerted effort by the state to persuade Latino respondents to select a standard race category and not mark "other race." Largely unsuccessful in this effort, the 2010 Census included modest changes to lower the percentage of "other race" responses. Respondents were instructed to answer both the Hispanic origin and race items and were explicitly told that "Hispanic origins are not races." Additionally, the last response category in the Hispanic origin question was reworded and lists of examples were provided to elicit a national origin response (Humes et al. 2011).[5]

Although the proposed change for the 2000 Census was ultimately rejected by the federal government, there was serious discussion about changing the Bureau's official position that race and ethnicity are separate concepts. Yet, the Hispanic proposal—the use of a combined race/ethnicity question where "Hispanic/Latino" is included in the list of races—lacked strong support among Latino organizations.[6] According to Rodriguez (2000: 160):

> Although the major, requisite Hispanic organizations were present at the hearings, few representatives of the Hispanic community testified. Likewise, there was little coverage of the issue in the Spanish- or English- language media and few public discussions elsewhere. When the Mexican Americans Legal Defense and Education Fund (MALDEF) and the National Council of La Raza (NCLR) testified at these hearings, MALDEF indicated that a recommendation on "whether or how to change the Census's Hispanic origin and race questions would be premature" (U.S. House Committee 1994b: 179). Both groups felt that the current Hispanic item should be retained; neither endorsed the proposal as presented.

Subsequently, when several research studies found that the combined format resulted in an undercount of Hispanics, the proposal was abandoned (Rodriguez 2000).

Despite polls showing a preference among Latinos for the combined question and the rise of "Latino/Hispanic" responses to survey questions using separate questions about ethnicity and race (see for example Campbell and Rogalin 2006; Golash-Boza and Darity 2008; Stokes-Brown 2006; 2009), Latino political organizations, including the National Council of La Raza and National Association of Latino Elected and Appointed Officials (NALEO), have been vocal in their support of the existing format (Suarez 2010). Recognizing that the census count is directly tied to representation, civil rights protections, and the allocation of federal aid, some argue that a separate question for Hispanic origin results in a more comprehensive count (Padgett 2010; see also Entwistle and Astone 1994). Still, many scholars argue that this strategy for enumerating the Latino population is problematic because it distorts Latinos' understanding of race and calls into question the analytic utility of this concept (Rodriguez 2000; Hirschman et al. 2000; Farley 2000; Hirschman 2004).

SELF REPORTS OF LATINO RACIAL IDENTITY: FOCUS GROUPS AND LNS FINDINGS

Although it is not my main intent to engage directly in a methodological debate about how best to measure race, my use of LNS (which like the census uses two separate questions rather than a single question) plants this research firmly in a particular "camp" and most importantly, in my assessment, acknowledges the role that the state plays in shaping racial identity (e.g. Omi and Winant 1994; Nobles 2000; Marx 1998; Anderson 1988; Haney-Lopez 2006). The use of this data also permits direct comparisons across multiple sources of data that also share this format. Yet the focus group interviews provide a rare and critical opportunity for participants to speak as candidly as possible about 1) how they define their racial identity on their own terms; 2) how they define that identity when forced to navigate the color line; and 3) their assessment of the political value of those identities. The use of this data in conjunction with the LNS data to explore questions of Latino identity enables important observations about the ways in which Latinos construct racial self understandings, showing that most Latinos simultaneously invoke race and ethnicity as separate and similar constructs depending on the context (see Fergus 2004).

Focus participants were first asked, "What race do you consider yourself?" None of the participants used standard racial categories like Black and White to describe themselves. Interestingly, two darker-skinned participants in the New York focus groups spoke in depth about feelings about being perceived as Black:

Man A (Mixed Latino, first group): A lot of people think I'm Black.
Interviewer: And you feel it necessary to straighten them out about that?
Man: Yeah, I do, I do. Most of my friends are [Black] and if I'm hanging around with a bunch of dark-skinned people they are going to assume that I am Black. So I tell people "no, I'm actually Puerto Rican and Dominican."

Man B (Dominican, second group): They always consider me, as you can see, African American—it gets me a little bit upset that they don't consider me Dominican. . . . It makes me mad.

There was consensus among the participants that standard racial categories were not terms they used to identify themselves because of their understanding of labels: the term Black means non-Hispanic Black/African American, whereas White refers to non-Hispanic Caucasians or Whites. Rather, most participants chose national origin labels like Puerto Rican, Mexican, Dominican, and Ecuadorian. Participants also self-identified as Chicano and Nuyorican. Chicano is a political and racial identity born out of the Chicano civil rights movement in the 1960s. Although the term was typically used as a pejorative for "Mexican American," political activists encouraged its adoption to transform its meaning, denoting a particular national origin and leftist political consciousness (Garcia Bedolla 2009: 74). Organizing in a wide range of states, including New Mexico, Colorado, Texas, and Illinois, activists sought to express their satisfaction with the responsiveness of the Democratic Party to address the needs of and unique issues facing Mexican American communities (Garcia and Sanchez 2008). By the mid-1970s, the movement began to lose political strength but its enduring legacy of pride in the Chicano culture remains deeply ingrained in many Latinos, regardless of whether they were active participants in the movement (Garcia and Sanchez 2008). As a result, the Chicano movement is widely regarded as institutionalizing a new political identity that has been adopted by some Mexican Americans as a racial identity—one that emphasizes indigenous roots and the celebration of and connection to Mexican history, culture, and language. Also born of the civil rights era, the Nuyorican movement is largely a literary and social movement that addresses the social, economic, and political marginalization of Puerto Ricans on the U.S. mainland. Although sometimes used pejoratively by Puerto Rican islanders, the term Nuyorican is often used by Puerto Ricans living in New York to denote a dual identity that stresses American identity and a strong cultural connection to the Puerto Rican mainland (Aparicio 1993). Thus, the use of this label signals a layered understanding that one's identification with the Puerto Rican community and lived experience in a specific context or location can be incorporated to create a new Rican-ness (e.g. Fergus 2004).

It is clear from these responses that national identification remains an anchoring identity for most Latinos (e.g. Itzigsohn and Dore-Cabral 2000). It also suggests that the American (and current academic) distinction between race and ethnicity is not clear to most Latinos, who have more fluid racial self understandings and see race and ethnicity as interchangeable. Yet at the same time, despite the nature of the question, a few participants were extremely aware that their response would be different depending on the context. This is consistent with identity literature, which suggests that because recognizing one's placement in the racial hierarchy is central to the process of incorporation into American society, some Latinos will adopt these identities to serve as a form of racial identification within the American racial stratification system (e.g. Oboler 1991; Rodriguez 1992, 2000; Rodriguez and Cordero-Guzman 1992). For example, after the first question was asked (self-racial identification), a male respondent in the third Chicago focus group asked, "Wait, so are we talking about how we consider ourselves in general or how we consider ourselves here in the U.S.?" His comments further illustrate this point:

> I say Chicano because it is my personal choice; growing up in Chicago and not knowing the Mexican culture and the people who come from Mexico, I don't relate to those cultural things. But I usually have no other option but to put "some other race."

Although this respondent views his racial identity as Chicano, he typically feels constrained to choose the "other" category to express his race. This feeling of constraint was echoed by almost every participant. In almost every group, participants engaged in a larger discussion about how people are automatically categorized by society more broadly. One male participant in the first New York focus group commented, "This country was built on racism and categorization. . . . People put you in a category." This comment signals an awareness that self identification is imposed by external influences. Similarly, when asked how they are perceived by most people in the U.S., most of the participants expressed a feeling of otherness—not White, not Black, but other. For example:

> We're perceived as Latinos, all Latinos because we all speak Spanish. (Mexican woman, first Chicago group)

> We are a minority group but I see Latinos everywhere—looks like majority to me. (Mexican woman, second Chicago group)

> Less than them . . . with the simple fact than you have a Hispanic last name and look like you speak Spanish. (Mexican man, second New York group)

The participants seemed very aware that language is used to categorize Latinos regardless of nationality and is used to discriminate against them. Feelings of imposition and constraint became even clearer when respondents were then asked a second question about race. Having had the opportunity to define themselves racially, participants were shown an enlarged print version of a census form and were asked, "Of the races specified on the census list, which best describes you?" Given this question, there was almost unanimous agreement that the best option was "other." Interestingly, no one chose Black. Only one participant (female) in the first Chicago focus group said "White"; she did so hesitantly and then started laughing with other participants. Once the laughter ended, another female participant turned to her and said, "Seriously, there is no other possible category—just other," and she nodded in agreement. An exchange between three participants from the third Chicago focus group demonstrates that

Latinos who chose the "other race" category often view their race as equivalent to their nationality (e.g. Rodriguez 2000) or hold a panethnic view of Latino identity:

Woman A (Mexican): It would have to be some other race, and I would write in Hispanic.
Woman B (Mexican): Yes, you would have no other choice but to put some other race. But I would write in Chicano because when you say Chicano you are still some sort of Mexican. Hispanic means you could be from anywhere like Puerto Rico.
Man A (Mexican): People think we are all alike but for us it does make a difference if we are Puerto Rican, Mexican, or Cuban.

These narratives suggest that some Latinos are consciously shifting their racial identification to "fit" the U.S. conceptualization of race, but are at the same time interpreting this conceptualization through their own frames.

There were a few participants for whom both questions (self racial identity and racial identity based on the census categories) solicited responses using panethnic terms. These participants refused to accept the other category, requesting that their race be recorded as Latino or Hispanic. In fact, one participant took great offense to the census question, staying after the session to make the point that the census is offensive to Latinos because it does not include Latino/Hispanic as a racial choice. These responses are consistent with findings from some quantitative studies (see Nicholson et al. 2005; Stokes-Brown 2006) and suggest that although Hispanic/Latino is technically an ethnic category, we cannot ignore some Latinos' perception of the category as a racial identifier.

There is little doubt that Latinos transcend and challenge the predominant racial categories. The LNS data, which is largely modeled after the census (i.e. closed-ended questions measuring race and Hispanic heritage separately), also confirms this, with almost two-thirds of respondents self-identifying as other race (see Table 1). This is much higher than in the 2000 Census, where 42 percent of Latinos identified as other (Logan 2003). Only 24 percent of the respondents self-identified as White, which is much lower than that reported in the census (50 percent). Less than one percent of respondents self-identified as Black. This percentage is much lower than the approximately 3 to 4 percent found in other data sources (e.g. Logan 2003). Far more respondents self-identified as multiracial (more than one race) than as Black. Of those respondents who chose more than one race, 81 percent selected White as one of their identities. The inclusion of the multiracial category is noteworthy because the data strengthens claims that multiracial identification is not uncommon among the Latino population (Lee and Bean 2004). It also highlights the role that states play in shaping and reinforcing identities and hierarchies (Marx 1998). The multiracial category is outside of the traditional racial scheme. Yet because the state

Table 2.1 Descriptive Results—Latino Racial Identity

Respondent racially identifies as	N	%
White	2249	22.9%
Black, African American, or Negro	75	.8
American Indian or Alaskan Native	141	1.4
Asian Indian	5	.0
Native Hawaiian or Pacific Islander	11	.1
Some other race (SOR)	6486	66.0
SOR_Latino[a]	(4875)	
Latino[b]	(2567)	
Multiracial (more than one race)	147	1.5
Refused	720	7.3
	9834	100%

Source: Latino National Survey/ Latino National Survey (LNS)—New England.
[a]Represents the number of other race Latinos who self-identified as Latino/Hispanic when asked to clarify their initial response.
[b]Represents the number of other race Latinos who self-identified as Latino/Hispanic when asked to clarify their initial response and gave a "yes" response to a separate question asking whether Latinos are a distinctive racial category in the U.S.

sanctions the option to select multiple categories, individuals who choose this category are recognized and accepted in the polity in a way that those who self-identify as other race are not (Kertzer and Arel 2002; Nobles 2000; see Masouka 2008: 256–257 for further discussion). Some Latinos who choose this category may perceive that this identifier signals a level of social, economic, and political privilege perhaps different or lower than that of those associated with membership in the majority group (White) but different and higher than the degree of privilege afforded to those who self-identity as part of another minority group (e.g. Masouka 2011). Given the number of respondents who chose White as one of their multiple racial identities, some may also perceive this category as an opportunity to connect with and express their mixed race heritage without giving up the privileges of Whiteness.

Following the standards set by the government, the race question in the LNS does not include Latino or Hispanic as an option. The sheer number of respondents who self-identify as other race strongly suggests that most Latinos reject the U.S. conceptualization of race, believing that standard census race categories do not fit them well. This leaves us with a significant percentage of respondents choosing a racial identity that is rather vague, presumes homogeneity, and is without much social and political meaning. One is then left wondering, "What does it mean to be some other race? Are all other race Latinos the same?"

The survey design adopted in the LNS provides a rare opportunity to examine this racial group in depth. Respondents who chose this category were probed by interviewers to explain what they meant by their choice. This small adaptation of the census has a strong impact, allowing respondents to express in their own words what "other" means, and provides detailed responses that can then be used to better understand who these Latinos are and how they differ from those in other Latino racial groups. As Table 2.1 shows, of those respondents who initially self-identified as some other race, approximately 75 percent used a panethnic identifier (Latino or Hispanic) to explain their initial response. I regard this category as the expression of a panethnic identity. Thus, in the absence of a Hispanic/Latino racial category in the race question, many Latinos choose this option to express their belief in shared cultural mores and experience among Latinos regardless of national origin (Oboler 1995; Padilla 1985). These respondents are identifying with a category they view as reflecting their Latin American and Caribbean origins, but without further clarification it remains unclear whether any of these respondents might be tapping into American conceptualizations of race where groups exist in a social hierarchy characterized by dominant and subordinate social relations between those groups (e.g. Marrable 1994). Might it be that for some, this category is best conceptualized as an indeterminate group identity that falls outside of the White/non-White race discourse and for others it is a non-White group identity firmly planted within (and yet challenging) the existing racial hierarchy (e.g. Trucios-Haynes 2000: 3; see also Muta 1999)? Fortunately, all survey participants were asked to respond yes, no, or maybe to the following question: "In the U.S., we use a number of categories to describe ourselves racially. Do you feel that Latinos/Hispanics make up a distinctive racial group in America?" The data shows that approximately 39 percent (2567) of the other race respondents who report their race to be Latino or Hispanic *also* believe that Latinos are a distinctive race category. If we place these identities on a scale with the general "other race" category at one end, the second "other race" category (SOR_Latino) falls in the middle of the scale and is conceptualized as an umbrella panethnic identity signaling a generalization of solidarity among Latinos but a high degree of racial ambiguity, and the third category (Latino) falls at the opposite end of the scale and is a *racialized* conceptualization of Latino other race identity.[7] For these other race respondents, there is seemingly little contradiction between their ethnic and racial group identities as they adopt a constructed non-White identity that has been imposed broadly on the group (Trucios-Haynes 2000).

The conceptualization of other race identity as a racialized non-White identity is also clear in the comments of several focus group participants. When asked whether Latinos make up a distinct racial group in the U.S., one woman (Puerto Rican) in the second Chicago focus group said, "Totally, yes. We stick to our own [national origin] groups in our neighborhoods, but we are all the same—Latinos." A male participant (Ecuadorian) in the same group said, "Yes. We are our own group. If I was just talking people would assume that I am Latino and I feel like I am bonded with people who are Latin American even though I am Ecuadorian." Yet the comments below from a Puerto Rican woman who also self-identified as other but does not believe Latinos are a distinct race are representative of the feelings expressed by other participants:

> We are all a little different. Even in Spanish there are many versions and there are different words for things from different countries. Plus, Hispanics move to different neighborhoods—Mexican, Dominican, Puerto Rican. We go by our nationality. (Second New York group)

Most of the focus group participants also agreed that they are consistently made aware of their self-ascribed race. For example:

> Every time you talk to someone people ask "where are you from?" And I say "I'm Mexican." (Mexican man, third Chicago group)

> I am very conscious of being Hispanic and I'm very aware of which places I can go at night and where I shouldn't go because of racial bias. (Puerto Rican man, second New York group)

Together with the conversations from the focus groups, the racial categories identified in the LNS provide a window into the complexity of Latino racial identity and reveal that the census plays a critical role in the process of racialization. Consistent with other studies (e.g. Logan 2003; Tafoya 2004), we see that few Latinos subscribe to the existing racial hierarchy, preferring instead to challenge the existing boundaries by self-identifying as other race. Furthermore, the findings from both the focus groups and LNS data suggest that Latinos who self-identify as "other" attach different meanings to their group membership, with some internalizing this identity as a panethnic identity and some internalizing it as a racialized identity.

By tailoring the discussion of Latino racial identity to six racial categories (White, Black, multiracial, and three categories of other race identity), this book moves us beyond the White-Black divide, recognizing both standard and innovative racial identification choices. Thus, we see that although racial identification reflects institutional efforts to classify populations, it can also reflect the efforts of groups to define themselves (e.g. Brubaker and Cooper 2000). This use of this data also indirectly speaks to the scholarly debate about how "best" to measure and classify the Latino population. A major criticism of the way the government currently measures race is that it does not adequately reflect self conceptions (e.g. Brown et al. 2007). As a result, most Latinos racially self-identify as "other," a term with little social and political meaning. The survey design adopted in the LNS provides a rare opportunity to examine other race Latinos in depth, clearly distinguishing other race Latinos who identify panethnically from those who identify racially. Thus, it is likely that Latinos who self-identify as other have vastly different understandings of the meaning of that identity, which might lead to distinct political attitudes and behaviors among these Latinos. This approach shows that it is possible to use externally imposed racial categories to examine the nuanced nature of Latino racial identities. The value of this methodological approach will be discussed in greater detail in the conclusion.

3 The Foundations of Latino Racial Identity

In an effort to explain the process by which identities are developed and maintained, scholars have long argued that race, as a sociologically constructed characteristic of individuals based on geographic heritage and phenotype, is constantly negotiated between the individual and society (Cornell and Hartmann 1998; Nagel 1995; Hirschman et al. 2000). Thus, although race may lack a scientific foundation, racial identification has vast social significance in that it reflects the efforts of institutions to classify populations and efforts of populations to classify themselves (Omi and Winant 1994; Nagel 1994; see also Williams et al. 1994). Creating and maintaining social stratification, racial identities are salient and embedded with meanings, and they define who is included in or excluded from the political system (e.g. Bonilla-Silva 1999).

Race in the American context has historically been used to distinguish between Blacks and Whites. The contemporary resurgence of Latino immigration has stimulated questions and concerns about Latino racial identity. Latin American notions of race have historically been based on a color continuum rather than a set of discrete categories. Thus, for Latinos with greater exposure to Latin American conceptions of race, racial self understandings may be more fluid and permeable than is true of the prevailing racial order. Recognizing that the Latino population has the potential to change our understanding of the color line and its meaning for U.S. society (Lee and Bean 2007; 2004), what factors influence how Latinos racially self-identify? Although a number of studies have explored the determinants of Latinos' racial self identification, here I present a composite theoretical model of Latino racial identity formation that incorporates features of established theoretical frameworks to contribute to a better understanding of Latino racial choice.

RESEARCH ON LATINO RACIAL IDENTIFICATION

A small but influential body of research has explored the complexity of Latino racial formation and concludes that several factors influence identify formation. National origin is highly influential, given that racial identification is shaped by the way in which race is construed in one's home country. The Latino population is comprised of peoples from numerous Latin American countries, and in the U.S., persons of Mexican origin form the largest group, followed by Puerto Ricans and Cubans (Guzman 2001; Pew Hispanic Center 2009). Furthermore, each of these groups has a unique historical and contemporary experience in the U.S. which is likely to influence the construction of one's racial identity. For example, Mexicans historically have been a target of discrimination and disenfranchisement and have used political organizations to mobilize and politicize grievances (Antunes and Gaitz 1975; Marquez and Jennings 2000; McLemore and Romo 1985). Puerto Ricans, who, whether born on the mainland or in Puerto Rico, are U.S. citizens by birth, have also faced discrimination but have historically expressed grievances through local social movements and activism, both of which tend to mobilize those who externalize power imbalances between groups and blame institutional barriers for their status in society (Marquez and Jennings 2000). Dominicans, who largely arrived in the U.S. after 1965, fleeing political, social, and economic instability, also face discrimination and prejudice due to their skin color (Itzigsohn and Dore-Cabral 2000). In contrast, Cubans (largely composed of middle- and upper-class political and economic refugees and their descendents) are the most structurally incorporated group, having achieved the greatest level of political power (particularly in Dade County, Florida), and are more likely to perceive that they face little to no discrimination than any other group, due in large part to Cuban immigrants receiving government-sponsored economic support as well as federal encouragement to obtain citizenship (DeSipio and Henson 1997; McClain and Steward 1995). Whereas Mexicans and Puerto Ricans are more likely to racially self identify as other, Cubans are most likely to choose a White racial category (Frank et al. 2010; Michael and Timberlake 2008; Vaquera and Kao 2006).

Skin color is also strongly related to definitions of race (Hischman et al. 2000). As a common marker that is used as a signifier of racial identification, skin color has varying cultural meanings depending on context (Hall 1998). Many Latin American and Caribbean countries have racially mixed populations due in large part to a long history of interracial marriage between indigenous populations, slaves, and colonizers. Furthermore, phenotype is linked to social class, as social hierarchies are organized around class and skin color rather than racial ancestry (Bonilla-Silva 2002; Massey 2007), and the preferred status of mixed racial origins in these countries means that mestizos and mulattos are not relegated to the bottom in a hierarchical system of racial preference. Once in the U.S., immigrant populations can, to some degree, choose among different identities, given their perceptions of how Americans identify them. In their study of Puerto Ricans, Rodriguez and Cordero-Guzman (1992) find that participants who believed Americans viewed them as White were more likely to self-identify as White. Cognizant of how skin color signifies a racial identification, some Latinos can use phenotype for establishing difference from non-Whites in the identification process (Fergus 2004; see also Waters 1994), whereas immigrants of color may be more constrained in their choices. Phenotypic variation becomes even more salient if one perceives that certain racial identities are synonymous with greater access to tangible and intangible benefits. Extant research on the Mexican American community has found that darker-skinned Latinos are more likely to be of a lower social class, have lower earnings, and live in poorer communities (Relethford et al. 1983; Mason 2004). Lighter-skinned Mexicans have better life chances, fairing far better than their darker counterparts in terms of education, occupation, housing, income, and political and economic power (e.g. Hakken 1979; Arce et al. 1987; Telles and Murguía 1990; Yinger 1991; Murguía and Telles 1996; Zweigenhaft and Domhoff 1998; but see Bohara and Davila 1992). Similar disparities in occupational status due to skin color have also been found among Cubans (Espino and Franz 2002).

The highest share of Black Latinos is found among Dominicans and Puerto Ricans, whereas Mexicans, Cubans, and South Americans are more likely to identify as White or other race (Logan 2003: 4). Dark-skinned Latinos are more likely than light-skinned Latinos to reject standard racial categories and identify as some other race in an effort to specifically reject a Black identity (Landale and Oropesa 2002: 236), whereas Latinos with light skin are more likely to self-identify as White (e.g. Frank et al. 2010; Michael and Timberlake 2008). Substantial Afro-Latino populations are also found in Columbia, Costa Rica, Nicaragua, Panama, and Venezuela (in addition to Cuba), where Black inhabitants trace their origins to African slaves imported in the eighteenth century to work in the Caribbean plantation economy. Emotional ties to these countries of origin, in conjunction with their system of racial categorization, may also predict Latino racial identity (see Itzigsohn et al. 2005).

Other factors found to be associated with Latino racial choices include age, gender, and socioeconomic status. Past research has found that differences in life experiences influence racial identification (e.g. Korgen 1998; see also Campbell and Rogalin 2006), as older Latinos are more likely to self-identify as White (Rodriguez 2000; Tafoya 2004). Although some scholars have found few gender differences with regard to the general issue of racial classification (i.e. Rodriguez 2000), others have found a higher rate of minority group self identification among Latino males (Campbell and Rogalin 2006). Socioeconomic status, as measured by educational attainment and income, also affects individual racial self identification in that Latinos with higher incomes are more likely to self-identify as White (Rodriguez 1992; Gomez 1998; Logan 2003). The effect of education is less clear. Whereas some research suggests that more-educated Latinos may be more aware of the issues surrounding their status as minorities and therefore retain a salient minority identity (e.g. Campbell and Rogalin 2006; Jimenez 2008; Agius Vallejo and Lee 2009), other studies suggest that educational attainment leads to a decline in social distance from Whites. For minorities, increased racial contact with Whites provides opportunities for interracial interactions and the adoption of culturally dominant definitions of race. Thus, a likely consequence of high educational attainment for some Latinos is the adoption of a White identity, in part because their access to resources increases the belief that it is unnecessary to identify with and be attached to specific groups in society to attain access to the political system (Campbell and Rogalin 2006). Using data from a 2002 national survey of Latinos, Golash-Boza and Darity (2008) found that highly educated and well-off Latinos are more likely to self-identify as White, yet found no statistically significant relationship between these variables and racial self identification using data from a nationally represented survey conducted in 1989/1990. Recognizing that the 2002 data does not include a variable for phenotype, the authors suggest that the strong relationship between social class and skin color might explain the differences in their findings.

Discrimination is a common experience for many members of minority groups in the U.S. Latinos have been subject to a long history of exclusion and discriminatory practices and these discriminatory experiences have been found to lead to positive outcomes for racial and ethnic groups. Discrimination, as a dimension of group consciousness, has been show to motivate political participation (e.g. Wong 2003; Stokes 2003; de la Garza and Vaughn 1984) and encourage support for policies or candidates that are perceived to be good for the group (e.g. Uhlaner 1991; Dawson 1994). Experiences with discrimination can facilitate an emotional attachment to others, as being discriminated against may encourage individuals to ally themselves with others as a means to combat discrimination and gain political influence. Societal conditions also promote the adoption of minority racial identity over that of the dominant group (Whites), particularly when individuals are treated by others is if they belong to a particular minority group (e.g. Tajfel 1978). Because social conditions and discriminatory treatment have unintended consequences of hardening the boundaries of racial identity, Latinos who have higher perceptions of discrimination are more likely to assume a non-White racial identity (Golash-Boza and Darity 2008; Landale and Oropesa 2002). Perceptions of a shared fate or commonality are also credited for facilitating Latinos' collective action (e.g. Sanchez 2006) and are likely to influence group identification. Latinos who perceive they have more in common with and feel linked to specific non-Latino racial groups are more likely to prefer those racial labels (Nicholson et al. 2005).

Existing research suggests that, over time, Latino immigrants and their descendants begin to accept and assume American cultural practices as their familiarity with their cultural heritage weakens (e.g. Miller et al. 1984; Branton 2007). Yet the degree to which one has been assimilated culturally into society is likely to influence identification choices. In addition to feeling strongly connected to their home country, immigrants often live in segregated communities which provide social distance from other groups (Malone et al. 2003). Thus, past research has found that Latinos born outside of the U.S. are more likely to identify as other race (Tafoya 2004). Generational status is also predictive of Latino racial choices, as U.S born children of immigrants self report more often as White than their immigrant parents (Tafoya 2004; Vaquera and Kao 2006; Lansdale and Oropesa 2002). Language, as a measure of acculturation, may influence racial self identification to the extent that English proficiency and weaker attachment to Spanish reflect a greater degree of cultural assimilation. In her study of ethnic self identification, Garcia Bedolla (2003) argues that language is an important part of Latinos' understanding of that identity. The same may be true for racial identity. The traditional acculturation hypothesis suggests that as groups integrate into mainstream culture, they become White and lose their cultural heritage (e.g. Gordon 1964). Language is an important part of socialization and connection to the larger community but is often one of the first cultural attributes to be lost in assimilation. In light of this relationship, it is possible that Latinos who speak English are more likely to self-identify as White (e.g. Yancey 2003; Gomez 1998), whereas those who desire to preserve Spanish-speaking skills are less acculturated and therefore less likely to self-identify as White.

A preliminary review of the LNS and focus group data reveals that most of the aforementioned factors are strongly correlated with Latino racial identity choices. Crosstabulations of the racial identity choices and national origin show that respondents of Cuban descent are most likely to self-identify as White (45 percent).[1] Dominicans (77 percent) and Mexicans (76 percent) are most likely to self-identify as other race. Interestingly, the results also show that respondents with ties to countries with significant Afro-Latino populations are the next group most likely to self-identify as White (32 percent). Of the national origin subgroups, Dominicans are unique in that they are the least likely to self-identify as White (19 percent) and most likely to self-identify as Black, although the percentage is still quite small (3 percent). This last finding is not entirely surprising, given our knowledge that Afro-Latinos are more numerous among the Dominican national origin population (e.g. Logan 2003).

Phenotype is an important feature for marking members as belonging to a racial group, and has been shown to be a strong predictor of the life chances of Latinos (e.g. Montalvo and Codina 2001; Gomez 2000). The extent to which individual racial identity is influenced by skin color is rather interesting to assess from the data. Latinos are phenotypically diverse, generally tracing their heritage to Spanish, African, and indigenous peoples. As one might expect, respondents with very light skin color are most likely to identify as White (36 percent). Yet, even among these respondents, a majority (63 percent) self-identify as other race. Interestingly, as is the case in many Latin American countries, there is evidence to suggest that respondents may self-identify as "whiter" than their phenotype might suggest because of the social benefits Whiteness offers (Duany 1998; Jones-Correa 1998; Rodriguez 2000). Using the 1989–1990 Latino National Political Survey, Forman et al. (2002: 72–74) found that although many Latinos self-identified as White and few as Black, interviewers' assessments of the respondents' skin color identified many Mexican, Puerto Rican, and Cuban respondents as having a dark complexion. Here we see that respondents who see themselves as having very dark skin reject a Black identity, choosing instead to identify as other race (72 percent) or as White (25 percent).

Turning to other demographic factors, the results show that age and gender are significantly related to racial identity. Older Latinos, particularly those 60 and older, are more likely to self-identify as White, whereas Latinos between the ages of 18 and 59 are more likely to identify as other race. A similar but weaker effect is observed for Latino men and women. Latinas (27 percent) are somewhat more likely to self-identify as White than are Latino males (23 percent) but both groups overwhelmingly self-identify as other race (71 percent for Latinas versus 74 percent for Latino males). The relationship between gender and racial identity is much stronger when examining the frequency distributions that include the racialized other race identity (Latino). Whereas a majority of women self-identify with the remaining other race identities, Latinas are almost equally as likely to self-identify as White (47 percent) than choose this particular other race identity (49 percent).

Latino racial self identity is also strongly associated with standard measures of socioeconomic status. Respondents with higher levels of income and education are more likely to self-identify as White than are poorer and less educated respondents. Interestingly, Latinos who earn less than $15,000 and Latinos who make over $65,000 are the wage earning groups most likely to self-identify as White. There is also a slight rise in multiracial self identification among Latinos who earn between $55,000 and $64,999. Moreover, there is a rather large jump in White identification when one's education level moves from a four-year degree to a graduate/professional degree. Although a majority of respondents in these two categories still self-identify as other race, the percentage of respondents who self-identify as White increases by 10 percentage points. This finding in particular provides some support for social whitening arguments, which claim that social class plays a significant role in racial identification in Latin America (e.g. Nutini 1997; Whitten and Torres 1998).

To explore whether racial identity choices are significantly related to perceptions of commonality, linked fate, and discrimination, I operationalize perceptions of commonality using two distinct variables, one measuring socioeconomic commonality and another measuring political commonality. Respondents were asked, "Thinking about issues like job opportunities, educational attainment, or income, how much do Latinos/Hispanics have in common with other racial groups in the U.S. today?" Respondents were also asked, "Now I'd like you to think about the political situation of Latinos/Hispanics in society. Thinking about things like government services and employment, political power and representation, how much do Latinos/Hispanics have in common with other racial groups in the U.S. today?" Percentage distributions of these indicators across modes of racial identity show that when it comes to socioeconomic and political competition, respondents who perceive they have more in common with Whites are more likely to self-identify as White. However, in most cases, perceived commonality with African Americans does not greatly increase the likelihood of self-identifying as Black or choosing one of the other race categories. The only exception is the relationship between African American socioeconomic commonality and the racialized other race identity (Latino). As feelings of commonality move from nothing to a lot, the percentage of respondents who choose this other race identity increases by 12 percentage points, from 42 percent to 54 percent.

Commonality is also assessed using questions that ask whether Latinos share a similar fate with one another and with African Americans. The results show that although racial self identification choice may be significantly associated with measures of linked fate, the relationship between linked fate with Blacks and racial identity choice is rather weak. Respondents who believe that Latinos' ability to "do well" is somewhat dependent upon Blacks' ability to "do well" are somewhat more likely to self-identify as other race, but the relationship is not statistically significant. Interestingly, as a sense of linked fate with Blacks increases, so too does the likelihood of self-identifying as other race, reaching 75 percent for respondents who said "some." Yet the likelihood of other race identification drops slightly to 70 percent for respondents who said "a lot." This pattern is much stronger and more consistent when we turn to Latino linked fate. Believing that the ability of one's national origin group (i.e. Mexicans) to "do well" depends on how other Latinos are doing is significantly related to having a greater likelihood of self-identifying as other race. However, just as with Black linked fate, the likelihood of self-identifying as other race slightly decreases at the highest level of shared linked fate.

Discrimination is measured using three distinct questions. Respondents were asked, "In the following questions we are interested in your beliefs about the way other people have treated you in the U.S. Have you ever been 1) unfairly fired or denied a job or promotion? 2) unfairly treated by the police? 3) unfairly prevented from moving into a neighborhood (vecindario or barrio) because the landlord or a realtor refused to sell or rent you a house or apartment? 4) treated unfairly or badly at restaurants or stores?" Affirmative responses were coded 1 and added together to create a discrimination scale that ranges from 0 (respondent has no experience with discrimination) to 4 (respondent has experience discrimination in all four areas). As experience with discrimination increases, so too does other race identification. Similar to Bonilla-Silva and Embrick's (2006) finding of the positive correlation between experiences of discrimination and Black identity, here a higher number of personal experiences with discrimination increases Black self identification (from 1 percent to approximately 3 percent). This pattern also holds true for the racialized other identity; the likelihood of choosing this identity increases from 47 percent to 69 percent as the degree of discrimination increases. A similar pattern emerges for multiracial identification as the respondent's experiences with discrimination increase from 0 to 3; however, the likelihood of multiracial self identification drops significantly at the highest level of discriminatory experiences (4). Respondents were also asked why they think they were discriminated against.[2] Respondents who believe that being Latino or their skin color was the reason for their experience are most likely to self-identify as other race. Yet, being discriminated against because of skin color slightly increases the likelihood of self-identifying as Black and multiracial.

Acculturation and assimilation into the U.S. is assessed using generational status and language proficiency, both of which are considered to be standard indicators (e.g. Alba and Nee 2003). First-generation Latinos include Latinos born outside the U.S. or on the island of Puerto Rico. Second-generation Latinos are those born in the U.S. to at least one foreign-born parent, and third- or higher-generation Latinos are those born in the U.S. to U.S.-born parents. Because they are more assimilated, Latinos whose families have long been in the U.S. and who are English dominant may be more likely to take on a White identity. However, although racial self identification may be associated with generational status, the relationship is not very strong. Multiracial self identification increases slightly as one moves from the first to the second generation, yet most Latinos, regardless of generation, are more likely to self-identify as other race. A stronger effect is observed for the language variables. The desire to maintain Spanish is often perceived as a way of holding on to and maintaining one's culture (e.g. Oboler 1995). Respondents who believe it necessary to hold on to the ability to speak Spanish are much less likely to self-identify as White than those who do not believe it very important to maintain their Spanish-speaking skills. Yet, at the same time we see that respondents who preferred to be interviewed in English are somewhat less likely to self-identify as White. Further analysis shows that 74 percent of those who preferred to be interviewed in English are native-born Latinos ($p < .000$). This suggests that although most native-born Latinos do not see themselves as part of the dominant racial group, they recognize that mastering English is critical to moving up in a society that tends to hold negative images of Latinos, particularly immigrants (e.g. Garcia Bedolla 2005). Finally, it is interesting to note that the desire to hold on to Spanish language skills strongly increases the likelihood of adopting the racialized other race identity.

WHAT FACTORS PREDICT LATINO RACIAL IDENTITY?

Whereas bivariate statistics help to reveal systematic relationships between modes of racial self identity and a wide range of factors, multinomial logistic regression models allow researchers to explore whether these factors make a difference in predicting racial identity choices (Long and Freese 2001). In Table 3.1, each column reports the likelihood that respondents prefer one racial category (Black, multiracial, or some other race) to a White racial identity. Here we can see some general patterns. First, national origin and phenotype are predictive of Latinos' racial choices. Mexicans and Dominicans are less likely to self-identify as White, choosing instead to self-identify as other race, whereas Cubans are more likely to self-identify as White than as other race. Skin color is also predictive of Latino racial choices, as Latinos with lighter skin tones are consistently more likely to self-identify as White than Latinos of darker hues. Although they are not representative of the population, it is interesting to note that all of the light-skinned focus group respondents self-identified as other race. When asked how she is perceived by most people in the U.S., one participant said, "Often times I am considered as White because I'm light-skinned and other places people talk Spanish to me straight up because they think I understand Spanish and I don't. Whether they believe it or not everyone judges people by the color of their skin." This comment further highlights the dynamic relationship between external racial categorization and Latinos' racial self identification. Latinos' racial self identification is affected by their classification by outsiders (on the basis of skin color), and how Latinos are categorized in everyday interactions helps to determine whether they accept or reject American racial categories.

Other demographic factors are also significantly associated with Latino racial choices. Latinas are much more likely than Latino males to view themselves racially as White, choosing this identification over Black and other race. Older Latinos are also more likely to self-identify as White than as other race.

Turning to the next set of indicators, we see that Latinos with higher levels of education are more likely to self-identify as White than as other race, whereas Latinos with higher incomes are more likely to identify as White than as Black. I also find that although intergroup perceptions, linked fate, and experiences with discrimination are believed to influence racial choices, overall just a few of these measures are significantly associated with Latino racial identity. In each of the focus group sessions, participants were asked, "Thinking about issues like job opportunities, educational attainment or income, how much do Latinos/Hispanics have in common with other racial groups in the U.S. today?" [socioeconomic commonality]. The responses by participants generally ranged from perceived intergroup commonality to intensified competition. For instance, one woman (mixed Latino) in the first New York focus group commented that "with Blacks, without a doubt,

Table 3.1 Predictors of Latino Racial Identity

	Black	Multiracial	Some other race
Demographic Characteristics			
Mexican	-.48 (.42)	.08 (.33)	.19 (.09)*
Cuban	.24 (.63)	-.30 (.59)	-.58 (.17)***
Puerto Rican	-.28 (.83)	-.81 (.78)	-.10 (.18)
Dominican	1.02 (.70)	.00 (.78)	.82 (.21)***
Ties to Afro-Latino country	-.23 (.79)	.49 (.52)	-.29 (.18)
Skin color (dark to light)	-.25 (.16)*	-.23 (.12)*	-.26 (.04)***
Female	-.76 (.35)*	-.18 (.25)	-.19 (.07)**
Age	-.02 (.01)	-.00 (.01)	-.02 (.00)***
Socioeconomic Status			
Income	-.22 (.10)*	.09 (.07)	.00 (.02)
Education	-.04 (.10)	.11 (.08)	-.07 (.02)***
Commonality, Linked Fate, and Discrimination			
Socioeconomic commonality with Blacks	.02 (.19)	-.05 (.15)	.10 (.04)*
Socioeconomic commonality with Whites	-.11 (.20)	.02 (.16)	-.15 (.04)***
Political commonality with Blacks	.14 (.21)	.19 (.16)	.02 (.04)
Political commonality with Whites	-.04 (.22)	.18 (.17)	-.05 (.04)
Linked fate with Latinos	.24 (.20)	-.00 (.14)	.07 (.04)*
Linked fate with Blacks	.10 (.18)	.07 (.13)	.01 (.04)
Discrimination (scale)	.07 (.21)	.43 (.13)***	.06 (.05)
Discrimination b/c R is Latino	.67 (.55)	-1.06 (.56)*	.28 (.14)*
Discrimination b/c R's skin color	1.48 (.63)**	-.41 (.66)	.29 (.23)
Acculturation			
Generation	-.02 (.24)	-.04 (.19)	-.26 (.05)***
English interview	.71 (.45)	.21 (.33)	.67 (.10)***
Keep Spanish language	-.18 (.25)	.04 (.22)	.20 (.07)**
Constant	-1.27 (1.59)	-3.26 (1.26)**	2.35 (.37)***

N = 4509
Log Likelihood = 2872.88
Pseudo R^2 = .070

Note: Estimates are multinomial logit coefficients. Standard errors are in parentheses.
*Significant at p<.05, **Significant at p<.01, ***Significant at p<.001

we have a lot in common." A man in the second Chicago focus group commented that the "U.S. was made for White people, so if they're fine we are going to be fine, it's built like that." Two Mexican men at the third focus group in Chicago had the following exchange:

> Of us minorities who has the most opportunity? The Blacks—because they have more information and there is worse racism again us. If it comes to a choice between us and Blacks, it is going to Blacks . . .

> Also because of language. I have been working here for 25 years but when a job came up to advance a Black guy who had less skills and knowledge than me he got the job because of language.

In the first Chicago focus group, the moderator and a Puerto Rican woman had a similar exchange:

> No, no, there is a lot of discrimination. Two people go for an interview—one White and one Latino—and even though the Latino is better qualified, if you speak with an accent as a Latino the White person gets the job.
>
> *Moderator:* How about Blacks?
> No, they treat us the same as they treat the African Americans—maybe even worse.

One participant ultimately objected to the question, suggesting that a sense of commonality is not possible on a group level:

> I don't know. . . . I guess that's just more on a personal level because if you want to succeed you put your best effort into getting what you want. It's encouraging to see someone else do well but if you want something you do it for yourself, you don't do it or get something because a whole group is doing it. (Puerto Rican woman, second Chicago group)

The LNS data suggests that Latinos who perceive socioeconomic commonality with African Americans are more likely to self-identify as other race than as White, whereas perceived socioeconomic commonality with Whites is positively associated with choosing a White racial identity over other race identity. A sense of linked fate with other Latinos is positively associated with other race identification.

The racial identity adopted by Latinos also depends, in part, on Latinos' experiences with discrimination and perceptions of discriminatory experiences. Whereas previous studies suggest that experiencing discrimination is a significant predictor of choosing a Black, other, or racialized Latino racial identity (Golash-Boza and Darity 2008), the results here show that discrimination leads to the adoption of a multiracial identity. Yet, the perceived reason for that discrimination leads to a different racial choice. Latinos who believe that skin color was the reason for a discriminatory experience are more likely to self-identify as Black than as White.

Acculturation also has a discernible effect on Latino racial choice, as a White racial identity is positively associated with distance from the immigrant experience. Respondents who believe it important to maintain their Spanish-speaking skills are significantly more likely to self-identify as other race than as White. The same is true for respondents who preferred to be interviewed in English. This last finding in particular suggests that the traditional assimilation model (where language assimilation leads to White identity) does not accurately reflect the Latino experience.

Using predicted probabilities to explain the probability that an individual with a given characteristic will select one of the four race categories (with continuous variables set at their means and nominal variables set at their model category (Tomz et al. 2003)), we see that although it is often presumed that there is a preference for whiteness (.23), most Latinos will self-identify as other race when asked to choose the racial category on the U.S. Census that best describes them (.75). This was also evident in the focus groups. Several respondents in one of the Chicago focus groups met this question with laughter, one in particular noting "on some forms [like application forms] they don't have anything for Hispanics, so you have no other choice but to put "some other race." In the first New York focus groups, all of the participants immediately self-identified as other race to the surprise of the moderator.

All Participants: [unanimously] Other.
Moderator: All of you?
All Participants: [Resounding] Yes!
Puerto Rican Woman: They don't have Puerto Rican, they don't have Latin or Latino! It has to be other.

These respondents expressed the general feeling that Latinos do not see themselves as fitting neatly into existing racial categories. The probabilities also show that the likelihood of self-identifying as Black (.01) or multiracial (.01) is quite low for most Latinos. This low rate of Black identity reporting suggests that Latinos are not assimilating as racialized minorities who see themselves as akin to non-Hispanic Blacks.

Overall, the findings show that Latino racial identity is conditioned by invariable characteristics like national origin and phenotype and more mutable factors. The adoption of a Black racial identity is significantly associated with skin color, gender, income, and phenotype as the source of perceived discrimination. Phenotype and discrimination are significant predictors of multiracial identity, whereas national origin, phenotype, gender, age, education attainment, socioeconomic commonality with Whites and Blacks, discrimination and linked fate, and all three measures of acculturation are associated with other race identification. The findings also demonstrate that most Latinos self-identify as other race, not seeing themselves as White or Black. Yet, we still know very little about a sizeable number of Latinos who choose this identification. If all other race Latinos are not the same, what factors are driving the distinct modes of other race identification?

Table 3.2 examines the predictors of racial identification for Latinos who self-identify as other race. In the first column, the dependent variable is an ordinal variable where 0 represents respondents who self-identified as *some other race only*; 1 represents other race respondents who said Hispanic or Latino after their initial choice *but do not believe Latinos are a distinct racial group*; and 2 represents other race respondents who said Hispanic or Latino to clarify their initial choice *and* believe Latinos make up a distinct racial group in the U.S.[3] Using ordered probit regression (Greene 2003), the results show that Mexicans, elderly Latinos, and Latinos farthest away from the immigrant generation are significantly less likely to adopt a racialized other race identity that challenges existing racial boundaries. Conversely, having a high income and feeling a sense of socioeconomic commonality with African Americans predict a willingness to assert a racialized panethnic identity.

The remaining columns in Table 3.2 also examine the predictors of racial identification for Latinos who self-identify as other race, exploring the likelihood that respondents will choose a specific other race identity (the general other race, SOR_Latino, or Latino). As discussed in Chapter Two, conceptually these categories represent a point on a continuum of racialized Latino identity. Whereas some other race is a general and broad category, the second category represents the expression of Latino panethnic identity, and the third represents a *racialized* conceptualization of Latino identity. Thus, the third category signals an increasing awareness *and* acceptance of these panethnic terms as a racialized identity. Each column represents a multinomial regression model where the other included categories are Black and multiracial and the reference category is White. Because all three categories share a primary racial identification, it is not possible to compare the relationships between all of these variables and independent variables in the same model. Therefore, I estimate regression models that compare a specific other race identification with other race variables.

Ultimately the results reveal fairly consistent predictors across each category. For example, Dominicans consistently are less likely to self-identify as White, whereas Cubans, lighter-skinned Latinos, women, and older Latinos are more likely to self-identify as White. Each measure of acculturation/ assimilation remains strongly predictive of racial identity. Socioeconomic commonality with Blacks, a sense of linked fate with other Latinos, and experiencing discrimination due to being Latino also consistently predict

Table 3.2 Predictors of Other Race Identity

	SOR (Scale)	SOR	SOR_Latino	Latino
Demographic Characteristics				
Mexican	-10 (.05)*	.19 (.09)*	.15 (.10)	.12 (.11)
Cuban	-.17 (.12)	-.58 (.17)***	-.62 (.18)***	-.90 (.22)***
Puerto Rican	-.17 (.11)	-.10 (.18)	-.17 (.19)	-.15 (.22)
Dominican	.08 (.10)	.82 (.21)***	.83 (.22)***	1.08 (.24)***
Ties to Afro-Latino country	.06 (.11)	-.29 (.18)	-.25 (.19)	-.37 (.22)*
Skin color (dark to light)	.02 (.01)	-.26 (.04)***	-.26 (.04)***	-.21 (.04)***
Female	.06 (.04)	-.19 (.07)**	-.14 (.08)*	-.16 (.09)*
Age	-.00 (.01)*	-.02 (.00)***	-.02 (.00)***	-.02 (.00)***
Socioeconomic Status				
Income	.03* (.01)	.00 (.02)	.00 (.02)	.02 (.03)
Education	.02 (.01)	-.07 (.02)***	-.07 (.02)***	-.04 (.03)
Commonality, Linked Fate, and Discrimination				
Socioeconomic commonality with Blacks	.04 (.02)*	.10 (.04)**	.11 (.04)**	.15 (.05)***
Socioeconomic commonality with Whites	-.02 (.03)	-.15 (.04)***	-.15 (.05)***	-.19 (.05)***
Political commonality with Blacks	.02 (.03)	.02 (.04)	.03 (.04)	.04 (.05)
Political commonality with Whites	-.03 (.04)	-.05 (.04)	-.05 (.04)	-.07 (.05)
Linked fate with Latinos	.00 (.02)	.07 (.04)*	.07 (.04)*	.09 (.05)*
Linked fate with Blacks	-.02 (.03)	.01 (.04)	-.01 (.04)	-.02 (.04)
Discrimination (scale)	-.00 (.03)	.06 (.05)	.03 (.05)	.10 (.06)*
Discrimination b/c R is Latino	.10 (.07)	.28 (.14)*	.29 (.14)*	.39 (.16)**
Discrimination b/c R's skin color	.09 (.11)	.29 (.23)	.35 (.24)	.41 (.25)*
Acculturation				
Generation	-.06 (.03)*	-.26 (.05)***	-.30 (.05)***	-.32 (.06)***
English interview	-.04 (.05)	.67 (.10)***	.39 (.10)***	.99 (.11)***
Keep Spanish language	.03 (.04)	.20 (.07)**	.21 (.07)**	.24 (.08)***
Constant/Cut 1	-.68 (.22)	2.35 (.37)***	2.30 (.39)	.84 (.44)*
Cut 2	.25 (.22)	-	-	-
N	3264	4509	3765	2645
Log Likelihood	-3458.38	-2872.88	-2618.14	-2043.50
Pseudo R2	.01	.07	.07	.10

Note: Estimates are OLS and multinomial logit coefficients. Standard errors are in parentheses.
*Significant at p<.05, **Significant at p<.01, ***Significant at p<.001

the rejection of a White identity, whereas perceived socioeconomic commonality with Whites consistently predicts the adoption of a White identity. There are, however, some important differences between the other race groups. Mexicans are more likely to self-identify as some other race, yet this predictor becomes insignificant in other models. Similarly, Latinos who experience greater instances of discrimination and Latinos who believe they face discrimination because of their skin color are more likely to adopt a racialized other race identity. Interestingly, whereas education is statistically significant in the first two models, education is no longer a significant predictor of the adoption of a White identity over a racialized other race identity. Having ancestral ties to a country with a significant Afro-Latino population also appears to affect racial choice, increasingly the likelihood of adopting a White identity over a racialized other race identity. Yet, this variable is statistically insignificant in other models.

Once again, predicted probabilities provide some real insight into the differences among these groups. The probability of self-identifying broadly as some other race is .75, which suggests that most Latinos prefer this race category. However, the likelihood of self-identifying as other race decreases as the category itself becomes more racialized. Although there is a small decline in the likelihood of adopting other race identity as one moves from the general identifier to the panethnic identifier (SOR_Latino = .69), the predicted probability of adopting the racialized other identity drops to .54. Thus, although the data in many ways suggests that most Latinos do not see themselves as White or Black, only a small majority of these respondents see themselves as a separate, distinctive race group.

NATIVITY AND LATINO RACIAL IDENTITY

The Latino population in the U.S. contains two main groups: immigrants (non-naturalized and naturalized) and the native born. Of the 9,834 respondents, 65 percent are foreign born. This degree of diversity in terms of nativity, in addition to the sheer size of the immigrant segment of this population, suggests that immigrants may possess a different set of orientations and reactions to the same situation and context than their U.S.-born counterparts. In an effort to better identify which factors influence Latino racial identification for both foreign- and native-born Latinos, Table 3.3 explores predictors of racial identity separately for U.S.-born and immigrant respondents. In addition to the independent variables used in previous tables, two additional control variables are included in the immigrant model: a variable measuring whether the respondent is a naturalized American citizen (coded 1 if yes, 0 if no) and a variable measuring demographic acculturation, specifically how long the respondent has been in the U.S. (Rodriguez 2000). More time in the U.S. provides more time for adaptation to U.S. culture and norms, making immigrants appear to others more "Americanized." Among immigrant respondents, Black and multiracial identification drops significantly—less than 1 percent of immigrants self-identify as Black (.05) or multiracial (.03). Therefore, the dependent variable used in this section is dichotomous where other race is coded 1, White is the base (and coded 0), and the models are estimated using logistic regression (Aldrich and Nelson 1984).

The first set of columns in the table present the odds of self-identifying as other race or White for U.S. and foreign-born respondents. Among the U.S.-born, being Cuban, older, female, having a lighter skin tone, higher levels of education, and stronger perceptions of both political and socioeconomic commonality with Whites is positively associated with adopting a White racial identity. Mexicans, Latinos who believe they were discriminated against because of their skin color, Latinos who feel a sense of linked fate with Blacks, English speakers, and Latinos who believe it is important to maintain Spanish-speaking skills are all more likely to self-identify as other race. Demographic characteristics, perceptions of commonality, discrimination, and acculturation are also significant predictors of racial choices for immigrant respondents. Immigrants from Cuba and other countries with substantial Afro-Latino populations, older immigrants, female immigrants, immigrants with lighter skin, those with higher levels of education, and Latino immigrants who feel socioeconomic commonality with Whites are significantly more likely to self-identify as White, whereas being Dominican, feeling a sense of socioeconomic commonality with African Americans, and being discriminated against for being Latino is positively related to self-identifying as other race. Also of interest is the variable measuring the language of the interview—it is a common predictor for both U.S.-born and immigrant respondents. That English-language dominant immigrants and native-born Latinos are more likely to self-identify as other race than as White indeed challenges assimilationist assumptions that the adoption of language leads to integration into the dominant group.

In addition to showing clear differences in racial identity formation for U.S.-born and immigrant Latinos, the set of significant variables predicting the adoption of these identities, although fairly consistent, does show some variation in the factors that predict other race identities. For example, among those who are foreign born, being female is positively associated with self-identifying as White than as other race but is a statistically insignificant predictor of racial identity in the other models. Similarly, among respondents born in the U.S., linked fate with Blacks is a significant predictor of a general other race identity only. Among foreign-born Latinos, identification with the most racialized other race identity is positively associated with a higher number of discriminatory experiences, being Dominican, the perception that discrimination occurred because the respondent is Latino, a desire to maintain Spanish, and perceived commonality with African Americans. When given the choice between this identity and a White identity, Mexican, Cuban, and immigrants from other countries

Table 3.3 Predictors of Other Race/White Identity by Nativity

	Some other race		SOR_Latino		Latino	
	U.S. born	Immigrant	U.S. born	Immigrant	U.S. born	Immigrant
Demographic Characteristics						
Mexican	.38 (.15)**	.02 (.11)	.47 (.16)**	-.08 (.11)	.48 (.17)**	-.12 (.13)
Cuban	-.72 (.31)**	-.68(.18)***	-.62 (.34)*	-.72(.19)***	-.56 (.35)	-.93(.24)***
Puerto Rican	.22 (.16)	-	.27 (.18)	-	.25 (.19)	-
Dominican	.09 (.45)	.87 (.23)***	.20 (.46)	-.83(.24)***	.15 (.49)	1.09(.26)***
Ties to Afro-Latino country	.23 (.59)	-.44 (.19)**	.16 (.63)	-.41 (.19)*	.30 (.65)	-.52(.22)*
Skin color (dark to light)	-.18 (.05)***	-.29(.04)***	-.16 (.06)**	-.29(.04)***	-.12 (.06)*	.25(.05)***
Female	-.18 (.11)*	-.17 (.09)*	-.17 (.12)	-.10 (.09)	-.14 (.13)	-.14 (.11)
Age	-.02 (.00)***	-.02(.00)***	-.02 (.00)***	-.02(.00)***	-.02(.00)***	-.02 (.00)***
Naturalized citizen	-	.10 (.11)	-	.10 (.11)	-	.07(.13)
Time in U.S.	-	.01 (.00)	-	-.01 (.00)	-	.00 (.01)
Socioeconomic Status						
Income	-.01 (.03)	-.00 (.03)	-.00 (.03)	.00 (.03)	.02 (.03)	.03(.04)
Education	-.15 (.04)***	-.04 (.02)*	-.13 (.02)***	-.05 (.03)*	-.09 (.04)*	-.02 (.04)

(continued)

Commonality/Linked Fate/ Discrimination					
SES commonality with Blacks	.06 (.07)	.12 (.04)*	.11 (.07)	.12 (.05)*	.13 (.08)*	.17 (.05)**
SES commonality with Whites	-.16 (.07)*	-.12 (.05)*	-.19 (.08)*	-.11 (.05)*	-.27 (.08)***	-.14 (.06)**
Political commonality with Blacks	.07 (.08)	.01 (.05)	.07 (.08)	.03 (.05)	.05 (.08)	.06 (.07)
Political commonality with Whites	-.12 (.07)*	-.08 (.05)	-.12 (.09)	-.09 (.06)*	-.10 (.08)	-.12 (.06)*
Linked fate with Latinos	.04 (.06)	.03 (.05)	.04 (.06)	.04 (.05)	.09 (.07)	.05 (.06)
Linked fate with Blacks	.09 (.06)*	-.00 (.04)	.08 (.06)	-.02 (.05)	.05 (.06)	-.03 (.05)
Discrimination (scale)	.03 (.06)	.06 (.07)	-.03 (.07)	.05 (.07)	.65 (.28)**	.18 (.07)*
Discrimination b/c R is Latino	.13 (.18)	.34 (.18)	.15 (.19)	.34 (.18)*	.23 (.20)	.46 (.20)**
Discrimination b/c R's skin color	.46 (.26)*	.21 (.34)	.49 (.27)*	.16 (.34)	.65 (.28)**	.19 (.39)
Acculturation						
English interview	.82 (.15)***	.52 (.13)***	.52 (.15)***	.26 (.14)*	.93 (.17)***	.82 (.15)***
Keep Spanish language	.28 (.08)***	.12 (.10)	.29 (.09)***	.14 (.11)	.29 (.09)***	.22 (.13)*
Constant	1.41 (.51)**	2.34 (.55)***	1.11 (.55)*	2.27 (.58)***	.10 (.59)	.63 (.69)
N	2069	3123	1570	2677	1325	1709
Log Likelihood	-1043.17	-1661.60	-898.135	-1527.13	-783.75	-1068.60
Pseudo R2	.08	.07	.08	.07	.10	.09

Note: Estimates are logistic coefficients. Standard errors are in parentheses.
*Significant at p<.05, **Significant at p<.01, ***Significant at p<.001

with substantial Afro-Latino populations, older immigrants, immigrants with lighter skin, and immigrants who feel political and socioeconomic commonality with Whites are more likely to self-identify as White.

CONCLUSION

Having explored the foundations of Latino racial identity, this chapter shows that Latinos choose to identify with particular race categories for both institutional and more personal social-psychological reasons. For example, the varied impact of educational attainment on the likelihood of adopting a White identity challenges the conventional whitening hypothesis. Highly educated respondents are more likely to self-identify as White than to adopt a general or panethnic other race identity. Yet the education variable is statistically insignificant in the model predicting the adoption of a racialized other race identity (Latino). Although not conclusive, this change in impact supports extant research that suggests that education can promote a racialized minority identity because well-educated minorities are more aware of the differences and realities in American society than are their less-educated counterparts (Portes 1984).

Latinos' experiences with discrimination have been shown to affect their racial choices (e.g. Golash-Boza and Darity 2008). Yet the results presented here provide a more nuanced understanding of how those experiences influence identity. Whereas the number of discriminatory experiences increases the likelihood that Latinos will self-identify as multiracial, phenotype as the perceived reason for discriminatory experiences increases the likelihood that Latinos will self-identify as Black. This perceived source of discrimination is also a significant predictor of a racialized other race identity. Latinos who perceived that being Latino is the reason for a discriminatory experience are more likely to self-identify as White than as multiracial, but are more likely to self-identify as some other race than as White. Thus, the inclusion of variables measuring perceived sources of discrimination further demonstrates the substantive impact of phenotype on racial identity choices.

This research also suggests that phenotype still matters for Latinos, shaping how they racially identify and view the world (e.g. Bailey 2001; Hall 1994; Arce et al. 1987; Golash-Boza and Darity 2008). Phenotype consistently predicts racial choices, as Latinos with lighter skin are consistently more likely to self-identify as White than Latinos of darker hues.[4] Yet another interesting contribution to the research on Latino racial identity rests in the gender differences found in the data. Latinas are more likely to self-identify as White than as Black or other race compared to their male counterparts. If beauty is a form of human capital that can enhance social relationships, then this finding might signal the enduring valorization of whiteness among Latinas as the marker of ideal beauty, and more broadly social success.

The Foundations of Latino Racial Identity 49

Overall, the findings show that in many respects Latinos conceptualize their identities in a much more complex way than the standard White-Black metric. The modal category of racial self identification is other race, yet what we see here is that all other race Latinos are not the same. Some choose this category to express panethnic identity. For others, choosing to self-identify as other race expresses a clear racialized identity. It is also important to note that a small but growing percentage of Latinos are choosing to self-identify as multiracial, a category of identity that denotes racial mixture *and* can be used to create distance from Blackness. This is yet additional evidence that many Latinos do not see themselves as either Black or White.

The growing presence of Latinos in the U.S. raises questions about whether this group can change the face of American politics. The degree to which Latinos can change the political landscape will be shaped in substantial measure by the degree to which Latinos become active in the political process, expressing clear policy positions and engaging in electoral activities—all of which is in itself strongly linked to group identity and consciousness (e.g. Stokes 2003; Stokes-Brown 2006; Sanchez 2006; Valdez 2011). If race, as a component of Latino identity, is politically significant, then efforts to understand Latino political behavior must place greater emphasis on the usefulness of this dimension of identity and its capacity to mobilize and facilitate political engagement. The next section of the book explores the role of racial identity for Latino politics, focusing on a wide range of political attitudes and behaviors. Chapter Four examines how racial self identifications affect orientations toward the political system. Chapter Five examines the link between Latino racial identity and partisanship. Chapter Six assess the extent to which racial identity influences political participation, and Chapter Seven examines the implications of Latino racial identity for public opinion. By assigning meaning and value to group membership, race shapes the distribution of resources that are central to achieve political power. Collectively, these chapters provide a better understanding of the degree to which Latino racial identity matters for Latino political incorporation.

4 Explaining Latino Political Orientations
The Role of Racial Identity

The linkage among race and political orientations has been a growing area of research as scholars examine differences in Americans' political orientations. Much discourse has focused on particular attitudes, including interest, trust, and efficacy. For example, we know that individuals who are interested in politics are more likely to be politically active (Campbell et al. 1960; Verba et al. 1995). Political trust is linked to political behavior in that high political trust often results in higher levels of political participation (Almond and Verba 1963; Stokes 1962). Efficacy is also a strong predictor of participation, as people who feel politically efficacious are more likely to pay attention to campaigns and elections, discuss politics, and vote (e.g. Abramson 1983; Abramson and Aldrich 1982; Campbell et al. 1960). Thus, it is clear that these types of attitudes reflect greater attachment to and interest in the U.S. political system, making them pivotal resources for political participation.

Several studies emphasizing the racial group differences between White and African Americans have found that African Americans are less likely than Whites to express trust and confidence in the government, particularly when it concerns government efforts toward achieving racial equality (Aberbach and Walker 1970; Abramson 1977, 1983). African Americans also tend to have lower levels of external efficacy than Whites because they have less political power (Bobo and Gilliam 1990). In an effort to expand our understanding of political orientations, research moving beyond the White-Black color line has found that Latinos tend to pay less attention to politics and have lower levels of internal efficacy (Jackson 2009) but are generally more trusting of the government than are Whites and African Americans (Abrajano and Alvarez 2007; Abrajano and Alvarez 2010; Jackson 2009).[1] However, as they become more acculturated, Latinos develop more pessimistic views of the government and society, becoming less trusting of government (Michelson 2001, 2003). Latinos are also more externally efficacious than Whites (Jackson 2009).

The goal of this chapter is to expand our understanding of Latinos' psychological connectedness to the American political system using the lens of race. Here I explore the role that race plays in Latino political attitudes and beliefs, arguing that the social implications attached to racial identity can foster distinct political attitudes and beliefs among Latino racial groups.

RESEARCH ON LATINO POLITICAL INTEREST, EFFICACY, AND TRUST

Political orientations measure citizens' subjective feelings about the political system: whether they know and care about politics, whether they desire to participate in politics, and whether they feel capable of affecting change in the political system (Burns et al. 2001). Political interest is a standard measure of psychological engagement in politics. Individuals who are interested in politics are more inclined to follow the news and discuss politics, which increases their knowledge about political affairs and their ability to understand political information (Neuman 1986; Nicholson et al. 2005). The literature on political engagement also addresses the extent to which actors express optimism about politics. Political efficacy is "the feeling that political and social change is possible, and that the individual citizen can play a part in bringing about this change" (Campbell et al. 1954: 187). Political efficacy is widely regarded as having two distinct dimensions: a personal sense of efficacy characterized by beliefs about one's perceived ability to effectively participate in politics (internal efficacy) and a system-oriented sense of efficacy characterized by one's beliefs about the responsiveness of the government to citizen demands (external efficacy) (Converse 1972; Craig et al. 1990; Lane 1959; Niemi et al. 1991). Also occupying a central position in democratic theory, political trust serves as a measurement of the government's ability to respond to people's normative expectations (Aberbach and Walker 1970; Hetherington 1998). The general decline in the level of trust Americans have in their local and national governments has several noted consequences, including a decline in perceived government effectiveness and support for government policies, and a decline individual political behaviors such as electoral participation (e.g. Michelson 2001; Hetherington 1998; Shingles 1981).

Although we know comparatively little about Latinos' political orientations to the American political system, several studies provide some insight into Latino political attitudes and beliefs. Using data from the 1999 Washington Post/Henry J. Kaiser Family Foundation/Harvard University National Survey on Latinos in America, Jackson (2009) finds that compared to Whites, Latinos have lower levels of political interest and lower levels of internal efficacy but are more externally efficacious. Michelson's (2000) study of Chicago Latinos finds lower feelings of internal political efficacy but higher levels of external efficacy among these Latinos. Focus group respondents most often expressed low levels of internal and external efficacy when asked to talk more broadly about political participation. For example:

No I don't vote because they don't identify with us so how are we suppose to identify with them? They don't make you feel part of the system so how can you identify with the political system? That is why I participate as little as possible. (Mexican woman, third Chicago group)

We don't make decisions—that's for the higher ups. What I say or do doesn't make a difference (Mixed Latino man, first New York group)

Higher levels of interest have been found to be associated with increased political participation among Mexicans (Leighley and Vedlitz 1999), Latino citizens in California, Florida, and Texas (Shaw et al. 2000), and Latinos in New York City (Hritzuk and Park 2000). Although Latinos are generally more trusting of government than other racial groups (e.g. Abrajano and Alvarez 2007; Jackson 2009), there are significant differences in political trust within the Latino population. Mexican American citizens and Puerto Ricans born in the U.S. are less trusting of government than Mexican noncitizens and Puerto Ricans born on the island of Puerto Rico (Michelson 2001). Cubans tend to be more trusting than Puerto Ricans and Mexicans tend to be less trusting than Puerto Ricans (Abrajano and Alvarez 2010). Immigrants who have not fully assimilated into American society tend to be more trusting of government than those who are more assimilated (Michelson 2001, 2003). Similarly, U.S.-born Latinos are less trusting of the government than naturalized Latinos (Hajnal and Baldassare 2001).

From a theoretical and practical standpoint, advancing our understanding of Latino political orientations is critical. It is well established that the development of a stable and effective democracy depends upon the orientations that people have to the democratic process (Almond and Verba 1963: 366). Thus, individuals' psychological attachment to government is often used as a measure of the health and vitality of society. The sheer size and growth of the Latino population in the U.S. suggests that greater knowledge of Latinos' political attitudes is necessary for a broader understanding of American political attitudes. Furthermore, given the link between psychological political connectedness and political participation, greater knowledge of Latinos' political attitudes may also help us better understand the conditions under which Latinos, who are now a sleeping giant in American politics, might be awakened to realize their full political strength. To the degree that racial group membership plays a role in Latinos' political socialization, racial identity may help shape Latinos' political beliefs, attitudes, and values. Thus, understanding how racial identity impacts political orientations could potentially be a missing piece of the puzzle that helps Latinos fully integrate into the U.S political system.

RACE AND LATINO POLITICAL ORIENTATIONS

A preliminary review of the data shows that Latino political orientations vary by racial identity. Respondents were asked, "How interested are you in politics and public affairs? Would you say you are very interested, somewhat interested, or not at all interested?" The question was coded to create a three-point scale ranging from not interested to very interested. Although Latinos from each racial group are most likely to be somewhat interested in politics, multiracial Latinos are most likely to be very interested in politics (32 percent), followed by Black Latinos (31 percent), White Latinos (25 percent), and other race Latinos (21 percent). Among other race Latinos, interest in politics increases slightly as other race identity becomes more defined. Whereas 21 percent of all other race Latinos are very interested in politics, 22 percent of other race Latinos who self-identify as Latino/Hispanic and 25 percent of other race Latinos who self-identify as Latino/Hispanic and believe Latinos are a distinct racial group express a strong interest in politics.

A total of three questions are used to measure political efficacy. The first two questions capture respondents' feelings of internal efficacy, measuring whether respondents agree strongly, agree somewhat, disagree somewhat, or disagree strongly with the statements "Sometimes politics and government seem so complicated that a person like me can't really understand what's going on" and "People like me don't have any say in what the government does." The last efficacy question measures whether respondents agree strongly, agree somewhat, disagree somewhat, or disagree strongly with the statement "People are better off avoiding contact with government." For all three questions, affirmative responses indicate lower levels of efficacy and dissenting responses indicate higher levels of efficacy. Crosstabulations reveal significant racial differences in internal and external efficacy. Black Latinos are the least efficacious, with 40 percent strongly believing that politics and government seem so complicated that they cannot really understand what's going on. Multiracial Latinos are most likely to strongly disagree with this statement (22 percent), followed by 21 percent of White Latinos, 20 percent of Black Latinos, and 19 percent of other race Latinos. Black Latinos are also most likely to believe that they have no say in what the government does. Whereas 46 percent of Black Latinos hold this opinion, only 34 percent of other race Latinos, 32 percent of White Latinos, and 25 percent of multiracial Latinos express this view. There is much less variation among respondents from different racial groups who feel most efficacious. Twenty-two percent of multiracial Latinos, 23 percent of White Latinos, and 24 percent of Black and other race Latinos strongly believe that they have a say in what the government does. Turning to the measure of external efficacy, crosstabulations show that almost half of all respondents in each group strongly disagree that people are better off avoiding the government. Multiracial Latinos are most efficacious (53 percent), followed by White Latinos (46 percent), other race Latinos (43 percent), and Black Latinos (41 percent). Conversely, Black (19 percent) and other race Latinos (18 percent) are more likely to agree with this statement than are White (15 percent) and multiracial Latinos (13 percent).

Turning to political trust, most of the focus group participants express extreme distrust of government and of politicians in particular. Many of the participants emphasized politicians' failure to follow through on promises and their disappointment with Latino politicians in particular:

> Our politicians have good intentions when they start; like the alderman in this neighborhood, they promise you everything but then where are they? Only when they need a vote. They only promise and no action. (Mexican man, third Chicago group)

> For me, it is important that they tell us the truth; that they not lie to us; that they not try to fool us. . . . They forget what their promises are and it is a lot of promises and no action. (Peruvian woman, first Chicago group)

> Politicians are so busy looking out for themselves that the ones on the bottom are getting crushed—the rest of us get nothing—and they give us a bad name. Last Sunday I went to the Bronx Pride in Katonah and they had tables up with signs asking to throw [Pedro] Espada [former state senator and majority leader] out, to vote him out. He cannot control his temper, so he gives us a bad name. (Puerto Rican woman, first New York group)

Two questions in the LNS data are used to measure political trust. Respondents were asked whether they agree strongly, agree somewhat, disagree somewhat, or disagree strongly with the statement "Government is pretty much run by just a few big interests looking out for themselves, and not for the benefit of all the people" (e.g. Michelson 2001). They were also asked how often they trust the government in Washington to do what is right: never, only some of the time, most of the time, or just about always. Both questions are ordered so that levels of trust rank from low to high. Whereas more than half (56 percent) of multiracial Latinos and approximately half of White and other race Latinos report trusting the government in Washington to do what is right some of the time, approximately a third of Black Latinos express this degree of trust. Black Latinos (37 percent) are much more likely than other racial groups (20 percent White Latinos; 19 percent other race Latinos; 14 percent multiracial Latinos) to never trust government to do what is right. Similarly, Black Latinos are also much more likely to believe that government is run by a few big interests. Sixty percent of Black Latinos hold this position, compared to 43 percent of White Latinos, 42 percent of other race Latinos, and 33 percent of multiracial Latinos. Of the respondents who strongly disagree with this statement, 15 percent of White, other race, and multiracial Latinos are most efficacious, compared to 12 percent of Black Latinos. There are also gaps in trust among other race Latinos. Those who adopt a racialized other identity are least trusting, with 45 percent believing that government is run by a few self-interested groups, as compared to 43 percent of those who adopt a panethnic other race identity.

In sum, the bivariate descriptive results suggest that racial identity influences Latino political orientations. Multiracial identity is positively associated with interest in politics and political efficacy, whereas Black identity is associated with lower levels of trust. Black and other race Latinos also tend to be less efficacious. Yet, although race appears to explain variation in Latinos' beliefs and views about government, additional theoretical approaches also inform our understanding of these attitudes. The remainder of the chapter is dedicated to developing and testing multivariate regression models to predict the development of Latino political attitudes, controlling for the effects of theoretically relevant variables that are expected to influence Latino psychological orientations.

Nationality, Phenotype, and Other Demographic Factors

People tend to learn basic political beliefs and values from various agents of socialization. Membership in a particular group can give people an important experience and perspective that shapes their view of political life. Although some research suggests that national origin identifications have little influence on some political orientations (Schildkraut 2005), other studies have found great diversity in Latino political beliefs (e.g. Abrajano and Alverez 2010; Jackson 2009). Thus, we might expect to significant differences in political attitudes among various Latino national origin groups.

Skin color has a direct and immediate effect on individuals, shaping their material well-being and social perceptions, and therefore may influence political orientations. Gender is yet another important social category that can be an important source of divergent political orientations. Extant research shows that Latinas and Latino males of Mexican descent differ significantly in their trust of the government (Michelson 2001), as Latinas are less trusting. However, older Mexicans tend to be more trusting of government to do the right thing. I expect to find, as suggested by extant research, that these factors also have an effect on political orientations.

Socioeconomic Status

Socialization theory also identifies schools as a major agent of socialization and thus a potential source of differences in political orientations. In addition to having their attitudes and beliefs shaped by the academic curriculum, those who attend college are often exposed to attitudes transmitted by faculty and other students, and as a result, hold fundamentally different views than those with lower levels of education. Research suggests that trust is highest for those in professional occupations and higher income groups (e.g. Alesina and La Ferrara 2002); therefore those with higher levels of socioeconomic resources might be expected to adopt psychological orientations that ultimately motivate their participation in the political system (Verba and Nie 1972).

Discrimination, Linked Fate, and Commonality

Perceptions of commonality and linked fate suggest that individuals can infer self interests from group interests more generally (e.g. Dawson 1994). The greater the extent to which Latinos see their economic and political opportunities tied to other groups, the more likely they are to adopt the attitudes and beliefs of those groups. Experience with discrimination may also affect Latinos' political attitudes and beliefs, causing them to feel less trusting and efficacious (e.g. Garcia Bedolla 2005; Michelson 2001, 2003; Portes and Rumbaut 1996). Thus, those who report being discriminated against repeatedly and report being discriminated against because of their ethnicity or skin color might be less efficacious and trusting than those who report no experiences of discrimination.

Acculturation/Assimilation

The degree to which one has fully assimilated into American society and the American political system may also influence political orientations. Language proficiency, as a measure of cultural adaptation or integration, has been linked to political trust, as English-dominant Latinos are less politically trusting than Spanish-dominant Latinos (Abrajano and Alvarez 2010; but see Jackson 2009). Language proficiency may also influence other political attitudes (e.g. Jackson 2009). Similarly, generational status is predictive of political orientations, as trust in government declines with one's generational status (Garcia Bedolla 2005). Significant difference in trust has been found between first-generation Latinos (who are much more trusting of the government) and later-generation Latinos (Abrajano and Alverez 2010). Among the Mexican population, later-generation Latinos are also more likely than first- and second-generation Latinos to hold pessimistic views about the political system (Garcia Bedolla 1999). Therefore, these measures are likely to be negatively associated with efficacy and trust but positively associated with political interest. One might expect Latinos' interest in politics to grow as they become more acculturated into and more experienced with American culture.

WHAT FACTORS PREDICT LATINO POLITICAL ORIENTATIONS?

The results presented in Table 4.1 from ordered probit regression models of political interest, political efficacy, and political trust show that racial

Table 4.1 Latino Racial Identity and Political Orientations

	Political Interest	Politics Complicated	No Say	Contact w/ Gov	Big Interests	Trust Gov.
Demographic Characteristics						
Black	-.22 (.19)	-.11(.18)	-.30 (.19)*	-.32(.18)*	-.27 (.19)*	-.30(.18)*
Multiracial	.31 (.15)*	.04 (.13)	.17 (.14)	.06(.15)	.38 (.14)**	.14 (.13)
Some other race	.01 (.04)	-.02 (.04)	-.00 (.04)	-.08 (.04)*	-.02 (.04)	-.03 (.04)
Mexican	.10 (.05)*	-.08 (.04)*	.00 (.04)	.00 (.04)	.00 (.04)	.08 (.04)*
Cuban	.14 (.09)*	.00 (.08)	-.02 (.04)	.09 (.08)	-.05 (.09)	.01 (.08)
Puerto Rican	.13 (.09)	-.10 (.08)	-.10(.09)	-.00(.09)	-.14 (.09)	-.00 (.08)
Dominican	.10 (.09)	-.14 (.09)	-.14 (.09)	-.08 (.09)	-.15 (.09)	.05 (.08)
Ties to Afro-Latino country	-.04 (.09)	-.01 (.02)	-.01 (.09)	.14 (.09)	.04 (.09)	.07 (.08)
Skin color (dark to light)	.01 (.02)	-.01 (.03)	-.01 (.02)	-.03(.02)*	-.03(.02)	.00 (.02)
Female	-.04 (.03)	-.11(.03)***	.00 (.03)	.07(.03)*	-.06(.03)*	-.07 (.03)*
Age	.01(.00)***	-.01(.00)***	-.01 (.00)**	.00(.01)	-.01(.00)***	-.00 (.01)
Socioeconomic Status						
Income	.07(.01)***	.03(.00)***	.00(.01)	.07(.01)***	-.02 (.01)**	-.00 (.01)
Education	.13(.01)***	.08(.01)***	.04(.01)***	.11(.01)***	-.03 (.01)**	.02 (.01)

(continued)

Explaining Latino Political Orientations   57

Table 4.1 (continued)

	Political Interest	Politics Complicated	No Say	Contact w/ Gov	Big Interests	Trust Gov.
Commonality/Linked Fate/Discrimination						
SES commonality w/Blacks	.02 (.03)	.01(.02)	-.04(.02)*	-.00(.02)	-.03 (.02)	.01 (.02)
SES commonality w/Whites	.02 (.04)	.02 (.03)	.02 (.01)	-.00 (.02)	.06 (.03)**	.07 (.02)***
Political commonality w/Blacks	.04 (.02)*	.00 (.02)	.03 (.02)*	.01 (.02)	-.01 (.02)	.02 (.03)
Political commonality w/Whites	.04 (.02)*	.02 (.03)	.03 (.02)*	-.01 (.02)	.02 (.03)	.02 (.02)*
Linked fate w/Latinos	.05 (.02)**	-.03 (.02)*	-.02 (.01)	.01(.02)	.03 (.02)*	.08 (.02)***
Linked fate w/Blacks	-.03 (.02)	-.04 (.02)*	-.01 (.02)	-.03(.02)*	.02 (.01)	.01 (.02)
Discrimination (scale)	.09(.02)***	-.00 (.02)	-.07 (.02)***	.01 (.02)	-.17(.02)***	-.11(.02)***
Discrimination—R is Latino	.02 (.06)	.03 (.06)	-.01 (.06)	-.03 (.06)	.03(.06)	-.04 (.06)
Discrimination—skin color	.08 (.09)	.05 (.09)	.00 (.09)	-.02 (.09)	-.14(.09)	.07 (.09)
Acculturation/Assimilation						
Generation	.03 (.02)	-.02 (.03)	-.05(.02)*	.01 (.02)	-.13 (.03)***	-.05 (.02)*
English interview	.09 (.04)*	-.02 (.04)	.09(.04)*	.04 (.05)	.12 (.04)**	.04 (.05)
Keep Spanish language	-.01 (.03)	-.10 (.03)***	-.04 (.03)	-.00 (.03)	-.03 (.04)	.01 (.03)
Cut 1	1.06 (.19)	-.86 (.18)	-.63 (.18)	-.45 (.18)	-.91 (.18)	-.50 (.17)
Cut 2	2.50 (.19)	-.13 (.18)	.01(.18)	.14 (.18)	-.15(.18)	.94 (.17)
Cut 3	—	.38 (.18)	.61 (.19)	.75 (.18)	.42 (.18)	1.64 (.18)
N	4363	4380	4319	4334	4262	4509
Log Likelihood	-4234.04	-5729.67	-5861.66	-5454.22	-5398.69	-5444.38
Pseudo R2	.07	.02	.01	.03	.02	.02

Note: Estimates are ordered probit coefficients. Standard errors are in parentheses.
*Significant at p<.05, **Significant at p<.01, ***Significant at p<.001

identity does indeed influence Latinos' political orientations. Multiracial Latinos are more likely than White Latinos to be interested in politics. They also tend to more trusting, disagreeing with the statement "Government is pretty much run by just a few big interests looking out for themselves, and not for the benefit of all the people."

Whereas multiracial Latinos tend to have more positive attitudes about government, the attitudes of Black Latinos tend to be much less positive. Black Latinos have lower levels of efficacy, believing that they don't have a say in what the government does and that people should avoid government. Not only are Black Latinos less efficacious, they are also less likely to trust government. Figures 4.1 and 4.2 show the impact of racial identification on both measures of political trust. Although a majority of respondents trust government "some of the time," Black Latinos are less likely than any other group to trust the government "just about always," and the predicted probability for Black Latinos who never trust government is almost double that for other Latino racial groups. Similar racial differences in political trust have been reported in other studies (e.g. Stokes-Brown 2009). Similarly, Black Latinos are more likely to believe that government is run by just a few big interests primarily concerned about themselves. Yet, whereas approximately 52 percent of Black Latinos believe this statement, only 27 percent of multiracial Latinos hold the same belief. Other race identity is also negatively associated with some political orientations, as these Latinos are more likely to believe that people are better off avoiding contact with the government.

The finding that Black Latinos are both less efficacious and less trusting of government suggests that these Latinos have a heightened awareness of

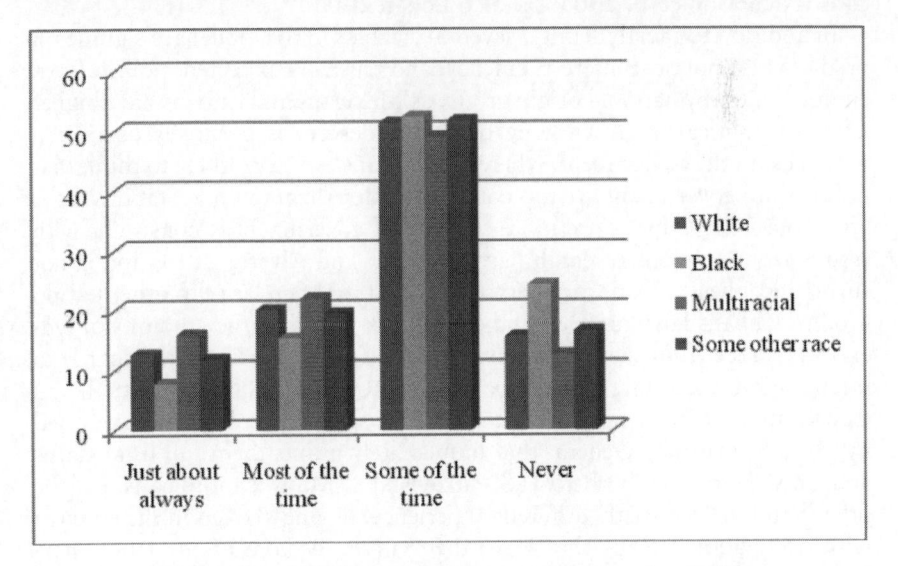

Figure 4.1 Predicted probability—trust government to do what is right.

60   The Politics of Race in Latino Communities

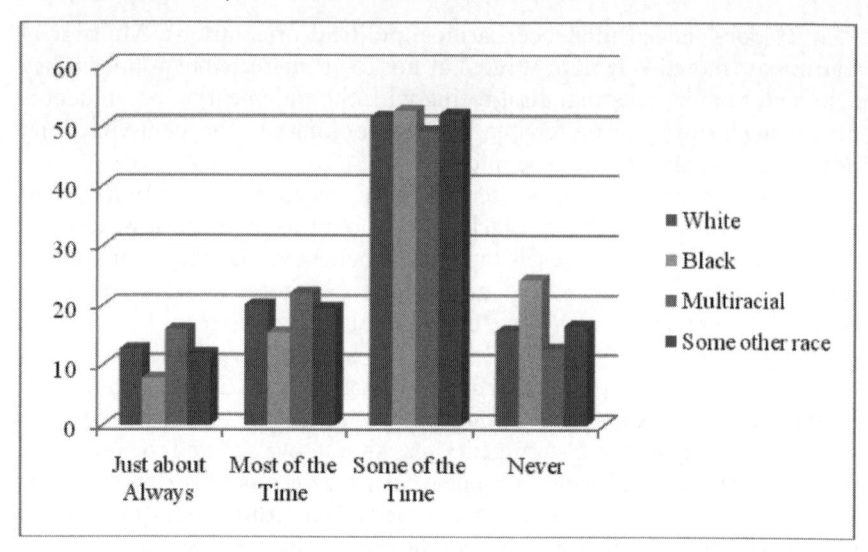

Figure 4.2 Predicted probability—government is run by a few big interests.

being outsiders to the political process. Similarly, non-Hispanic Blacks also tend to express less trust in the political system and have lower levels of external efficacy (e.g. Aberbach and Walker 1970; Abramson 1977, 1983; Bobo and Gilliam 1990). That Black Latinos have distinctly different attitudes about government than other Latinos and that their attitudes are less positive than those of White Latinos further enhances a general perception of commonality and closeness among Black Latinos and African Americans (Nicholson et al. 2005; see also Logan 2003).

In addition to racial identity, several variables in the model are significant predictors of political interest, efficacy, and trust. As expected, political orientations vary by national origin group, as Mexicans and Cubans have higher levels of political interest. Being of Cuban descent is positively correlated with trust in the government, whereas Mexicans are more likely to think that politics and government are too complicated for them to understand what is going on. That Cubans are more trusting of government is consistent with results from previous research (e.g. Abrajano and Alverez 2010) and is not surprising, given Cubans' privileged status in the U.S. relative to other Latino groups. Cubans have received and continue to receive large amounts of federal assistance from the federal government (Garcia 1996). With regards to immigration, according to the Pew Hispanic Center (2006: 2), "virtually all Cuban migrants have been admitted under a special parole power exercised by the U.S. Attorney General that immediately grants them full legal status and puts them on a path to U.S. citizenship." Many Dominicans, on the other hand, have a vastly different experience, having arrived in the country with occupational skills that leave them at the bottom of the labor market and exposed to social stigmatization (Itzigsohn 2009; Hernandez 2002).

This may help explain why being of Dominican descent is also negatively associated with political efficacy, as Dominican respondents are more likely to believe that they have no say in what the government does.

Education is an important predictor of Latino orientations. Respondents with higher levels of education are more likely to have higher levels of political interest and efficacy, believing that they have a say in what the government does and that people should not avoid contact with the government. However, well-educated Latinos are less trusting, believing that government is run primarily by just a few big interests looking out for themselves, and not for the benefit of all the people. Income and age are highly predictive of political orientations, as both affluent and older respondents are more likely to be politically interested and believe that government is run by a few big interests than are poor and young respondents. However, whereas affluent Latinos believe people should have contact with the government, older respondents are more likely to believe that they do not have any say in what the government does. Gender is also predictive—Latinas express lower levels of trust yet they are much less likely than Latino males to believe that people should avoid contact with government.

Also significant in predicting political orientations are commonality, linked fate, and discrimination. Whereas Latinos who feel a sense of socioeconomic commonality with African Americans believe they have less say in what government does, those who feel political commonality with Blacks are efficacious and are more likely to be interested in politics. Socioeconomic commonality with Whites is positively associated with political trust, as these Latinos are less likely to believe that government is run by a few big interests looking out primarily for their own interests and are more likely to trust the government in Washington to do what is right. Political commonality with Whites not only predicts higher levels of trust but is also positively associated with political interest and internal efficacy. Linked fate and discrimination influence political orientations, as Latinos who believe their fate is linked to that of other Latinos are politically interested, have lower levels of internal efficacy (politics is too complicated), and are more trusting. A sense of linked fate with Blacks and experiencing discrimination is negatively associated with many of the dependent variables. Latinos who perceive that their fate is linked to Blacks are more likely to believe that politics is too complicated and that people should avoid contact with government. Although an increased number of discriminatory experiences increase political interest, it predicts lower levels of efficacy and trust.

Lastly, English language use and generational status, as measures of assimilation and acculturation, have opposing effects. English language use is a positive and significant predictor of political interest and efficacy, whereas being farther away from the immigrant experience points to lower levels of efficacy and trust. This last finding is in line with Melissa Michelson's finding that Latinos most familiar with the political system are likely to become disaffected and cynical and lack reasons to participate (2003).[2]

Table 4.2   Other Race Identity and Political Orientations

	Some other race	SOR_Latino	Latino
Political interest	.01 (.04)	.00 (.04)	.00 (.05)
Politics complicated	-.02 (.04)	-.02 (.04)	-.04 (.05)
No say	-.00 (.04)	-.01 (.04)	-.03 (.05)
Contact with government	-.08 (.04)*	-.09 (.04)*	-.12 (.05)**
Big interests	-.02 (.04)	-.01 (.04)	-.07 (.04)*
Trust government	-.03 (.04)	-.05 (.04)	-.09 (.04)*

Note: Each column represents coefficients from an ordered probit regression model that includes the independent variables listed in Table 4.1. Standard errors are in parentheses.
*Significant at p<.05, **Significant at p<.01, ***Significant at p<.001

Recognizing the diversity among Latinos who self identify as other race, Table 4.2 explores patterns of difference in political attitudes among these three groups. Included in the table is the coefficient for the variables of interest (other race identity) from regression analyses which include the independent variables listed in Table 4.1. Here we see further evidence for disaggregating this category, as there are key differences in political attitudes among other race Latinos. As this identity becomes racialized for respondents, we see that other race Latinos who self identify as Latino/Hispanic and believe Latinos are a distinct racial group not only believe that people should avoid contact with government, but are also less trusting. This suggests that as Latinos begin to view themselves as part of a unique racial classification that explicitly references their Latin American ancestry, they become more cynical about American government.

RACIAL IDENTITY AND POLITICAL ORIENTATIONS AMONG IMMIGRANT LATINOS

Because Latino immigrants make up a significant portion of the U.S. Latino population and therefore represent a growing number of people in U.S., attention to their incorporation into the U.S. political system is critical to the understanding of future developments in American politics. With this in mind, Table 4.3 examines the predictors of political orientations among this population. In addition to the variables reported in Table 4.1, I include two additional controls: a variable measuring whether the respondent is a naturalized American citizen and a variable measuring how long the respondent has been in the U.S. Here we see that multiracial Latinos are more likely to be interested in politics and more efficacious than are White Latinos. Black and other race Latinos hold more negative opinions, as respondents in both groups are less likely to trust government. That racial identity is a significant factor shaping political orientations in both the total sample and the foreign-born sample suggests that there is something unique about Latinos' experiences with government and politics in the U.S. on the basis of race. Overall, multiracial Latinos appear to feel more connected to politics and more empowered, believing that government is responsive to their concerns and needs. Feeling marginalized by both society and governmental institutions, Black and other race Latinos express cynicism and distrust over the government's ability to make sound and meaningful decisions that impact their lives.

Many of the patterns found in the full sample for the remaining variables are also present in the immigrant sample. For example, as in the full model, Mexicans have higher levels of political interest but are more likely to think that politics and government are too complicated for them to understand what is going on. Being of Dominican descent is also negatively associated with political efficacy, as Dominican respondents are more likely to believe that they have no say in what the government does. Yet here we see that Dominican immigrants are also more likely to think that politics is too complicated and are more likely to believe that government is run by a few big interests. Among immigrants, being Cuban and having ties to other countries with significant Afro-Latino populations are positive predictors of external efficacy.

Turning to other demographic variables, gender and age are significant predictors of efficacy and trust, as Latinas are more likely to believe that politics is too complicated and that government is run by a few big interests, and older Latinos are more likely to be interested in politics. Older Latinos are also more trusting, disagreeing with the statement that government is run by a few big interests. Interestingly, it is also worth noting that among immigrants skin color is a significant predictor of political interest and trust, as lighter-skinned Latinos are more likely to be interested in politics and more likely to believe that big interests dominate politics. Education and, to a lesser extent, income are also strongly associated with Latino immigrants' orientations toward politics.

Also significant in predicting political orientations among immigrants are commonality, linked fate, and discrimination. Political commonality with Whites, in particular, is associated positively with political interest, whereas socioeconomic commonality with Whites is positively associated with political trust. As in the full model, an increased number of discriminatory experiences is a positive predictor of political interest, but predicts lower levels of efficacy and trust. Whereas linked fate has less impact among immigrants than among both foreign- and native-born Latinos, linked fate with Latinos is positively associated with political interest and trust but negatively associated with efficacy.

Language, being naturalized, and the length of time in the U.S. also predict Latino immigrants' orientations toward politics. English language use is a positive and significant predictor of political efficacy and trust, whereas those who desire to maintain Spanish are more likely to think that politics is too complicated for them to understand what is going on. Interestingly,

Table 4.3 Latino Racial Identity and Political Orientations among Immigrants

	Political Interest	Politics Complicated	No Say	Contact w/Gov.	Big Interests	Trust Gov.
Demographic Characteristics						
Black	-.06 (.24)	-.06(.24)	-.21(.24)	-.40(.24)*	-.26 (.24)	-.43(.23)*
Multiracial	.33 (.17)*	-.04 (.16)	.18 (.17)	.02(.18)	.36 (.16)**	-.03 (.16)
Some other race	.07 (.05)	-.01 (.05)	.00 (.05)	-.05 (.04)	-.01 (.04)	-.09 (.05)**
Mexican	.10 (.05)*	-.13 (.05)**	.00 (.05)	.01(.04)	.04 (.05)	.08 (.05)
Cuban	.11 (.09)	-.02 (.09)	-.05 (.09)	.21(.10)*	-.04 (.09)	-.03 (.09)
Dominican	.08(.10)	-.15 (.09)*	-.26 (.10)**	-.03 (.09)	-.16 (.10)*	.05 (.09)
Ties to Afro-Latino country	-.00 (.09)	-.01 (.09)	-.10 (.09)	.25(.09)**	.01 (.09)	.03 (.08)
Skin color (dark to light)	.04 (.02)*	-.00 (.03)	-.00 (.02)	-.02 (.03)	-.04(.02)*	-.01 (.02)
Female	-.05 (.04)	-.09(.04)*	-.02 (.04)	.02 (.04)	-.07(.03)*	-.03 (.04)
Age	.01(.00)***	-.01(.00)*	-.00 (.01)	.01(.00)*	-.01(.00)*	-.00 (.01)
Naturalized citizen	-.16(.05)***	.03 (.05)	-.17 (.05)***	-.02(.05)	.03 (.05)	.03(.05)
Time in U.S.	.00 (.01)	-.00 (.01)	-.01 (.00)**	.01(.00)	-.01(.00)***	.00 (.01)
Socioeconomic Status						
Income	.05(.01)***	.03(.00)*	-.00(.01)	.07(.01)***	-.03 (.01)**	-.00 (.01)
Education	.12(.01)***	.07 (.01)***	.03 (.01)**	.10(.02)***	-.02 (.01)*	.02 (.01)*

(continued)

Explaining Latino Political Orientations

Commonality/Linked Fate/Discrimination					
SES commonality w/Blacks	.03 (.02)	.02 (.03)	-.03 (.02)	-.04 (.02)	-.01 (.02)	.03 (.02)
SES commonality w/Whites	.00 (.02)	.02 (.04)	.03 (.02)	-.00 (.02)	.04 (.02)*	.06 (.02)**
Political commonality w/Blacks	.03 (.02)	.00 (.02)	.03 (.02)	.03 (.02)	-.01 (.02)	.02 (.03)
Political commonality w/Whites	.05 (.03)*	.00 (.03)	.00 (.03)	-.03 (.02)	.03 (.04)	.02 (.03)
Linked fate w/Latinos	.05 (.02)**	-.03 (.02)	-.02 (.01)	.02 (.03)	.04 (.02)*	.09 (.02)***
Linked fate w/Blacks	-.03 (.02)	-.03 (.04)	-.01 (.02)	-.02 (.03)	.01 (.02)	.01 (.02)
Discrimination (scale)	.07 (.03)*	-.02 (.03)	-.05 (.03)*	.03 (.04)	-.13 (.03)***	-.09 (.03)***
Discrimination—R is Latino	.06 (.07)	.00 (.07)	-.07 (.08)	-.07 (.08)	.05 (.07)	-.05 (.07)
Discrimination—skin color	-.04 (.14)	.02 (.13)	-.18 (.13)	-.23 (.14)*	-.20 (.14)	.11 (.13)
Acculturation/Assimilation					
English interview	.01 (.06)	-.00 (.06)	.16 (.05)**	-.14 (.05)**	.30 (.06)***	.10 (.05)*
Keep Spanish language	.04 (.05)	-.12 (.05)**	-.06 (.05)	-.01 (.04)	.02 (.04)	.01 (.05)
Cut 1	.86 (.28)	-.91 (.26)	-1.09 (.27)	-.69 (.27)	-.31 (.27)	-.42 (.25)
Cut 2	2.29 (.28)	-.20 (.26)	-.46 (.27)	-.10 (.27)	-.44 (.27)	1.01 (.26)
Cut 3	-	.30 (.27)	.12 (.27)	.54 (.27)	1.00 (.27)	1.62 (.26)
N	3081	3079	3035	3057	2992	3195
Log Likelihood	-3017.12	-4032.98	-4107.09	-3959.30	-3896.81	-3905.65
Pseudo R2	.05	.01	.01	.03	.02	.01

Note: Estimates are ordered probit coefficients. Standard errors are in parentheses.
*Significant at p<.05, **Significant at p<.01, ***Significant at p<.001

being naturalized and being in the U.S. for longer periods of time negatively predict these political attitudes, as naturalized immigrants are less interested in politics and less likely to believe they have a say in what the government does. Similarly, long-time residents in the U.S. are also less likely to believe they have a say in what the government does and are more likely to believe that government is run by a few big interests looking out for themselves. There are also key differences in political orientations among other race immigrants. Other race immigrants who believe Latinos are a distinct racial group in the U.S. express a distrust of government and lower levels of external efficacy.

CONCLUSION

Political orientations are pivotal resources for electoral participation (e.g. Campbell et al. 1960; Almond and Verba 1963; Stokes 1962; Verba and Nie 1972; Abramson and Aldrich 1982; Abramson 1983) yet few studies explore the role of identity in shaping political orientations. Here we see that there are significant differences in political attitudes across Latino racial groups. Multiracial Latinos hold positive attitudes about government, whereas Black Latinos express a higher level of mistrust and doubt about their capabilities as political actors. Latinos who self-identify as other race are also generally less positive regarding their ability to bring about political change, and become increasingly more cynical as they view themselves as a part of a distinct racial group in the racial hierarchy.

These results provide a unique perspective through which to better understand Latinos' psychological connectedness to the American political system. It has been argued that generational distinctions among Latinos and the steady influx of foreign-born Latinos to the U.S. may explain why, over time, Latinos have become more politically trusting than non-Hispanic Whites and Blacks (Abrajano and Alvarez 2010). I do find evidence that generational status matters; however, this study's findings may support yet another narrative. That most Latinos self-identify as White or other race may also account for Latinos' higher level of political trust. Yet, should more other race Latinos over time see themselves as belonging to a distinct racial category, the political attitudinal profile of Latinos compared to non-Hispanic Whites and Blacks may change.

Using race as a foundation to explore Latinos' psychological attachment to government, we see important intragroup differences in political attitudes. Consequently, the extent to which Latinos express positive feelings about government and their ability to impact the political process is shaped by the way in which they conceptualize themselves in the existing racial order. In addition to interest, efficacy, and trust, Latinos' attachment to the political system can also be measured by partisan ties. In the next chapter, I explore the extent to which partisanship is shaped by racial identity.

5 Racial Identity and the Politics of Latino Partisanship

Partisanship has long been a central organizing concept in the study of American political behavior. Early studies of electoral behavior examined political behavior in terms of the individual characteristics of voters and found that characteristics such as age, gender, education, income, occupation, religion, and race are all significant determinants of political behavior (Lazarsfeld et al. 1944; Berelson et al. 1954). In their seminal work, *The American Voter*, Campbell et al. (1960) found that partisanship, a psychological attachment to a political party, also shapes political attitudes and behaviors. Using a socio-psychological approach, the authors presented voting as the outcome of a sequence of influential factors. Illustrating this point through a "funnel of causality," they argue that partisan attachment results from the process of socialization, stemming from childhood and reflecting the influences of family and social environment. Partisanship is therefore fixed and one of the most influential determinants of political behavior, predicting participation among the general population (e.g. Conway 1991; Rosenstone and Hansen 1993) and among racial and ethnic groups (e.g. Lien 1994; Uhlaner 1996; Kam and Ortiz 1998).

There is strong agreement among scholars that social group identity directly influences partisanship. Despite classic and more recent research that affirms the importance of group identity as a key determinant of partisanship (e.g. Lewis-Beck et al. 2008), we know relatively little about the acquisition of partisanship by Latinos. Extant research suggests that several factors, including national origin, education, issue positions, and political ideology, exert an independent effect on Latino party identification (e.g. Alvarez and Garcia Bedolla 2003; Uhlaner and Garcia 2001). Although these studies provide important information about the foundations of Latino partisanship, much less is known about race and its influence as an individual-level determinant of Latino partisan identity.

This chapter examines the relationship between race and the acquisition of political partisanship, arguing that because group identity can play a significant role in attitude formation (e.g. Conover and Feldman 1984; Gurin et al. 1980), it is possible that racial self identification within the Latino community will shape the development of partisan attachments. We saw in

Chapter Four that racial group attachment among Latinos influences the acquisition of political orientations. Therefore, if Latino racial identity is salient and politically relevant, we might expect racial identity to also be a significant predictor of the direction and strength of partisanship.

RESEARCH ON LATINO PARTISANSHIP

Partisanship, the sense of belonging or attachment that one feels for a political party, has long been a central issue in the study of American politics. Partisanship is typically evaluated along two dimensions—the strength of reported partisan attachment and the direction of that attachment (Campbell et al. 1960; Converse 1976). A central question regarding the nature of partisanship focuses on the way in which attachments to parties are developed. The Michigan school of thought, developed by Angus Campbell and colleagues, is a social-psychological view of partisanship that suggests that individuals are socialized to attach to a specific party early in life as part of the pre-adult socialization process (see also Beck and Jennings 1991). That attachment is then stable in direction and increases in strength over time (see also Converse 1969, 1976). Alternatively, the Downsian school takes an economistic view of partisanship, grounded in rational choice theory. As rational actors with limited information, individuals are likely to be attracted to candidates who share their beliefs and are strongly committed to issues they care about (Rabinowitz and Macdonald 1989). Thus, they use party labels as cues to choose among candidates. Selecting representatives that fit their personal interests, voters rank preferences and always choose the highest-ordered preference (Downs 1957: 6). Given this perspective, party identification is more dynamic and malleable than Campbell and his colleagues suggest (e.g. Fiorina 1981; Markus and Converse 1979; McKuen et al. 1989). Although political attachments are often formed early, other agents can change the nature and strength of party identification.

Extant literature on Latino partisanship shows that Latinos align themselves more frequently with the Democratic Party (Cain et al. 1991; Uhlaner and Garcia 2001). Using a nationally representative sample of likely Latino voters in the 2000 elections, Alvarez and Garcia Bedolla (2003) find that approximately 57 percent of likely voters identified as Democrats, 24 percent identified as Republicans, and 13 percent identified as Independents. The Democratic Party also gained an advantage in party identification (and voting) among Latinos in the 2006, 2008, and 2010 elections (Lopez and Taylor 2009; Pew Hispanic Center 2010). Other data sources, including the LNS, suggest that although Latinos are more likely to be Democratic than Republican, they are just as likely to not feel attached to any party.[1] Approximately 36 percent of the LNS respondents considered themselves Democrats compared to 11 percent Republican, 17 percent Independent, and 36 percent nonidentifiers. However, Latinos are a diverse group, coming from dozens of countries with distinct cultural traits and traditions. As a result of this diversity in origin and experience in the U.S., Latinos are much less cohesive than African Americans, who are overwhelmingly Democratic. For example, Cubans, in general, are much more likely than other Latino national origin groups to assume Republican affiliations, in part because the Republican Party is perceived to be a stronger critic of the Castro regime in Cuba (e.g. Alvarez and Garcia Bedolla 2003; Cain et al. 1991). Most Mexicans, Puerto Ricans, and Central Americans identify as Democrats (e.g. Alvarez and Garcia Bedolla 2003). When asked which party they most associate themselves with, LNS respondents of Mexican and Puerto Rican descent were much more likely to chose the Democratic Party over the Republican Party.

Comments from two focus group participants highlight Latino ties to the Democratic Party:

> You know the last election for city council—I went around doing petitioning and stuff like that and I'm representing [Fernando] Cabrera [who is of Dominican and Puerto Rican heritage] and saying vote for him. One question that stood out the most was "Is he of the Democratic Party? Oh, I'll vote for him." First they notice the last name—he's Spanish—good! Then he is a Democrat, I'll vote for him. An association between race and party does exist. (Puerto Rican man, second New York group)

However, an exchange in the same group and comments from a participant in one of the Chicago focus groups highlight Latinos' willingness to adopt a more candidate-centered approach to elections:

> When I lived in Puerto Rico, I belonged to the Republican Party but when I came here I decided I would go by the individual, not by the party. (Puerto Rican woman, second New York group)

> That's right, that's the right approach. Every candidate has some good qualities and you have to look for the best, regardless of party. (Puerto Rican man, second New York group)

> I don't personally think this but there are some people who say 'oh because they are Democrats and they have a Hispanic name, I'll vote for them'. . . . but it's not always a good idea. . . . .(Mexican woman, second Chicago group)

Party preference is also significantly related to length of residency, generation, and citizenship status (e.g. Alvarez and Garcia Bedolla 2003; Cain et al. 1991; Wong 2000). Newly arrived immigrants tend not to identify with either majority party (Hajnal and Lee 2006). However, the longer they live in the U.S., the more likely they are to attach themselves to a major party, primarily the Democratic Party (Cain et al. 1991; Uhlaner and Garcia 2001; Wong 2000). Similarly, Alvarez and Garcia Bedolla (2003) find that time in the U.S. is associated with greater identification with the Democratic Party for Mexicans and Puerto Ricans, but with stronger identification with the Republican Party for Cubans. This positive correlation between Democratic partisanship attachment and length of time in the U.S. is also evident in the LNS data. Although most Latinos (49 percent) in the country less than 20 years identify with no political party, 26 percent identify as Democrats. Democratic affiliation increases to 39 percent for Latinos in the country more than 20 years but less than 40 years, 53 percent for those here more than 40 years but less than 60 years, and 65 percent for those in the country more than 60 years. Patterns of partisanship, particularly among Independents, are influenced by the degree of acculturation Latinos experience in the time that they are in the U.S. (Hajnal and Lee 2004). Barreto and Pedraza (2009) also find that, in addition to years lived in the U.S., strength of ethnic identification and degree of perceived discrimination influence Latino party preferences.

Whereas Anglo partisanship is heavily influenced by socioeconomic status, Latino partisanship appears to be more heavily influenced by social and political factors, including political ideology and policy issue preferences (Alvarez and Bedolla 2003; Uhlaner and Garcia 2001). Latinos with liberal attitudes about abortion, affirmative action, school vouchers, and government-funded health insurance are more likely to be Democrats than Republicans (Alvarez and Garcia Bedolla 2003: 41). Finally, it is worth noting that extant research has also given attention to the influence of religion in Latino politics and found that affiliation with evangelical and mainline Protestant denominations increases identification with the Republican Party (Kelly and Kelly 2005; but see Garcia Bedolla et al. 2006).

Understanding the sources of partisanship in the Latino community is particularly important for several reasons. First, the growth and size of the Latino population makes this group a potentially viable political force. Based upon demographic trends, both political parties often try to appeal to Latino voters, with Democrats appealing to issues such as immigration and Republicans courting Latinos with socially conservative appeals. Yet, the degree to which political parties engage and mobilize Latinos is questionable. As Hajnal and Lee (2011) point out, parties are the primary gateway through which individuals are mobilized to participate (Rosenstone and Hansen 1993). However, when parties fail to raise political awareness or affirm group attachments, Latinos are less inclined to align themselves with a political party. They go on to argue that

> if parties are the main institutional force driving the political incorporation of the minority community, the widespread disconnect with today's parties implies that America's newcomers and its other

minorities could be falling through the cracks. One of the putative results of this underwhelming partisan presence in the everyday lives of America's minorities is equally disappointing rates of political participation. . . . This under-participation is also reflected in gross underrepresentation among the nation's elected officials. Despite the nation's vast demographic transformation, the political leadership of the United States remains overwhelmingly White. (Hajnal and Lee 2011: 16)

If political parties play a central role in the process of political incorporation, as these authors suggest, then research on the adoption and direction of partisanship among Latinos is critically necessary to assess the extent to which Latino group interests are represented and met in public-policy making.

Theoretically, it has also been suggested that the salience of distinct social identities has been overlooked in accounts of party identification (Hajnal and Lee 2011). Although racial identity may not be most Latinos' primary social identity, Latinos live with the reality that racial constructs have significant implications for their life chances. Insofar as racial identity plays a role in the socialization process, it may influence their psychological attachment to political parties, making this identity an overlooked dimension of Latino partisan choice.

RACE AND LATINO PARTISAN PREFERENCES

A preliminary review of the data reveals that, in general, Latino partisanship varies somewhat by racial identity, yet the differences are generally modest. Respondents were asked, "Generally speaking, do you usually consider yourself a Democrat, a Republican, an Independent, some other party, or what?" This question was coded to create a four-point scale where Democrats are coded 1, Republicans are coded 2, Independents are coded 3, and unaffiliated and undecided respondents (nonidentifiers) are coded 4. As found in other research, Latinos have a fairly strong connection to the Democratic Party. About a third of respondents from all Latino racial groups reported a Democratic affiliation. Thirty-six percent of White Latinos self-identified as Democrat, compared to 39 percent of Black Latinos, 41 percent of multiracial Latinos, and 38 percent of other race Latinos. Democratic affiliation is particularly high (43 percent) among other race Latinos who report their race to be Hispanic/Latino and believe that Latinos are a distinctive racial category (Latino). However, it is important to note that although Latinos are more likely to self-identify as Democrat than Republican, almost a third of the respondents in each racial group also reported that they were affiliated with no political party. This percentage is almost six times the size of the percentage reported in the 2000 Latino Voter Survey (Alvarez and Garcia Bedolla 2003). A significant percentage of nonidentifiers (regardless of race) are respondents who were born outside of the U.S. Overall, these results support recent research that shows that the number of Independents and nonaffiliated Latinos is considerable (e.g. Hajnal and Lee 2004).

Although many respondents have not yet formed partisan attachments, other race Latinos who adopt a racialized understanding of that identity (Latino) and multiracial Latinos are somewhat less likely to be nonidentifiers (27 percent and 29 percent, respectively). Interestingly, the results also show that Black Latinos are somewhat less likely to be Independents and are much less likely to report Republican affiliation (7 percent) compared to other Latino racial groups (13 percent of White Latinos, 16 percent of multiracial Latinos, and 10 percent of other race Latinos). Conversely, the difference or gap in Independent and Republican affiliation (as compared to Democratic affiliation) is much smaller for multiracial and other race Latinos.

To measure the strength of respondents' partisan attachments, Democratic and Republican respondents were asked to identify themselves as strong or weak, and Independent respondents were asked to identify themselves as closer to the Republican or Democratic Party. From these questions, I created a five-point scale coded 4 for strong Democrats or Republicans, 3 for weak Democrats or Republicans, 2 for leaning Democrats and Republicans, 1 for Independents, and 0 for all others.[2] Cross-tabulations reveal that approximately 25 percent of all respondents are strong partisans, 22 percent are weak partisans, 9 percent are leaning partisans, 8 percent are pure Independents, and 36 percent are nonidentifiers. Although a substantial percentage of respondents are nonidentifiers, partisanship does vary somewhat by race. Black Latinos are most likely to be strong partisans, primarily of the Democratic Party (32 percent), followed by White Latinos (28 percent), multiracial Latinos (26 percent), and other race Latinos (25 percent). Interestingly, the results also suggest that the strength of partisanship increases somewhat as other race identity becomes more defined, moving from a general other race identity to panethnic and racialized other race identities (25 percent, 24 percent, and 27 percent respectively).

Overall, the bivariate descriptive results suggest that racial identity influences the acquisition of partisanship. Democratic affiliation is highest among other race Latinos who report their race to be Hispanic/Latino and believe that Latinos are a distinctive racial category, and among multiracial Latinos. Republican affiliation is highest among multiracial Latinos (16 percent), followed by White Latinos (13 percent) and other race Latinos (10 percent). Racial identity is also correlated with the strength of partisan attachments. Black Latinos are more likely to be strong partisans, identifying strongly with the Democratic Party. Yet to fully understand the degree to which racial identity predicts the acquisition and strength of partisanship, multivariate models are needed to test simultaneously the impact of racial identity and other theoretically relevant variables.

Nationality, Phenotype, and Other Demographic Factors

Although most Latinos report relatively weak partisan attachments (Barreto and Woods 2005; Cain et al. 1991; Uhlaner and Garcia 2002; de la Garza et al. 1992), Mexicans, Puerto Ricans, El Salvadorans, Guatemalans, and Dominicans are predominantly Democrats, and Cubans are predominantly Republicans (Hajnal and Lee 2004). The strength of partisan attachment increases with age, often as a result of an individual becoming more active within the community and associating with social groups that have partisan ties (Campbell et al. 1960). Age and gender have an independent effect on Latino partisanship, as women and older Latinos are more Democratic than men (Barreto and Pedraza 2009; see also Alvarez and Garcia Bedolla 2003; Kelly and Kelly 2005).

Socioeconomic Status

The development of political views and participatory behavior is commonly tied to socioeconomic status. Although some studies suggest that conventional socioeconomic measures do not explain Latino partisanship (e.g. Coffin 2003; Alvarez and Garcia Bedolla 2003; but see Garcia Bedolla et al. 2006), I test whether Latino partisanship is also influenced by one's level of educational attainment and income. Given that differential rates of economic progress influence the acquisition of party preferences, one might expect Latinos with higher incomes to be more supportive of the Republican Party. Thus, it is possible that as Latinos' material well-being improves so does their support for Republicans (Cain et al. 1991: 397).

Discrimination, Linked Fate, and Commonality

The perception that racial discrimination exists in society and that these inequalities are based on ethnicity and phenotype may facilitate racial group attachment, which could lead to distinct partisan attachments. Experiencing discrimination is highly predictive of Latino political behavior, including various forms of political participation and policy preferences (e.g. Stokes 2003; Pantoja et al. 2001; Sanchez 2006; Branton 2007). Examining partisanship among Latinos and Asian Americans, Cain et al. (1991: 394) argue that groups that experience discrimination and perceive unequal opportunities are more likely to identify as Democrats, given the Democratic party's image of being more supportive of policies that favor disadvantaged groups. Using data from the LNS, Barreto and Pedraza (2009) also found that experiencing discrimination increases the probability of Democratic partisanship. Previous research has also found that the greater the perceived link between one's own fate and the fate of a racial group, the more politically salient that racial identity becomes (e.g. Dawson 1994). Thus, feelings of linked fate and various types of commonality with established groups in the racial hierarchy may also exert a powerful influence on the acquisition of partisanship.

Acculturation/Assimilation

The traditional acculturation hypothesis suggests that as groups integrate into mainstream culture, they lose their cultural heritage (e.g. Gordon 1964). Language is often one of the first cultural attributes to be lost. English-language dominant Latinos, presumably farthest removed from the immigrant experience, may be more likely to identify as Democrat when compared to less acculturated Latinos. Thus, one might expect to find that language competence is highly predictive of Latino partisanship. Native-born and foreign-born Latinos also differ significantly in their partisan attachment, as foreign-born Latinos are more likely to lean toward political independence and their eventual attachments will be influenced by their policy preferences and the historical political experiences of their national origin group (Alvarez and Garcia Bedolla 2003: 45).

Finally, extant research also suggests that political knowledge, political interest, and political ideology all shape partisanship (Campbell et al. 1960; see also Kelly and Kelly 2005). Increased interest in politics and knowledge is highly correlated with partisan identification, and having a strong ideological base links people to a particular political party.

WHAT FACTORS PREDICT THE DIRECTION OF LATINO PARTISANSHIP?

The multinomial logistic regression models presented in Table 5.1 report the likelihood that a respondent will identify as Republican, Independent, or a nonidentifier relative to identifying as Democrat. Here we see that multiracial Latinos are significantly more likely to be Republican than Democrat, controlling for all other factors. This finding is particularly interesting as it stands in opposition to research which suggests that multiracial Latinos mirror their monoracial counterparts in terms of political party preference (see Masuoka 2008). Here I also find that Black Latinos are more likely to be nonidentifiers than Democrats, controlling for all other factors. This finding is somewhat surprising in light of other findings from the data. Additional crosstabulations show that Black Latinos are more likely than other Latino racial groups to believe that their fate is highly linked with African Americans (48 percent compared to 39 percent of White Latinos, 40 percent of multiracial Latinos, and 35 percent of other race Latinos). This greater sense of linked fate, in conjunction with 1) the perception among most Latinos that the Democratic Party and its policies are more favorably inclined toward minorities (e.g. McDaniel and Ellison 2008), and 2) the reality that an overwhelming percentage of African Americans

Racial Identity and the Politics of Latino Partisanship

Table 5.1 Predicting the Direction of Latino Political Partisanship

	Outcome for Republican (y=1)	Outcome for Independents (y=2)	Outcome for Nonidentifiers (y=3)
Demographic Characteristics			
Black	.21 (.82)	.69 (.62)	1.15 (.66)*
Multiracial	.74 (.39)*	.22 (.43)	.69 (.46)
Some other race	-.00 (.15)	.05 (.13)	.11 (.14)
Mexican	.02 (.17)	.21 (.15)	-.06 (.15)
Cuban	1.26 (.27)***	.85 (.26)***	.06 (.32)
Puerto Rican	.27 (.29)	-.11 (.30)	-.50 (.36)
Dominican	-.31 (.36)	-.23 (.29)	-.50 (.30)*
Ties to Afro-Latino country	.12 (.31)	-.33 (.29)	-.28 (.32)
Skin color (dark to light)	.16 (.06)	.07 (.05)	.03 (.05)
Female	-.19 (.13)	-.22 (.10)*	.13 (.12)
Age	-.01 (.00)*	-.02 (.00)***	-.03 (.00)***
Socioeconomic Status			
Income	.07 (.03)*	.00 (.03)	-.11 (.03)***
Education	.00 (.09)	.01 (.03)	-.07 (.03)*
Commonality/Linked Fate/ Discrimination			
SES commonality w/Blacks	-.11 (.08)	-.05 (.06)	-.07 (.06)
SES commonality w/Whites	.17 (08)*	.08 (.07)	.07 (.08)
Political commonality w/Blacks	-.11 (.08)	-.05 (.07)	-.04 (.07)
Political commonality w/Whites	.12 (.09)	.14 (.07)*	.04 (.07)
Linked fate w/Latinos	-.06 (.07)	-.08 (.06)	-.08 (.06)
Linked fate w/Blacks	-.14 (.07)*	-.12 (.05)*	-.08 (.07)
Discrimination (scale)	-.18 (.09)*	.05 (.07)	-.05 (.08)
Discrimination—R is Latino	.00 (.23)	-.20 (.18)	-.02 (.21)
Discrimination—skin color	-.00 (.34)	-.53 (.30)*	.07 (.31)
Acculturation/Assimilation			
Generation	.01 (.09)	-.18 (.08)*	-.20 (.09)*
English interview	.19 (.16)	-.58 (.14)***	-.75 (.16)***
Keep Spanish language	-.34 (.11)***	-.09 (.11)	-.05 (.13)
Political interest	.11 (.10)	-.18 (08)*	-.32 (.09)***
Political ideology	-.32 (.03)***	-.00 (.02)	-.12 (.03)***
Political knowledge	.12 (.07)*	.12 (.05)*	.19 (.06)***
Constant	.73 (.71)	-1.39 (.63)*	2.59 (.71)***

N = 2591
Log Likelihood = -3023.11
Pseudo R2 = .10

Note: Estimates are multinomial logit coefficients. The reference category is Democrat. Standard errors are in parentheses.
*Significant at p<.05, **Significant at p<.01, ***Significant at p<.001

align themselves with the Democratic Party, leads me to expect a greater likelihood of Democratic affiliation among these Latinos. The preference for nonidentification can be largely explained by the nativity and generational status of Black Latinos in the data. Fifty-five percent of the Black Latino respondents are foreign-born. This runs contrary to census data that finds that Black Latinos are much less likely to be immigrants than Latinos from other racial groups (Logan 2003). Thus, overrepresentation of Black Latino immigrants begins to explain the lack of attachment found here to the Democratic Party.

Other general patterns are clear from the results. First, national origin is highly predictive of partisanship. As other studies show, Cubans are more likely to be Republican (Alvarez and Garcia Bedolla 2003; Uhlaner and Garcia 2001). They are also more likely to be Independents than Democrats. We also see that Dominicans are also more likely to be Democrats than nonidentifiers. Regarding other demographic factors, we see that Democratic partisan attachment increases with age: older Latinos are significantly more likely to be Democrats than Republicans, Independents, or nonidentifiers. Interestingly, phenotype along with income are significant predictors of partisanship, as lighter-skinned Latinos and wealthy Latinos are more likely to self-identify as Republicans than as Democrats. Yet affluent and highly educated Latinos are more likely to identify as Democrats than have no attachment to any parties. Experiences with discrimination and intergroup perceptions are also significant predictors of Latino partisanship. Feeling commonality with Whites is predictive of self-identifying as Republican or Independent. Respondents who believe their fate is linked to African Americans are more likely to self-identify as Democrats than as Republicans or Independents. Given the public perception that the Democratic Party is the party for minorities, particularly African Americans (e.g. McDaniel and Ellison 2008), this finding is not very surprising. Other indicators of connectedness such as political commonality are also positively associated with the acquisition of political independence. Perhaps also not surprising is the statistically significant positive relationship between discrimination and Democratic partisanship. Controlling for all other factors, Latinos who have experienced some level of discrimination are more likely to identify as Democrat than Republican. Yet it is worth noting that the belief that discrimination is due to skin color is positively associated with the acquisition of political independence over Democratic Party identification.

Lastly, standard measures of acculturation and political factors have an independent effect on Latino party identification. Preferring to be interviewed in English (as a measure of language proficiency) is highly predictive of partisan attachment, as English speakers are more likely to be Democrats than Independents or nonidentifiers. Yet at the same time, respondents who desire to preserve Spanish language skills are also more likely to identify as a Democrat than as Republican. Generational status is also significant, as

Racial Identity and the Politics of Latino Partisanship 77

Table 5.2 Political Partisanship and Other Race Identity

	Some other race	SOR Latino	Latino
Republican	-.00 (.14)	.03 (.15)	.04 (.18)
Independent	.05 (.13)	.01 (.13)	-.04 (.15)
Nonidentifier	.11 (.14)	.10 (.14)	-.01 (.16)
N	2591	2186	1582
Log Likelihood	-3023.11	-2557.76	-1803.34
Pseudo R2	.10	.10	.11

Note: Each column represents coefficients from a multinominal regression model where the dependent variable is a categorical variable that includes the following categories: Republican, Independent, Nonidentifier, and Democrat (base category). The model also includes other race variables and independent variables listed in Table 5.1. Standard errors are in parentheses. *Significant at p<.05, **Significant at p<.01, ***Significant at p<.001

Latinos farthest away from the immigrant experience are more likely to be Democrats than Independents or nonidentifiers. As expected, most of the political variables are significant—ideologically, liberals are more likely to be Democrats than Republicans or nonidentifers (e.g. Uhlaner et al. 2000). Those most interested in politics and with greater levels of political knowledge are more likely to be Democrats than Independents or nonidentifiers. Political knowledge is also positively associated with a greater likelihood of Democratic partisanship over Republican partisanship.

Although the most common racial category chosen by Latino respondents is other race, there are important differences among respondents who choose this identifier. For some, this racial option is synonymous with pan-ethnic identification, whereas for others this option is meant to signify their acceptance of Latino identity as a formalized racial category within the U.S. racial hierarchy. The relationship between political partisanship and each form of other race identity is examined in Table 5.2. Although their identity holds different meanings for other race respondents, here we see no real difference in the foundations of partisan attachment. For each group, racial identity is not a significant predictor of partisanship. This is true for even the racialized other race respondents (Latino).

RACIAL IDENTITY AND THE DIRECTION OF PARTISANSHIP AMONG IMMIGRANT LATINOS

Given the substantial immigrant segment of the Latino population, I also examine the influence of racial identity on Latino partisanship for non-native respondents to gain a better understanding of how these Latinos are socialized into the political system. The results presents in Table 5.3 show

Table 5.3 Predicting the Direction of Latino Political Partisanship among Immigrants

	Outcome for Republican (y=1)	Outcome for Independents (y=2)	Outcome for Nonidentifiers (y=3)
Demographic Characteristics			
Black	.56 (.91)	.72 (.74)	.42 (.81)
Multiracial	.37 (.59)	.23 (.51)	.63 (.54)
Some other race	-.01 (.19)	.10 (.15)	.12 (.16)
Mexican	.26 (.22)	.32 (.16)*	.07 (.16)
Cuban	1.39 (.30)***	1.00 (.29)***	.22 (.34)
Dominican	-.08 (.37)	-.10 (.31)	-.29 (.31)
Ties to Afro-Latino country	.28 (.33)	-.38 (.31)	-.32 (.33)
Skin color (dark to light)	.13 (.08)*	.07 (.06)	-.00 (.06)
Female	.12 (.16)	-.02 (.13)	.31 (.13)*
Age	-.00 (.01)	-.02 (.00)***	-.01 (.00)*
Naturalized citizen	-.17 (.20)	.17 (.15)	.57 (.17)***
Time in U.S.	-.00 (.01)	-.00 (.01)	-.02 (.00)**
Socioeconomic Status			
Income	.06 (.05)	.02 (.04)	-.05 (.04)
Education	.02 (.06)	.01 (.04)	-.08 (.04)*
Commonality/Linked Fate/ Discrimination			
SES commonality w/Blacks	-.15 (.09)	-.01 (.07)	-.10 (.07)
SES commonality w/Whites	.05 (.10)	.03 (.07)	.10 (.08)
Political commonality w/Blacks	-.11 (.10)	.00 (.08)	-.00 (.08)
Political commonality w/Whites	.22 (.11)*	.11 (.08)	.00 (.08)
Linked fate w/Latinos	.00 (.09)	.05 (.08)	-.07 (.06)
Linked fate w/Blacks	-.09 (.08)	-.15 (.07)*	-.13 (.07)*
Discrimination (scale)	-.05 (.12)	.11 (.08)	.01 (.09)
Discrimination—R is Latino	-.04 (.30)	-.62 (.24)**	-.16 (.23)
Discrimination—skin color	-.13 (.50)	-.83 (.42)*	-.26 (.41)
Acculturation/Assimilation			
English interview	.27 (.22)	-.36 (.18)*	-.11 (.20)
Keep Spanish language	-.00 (.20)	-.17 (.16)	-.11 (.16)
Political interest	.05 (.12)	-.25 (.09)**	-.32 (.09)***
Political ideology	-.20 (.04)***	.05 (.03)	-.09 (.03)**
Political knowledge	.10 (.09)	.14 (.07)*	.15 (.07)*
Constant	-1.27 (1.14)	.23 (.89)	1.10 (.92)

N = 1811
Log Likelihood = -2177.52
Pseudo R2 = .08

Note: Estimates are multinomial logit coefficients. The reference category is Democrat. Standard errors are in parentheses. *Significant at p<.05, **Significant at p<.01, ***Significant at p<.001

that, other conditions being equal, national origin, gender, age, perceptions of commonality, measures of acculturation, experiences with discrimination, being naturalized, length of time in the U.S., and political variables (interest, ideology, and knowledge) are all significantly associated with the acquisition of Latino partisanship. In relative terms, being Cuban, having a lighter skin color, feeling political commonality with Whites, and being ideologically conservative are positively linked to the adoption of Republican partisanship. Mexicans, Cubans, and Latinos who have higher levels of political knowledge are drawn to political independence over Democratic partisanship, whereas old age, experiences of discrimination, linked fate with African Americans, and lower levels of political interest are significantly associated with Democratic partisanship. And when given the choice of Democratic partisanship vs. nonidentifier, women, younger Latinos, Latinos with lower levels of education, those who do not feel a sense of linked fate with African Americans, ideologically conservative Latinos, those with higher levels of political interest and political knowledge, those who have spent fewer years in the U.S., and naturalized respondents are more likely to choose nonidentification. Ultimately, the results show that the acquisition of partisanship is not associated with racial identification. It is worth noting that this is also true of multinomial logistic regression models predicting the direction of partisanship that included other forms of other race identity (SOR_Latino and Latino). Thus, although these identities exist and can be socially and politically relevant, here we see that Latino immigrants do not rely on them to inform this political choice.

WHAT FACTORS PREDICT THE STRENGTH OF LATINO PARTISANSHIP?

To explore whether racial identity influences the strength of partisan identification with political parties, a five-point scale of partisanship strength ranging from nonidentifier (0) to strong Democrat or Republican (4) is used as the dependent variable. Model I includes all respondents and Model II is restricted to immigrants. The results from the ordered probit regression models presented in Table 5.4 show racial identity is generally not linked with a higher likelihood of becoming a strong partisan. This is also true of the models predicting partisan strength that include distinct forms of other race identity. The lone exception is a statistically significant relationship between the general some other race identity and partisan strength among immigrants. The fact that this relationship is negative and statistically significant for the general identity and not significant when this identity is further defined suggests that for many other race Latinos, sustained party polarization on race and racial issues impacts their political allegiance. Being immigrants, many of these respondents are presumably less comfortable with the practice of racial classification

80   The Politics of Race in Latino Communities

Table 5.4   Predicting the Strength of Latino Political Partisanship

	All respondents	Immigrants
Demographic Characteristics		
Black	-.22(.26)	-..08 (.31)
Multiracial	-.14 (.16)	-.22 (.21)
Some other race	-.04 (.05)	-.15 (.06)*
Mexican	-.02 (.06)	-.07 (.08)
Puerto Rican	.12 (.11)	-
Cuban	.08 (.10)	.00 (.11)
Dominican	.30 (.12)**	.24 (.12)*
Ties to Afro-Latino country	.11 (.12)	.14 (.12)
Skin color (dark to light)	-.00 (.02)	.01 (.03)
Female	-.00 (.04)	-.07 (.05)
Age	.02 (.00)***	.01 (.00)***
Naturalized citizen	-	-.26 (.06)***
Time in U.S.	-	.01 (.00)*
Socioeconomic Status		
Income	.05 (.01)***	.02 (.01)
Education	.02 (.01)	.03 (.01)*
Commonality/Linked Fate/Discrimination		
Socioeconomic commonality with Blacks	.01 (.02)	.01 (.03)
Socioeconomic commonality with Whites	-.02 (.03)	-.02 (.03)
Political commonality with Blacks	.01 (.03)	-.00 (.03)
Political commonality with Whites	-.02 (.04)	-.00 (.03)
Linked fate with Latinos	.02 (.03)	.01 (.03)
Linked fate with Blacks	.02 (.03)	.06 (.03)**
Discrimination (scale)	-.01 (.03)	-.01 (.03)
Discrimination—R is Latino	.02 (.08)	.13 (.10)
Discrimination—skin color	.03 (.11)	.18 (.16)
Acculturation/Assimilation		
Generation	.10(.03)**	-
English interview	.36 (.06)***	.15 (.07)*
Keep Spanish language	-.02 (.04)	.07 (.06)
Political interest	.19 (.03)**	.17 (.04)***
Political ideology	.01 (.02)	.00 (.01)
Political knowledge	-.06 (.02)**	-.04 (.03)
Cut 1	.43 (.25)	.15 (.36)
Cut 2	.73 (.25)	.47 (.36)
Cut 3	1.14 (.25)	.87 (.36)
Cut 4	1.90 (.25)	1.61 (36)
N	2591	1811
Log Likelihood	-3708.52	-2666.22
Pseudo R2	.05	.05

Note: Estimates are ordered probit coefficients. Standard errors are in parentheses. *Significant at p<.05, **Significant at p<.01, ***Significant at p<.001

in the U.S., as it is different from that practiced in most Latin American countries. Furthermore, having rejected standard racial categories, one might argue that the individuals in this category who do not conceptualize this identity as a panethnic or racial identity are in essence rejecting existing U.S. social norms about race (e.g. Masuoka 2011). To the extent that the White-Black racial divide remains the driving force in American politics and therefore mainstream political parties (e.g. Fraga and Leal 2004), it is conceivable that other race Latinos who do not conceptualize that identity as panethnic or racial would feel little reason to become invested in racially polarized political parties.

Predicted probabilities provide some support for this perspective. Among Latinos who self-identify as other race, the predicted probability of self identification as a strong partisan is .25 and increases slightly as the remaining other race identities narrow how respondents conceptualize that identity. Among other race Latinos who conceptualize that identity as a panethnic identity (SOR_Latino) the probability of being a strong partisan .27, and the probability is .30 for other race Latinos that hold a racialized conceptualization of other race identity (Latino).

In the full model, national origin, age, income, generational status, language proficiency, political knowledge, and political interest are significant predictors of stronger partisanship. Older, wealthier, and politically interested Latinos are significantly more likely to be strong partisans than are younger, poorer, and disinterested Latinos. Latinos of Dominican descent, those farther away from the immigrant experience, and respondents who were interviewed in English are also more likely to be strong partisans. Conversely, those with greater political knowledge are significantly more likely to be weak partisans. Among immigrants, national origin, gender, age, linked fate, language proficiency, and political interest are positively associated with stronger identification with major parties. Whereas being naturalized is negatively linked to strong partisanship, having lived in the U.S. for a long time contributes to the development of strong partisan attachments.

CONCLUSION

Partisanship is often noted as one of the most important influences on political behavior, consistently predicting modes of political participation. The research on the development of Latino partisanship is an important first step toward understanding Latino political participation and gaining insight into how they are incorporated into the political system. Although race is a significant predictor of partisanship among non-Hispanic Whites and Blacks, the multinomial regression results generally identify few instances of racial identity influence, suggesting that in this context, Latino racial identity lacks strong political importance. Yet, I do find that multiracial Latinos are significantly more likely to identify as Republicans than as Democrats, controlling for all other factors. This is particularly interesting, considering that most Latinos are presumed to lean Democratic. I also find that among immigrants, other race identification negatively impacts the strength of partisan identification. Finally, it is also important to note that although many factors, including national origin, experiences of discrimination, and acculturation, influence the development of Latino partisanship more broadly, the process of partisan acquisition is somewhat different for immigrants. For example, whereas there is no significant gender difference in the strength of Latino partisanship more broadly, gender plays a much larger role in shaping partisan strength for immigrants. These differences further highlight the need to give greater attention to immigrants' political experiences.

Although it is clear that other factors are more likely to affect the direction and strength of partisanship, this research adds to our general understanding of racial identity and its impact on Latino politics, specifically the degree to which this identity plays a role in Latinos' integration into American political parties. In the next chapter, I continue to explore the effects of racial identification on politics, examining the political significance of racial self-identity formation and its influence on Latino political participation across electoral and nonelectoral activities.

6 The Impact of Race on Latino Political Participation

In the study of Latino politics, there is one question that remains of great interest to scholars and practitioners alike: what factors influence political participation? Traditional studies of political participation emphasize the importance of socioeconomic status in determining whether individuals will participate in politics (Berelson et al. 1954; Verba and Nie 1972; Wolfinger and Rosenstone 1980; Rosenstone and Hansen 1993; Verba et al. 1995). Focusing on the means of the individual, resource-based explanations hold that education and income drive political participation, as persons with higher levels of schooling and income are more likely to be politically involved. These factors are indeed predictive of Latino political activism—affluent and highly educated Latinos are more likely to participate (e.g. Hero and Campbell 1996; DeSipio 1996; Arvizu and Garcia 1996). Much of the literature on Latino politics also emphasizes the impact of nativity (Verba et al. 1995; DeSipio 1996; Leal 2002; Baretto and Munoz 2003); mobilization (e.g. Rosenstone and Hansen 1993; Shaw et al. 2000; Michelson 2003, 2006), and political context (e.g. Barreto et al. 2004; Bishin et al. 2005).

Yet another avenue of research in the study of Latino political participation is the political and social consequences of group identity. Within the Latino population, national origin is highly predictive of political participation (de la Garza et al. 1992; DeSipio 1996). Studies that separately examine Latino national origin groups have found that there are seminal political differences among the groups. For example, Cubans have a higher propensity to vote than Mexicans and Puerto Ricans but are less likely to be involved in alternative forms of political participation (Wrinkle et al. 1996; see also de la Garza et al. 1992; Garcia and Sanchez 2004; Highton and Burris 2002). Yet another avenue of research is the role of identity and consciousness as group-based resources and their effect on political participation (e.g. Garcia Bedolla 2005; Sanchez 2006). Latinos, when stimulated by a sense of commonality and linked fate and of panethnic identification, are more likely to participate in a wide range of political activities, including voting (Stokes 2003).

This chapter assesses the extent to which racial identification influences Latinos' propensity to participate in politics. Political participation is broadly characterized by the action people use to influence the structure of government, the selection of government officials, or the policies of government (Conway 2000). Participation in elections is a two-step process that requires both citizenship and the act of registering to be eligible to vote. Voting is the most common political act and most often recognized as a critical indicator of political incorporation. Yet, political participation extends beyond voting, allowing both citizens and noncitizens to be a part of the body politic and affect change. Latino noncitizens often participate in the political process and work collectively to solve issues in many other ways, such as volunteering, attending meetings and rallies, and participating in civic groups (e.g. Barreto and Munoz 2003; Highton and Burris 2002; Garcia Bedolla 2005). Thus, to better understand Latino political participation, here I explore whether racial identity can facilitate participation in the electoral arena and in nonelectoral political activities.

RESEARCH ON LATINO POLITICAL PARTICIPATION

Much of the literature on political participation has focused on racial and ethnic differences in political activity. Although Latinos tend to participate politically through a broad range of political activities, political participation is lowest among Latinos when compared with non-Latinos (Hero and Campbell 1996; see also Jennings 1993; McClain and Stewart 1995). This is due in part to low rates of naturalization among Latino immigrants, which severely limit Latino voting power (DeSipio 1996; Shaw et al. 2000). Many Latinos also lag behind Whites and African Americans when considering dominant factors closely linked to voting in elections, such as socioeconomic status and age.

Moving beyond the standard model of participation, additional theories of political participation focus on political attitudes, political mobilization, and cultural factors. These are all thought to drive down the cost of registering and going to the polls. Participation depends upon political engagement, a psychological orientation toward politics (Almond and Verba 1963; Verba and Nie 1972; Verba et al. 1995). Thus, political attitudes like efficacy, interest, and political trust are positively correlated with Latino political participation (Leighley and Vedlitz 1999; Rosenstone and Hansen 1993; Hritzuk and Park 2000). Mobilization is also closely linked to Latino participation. Being contacted by a political party or group has long been shown to increase voting and other types of participation in the U.S. (Dahl 1961; Rosenstone and Hansen 1993; Verba et al. 1995). Being mobilized is a significant and positive predictor of overall participation levels among Latinos, even when other potential influences are taken into account (Leighley 2001; Hritzuk and Park 2000). Coethnic mobilization is particularly salient, as Latinos who report being encouraged to vote by a non-Latino individual or group were no more likely to have voted but those who reported being encouraged to register to vote by a Latino candidate or political organization were more likely to have participated (Shaw et al. 2000). Door-to-door Latino voter mobilization is also effective in encouraging Latino voters to participate (Michelson 2003, 2006). Extant research also suggests that cultural factors influence the political activity of Latinos. Nativity influences Latino electoral and nonelectoral participation, as foreign-born Latinos are much less likely to register, vote, and participate in civic activities than are U.S.-born Latinos (e.g. de la Garza and DeSipio 1997; Verba et al. 1995; DeSipio 1996; but see Pantoja et al. 2001). Latinos who have lived longer in the U.S. are also more likely to participate in politics (e.g. Arvizu and Garcia 1996; Highton and Burris 2002).

Understanding the political involvement of Latinos is crucial for assessing the degree to which groups achieve political power. The more involved and active a group is, the more likely it is that the group will be represented in policy making in government and will have the ability to influence public-policy outcomes. Thus, being politically involved facilitates and enhances not only Latino political representation (representation of minorities on policy-making bodies) but also the ability of those representatives as part of governing coalitions to advance the goals and interests of the group (e.g. Browning et al. 2003). Although it has been argued that for Latinos to be incorporated and empowered they must develop a positive attachment to their group (e.g. Garcia Bedolla 2005), Latinos have many options in deciding how to identify, which then begs the question: which forms of group identity are most relevant to politics? In her study of Latino identity and political participation, Natalie Masuoka (2008) concludes that a racialized group identity most strongly encourages political participation. Yet only those who rejected traditional census race categories and gave the response of Latino/Hispanic as their race are treated as having a racial identity. Similarly, in her study of Latino political participation, Zulema Valdez (2011) also finds that racial group identity influences political action and, like Masouka, uses Latino/Hispanic responses as the sole measure of Latino racial identity.[1] Taking into account the reality that Latinos self-identify with a wide range of racial groups, the research presented here reaffirms these and other works that highlight the salience of shared racial identity in the Latino community. However, a central goal is to explore with greater specificity and depth the degree to which distinct racial identities encourage participation (see also Stokes-Brown 2006; Stokes-Brown 2009).

RACE AND LATINO POLITICAL PARTICIPATION

A preliminary review of the data shows that the type of political activities and the extent to which Latinos engage in those activities are influenced by racial identity. Respondents who are citizens of the U.S. were asked if they were registered to vote and if they voted during the 2004 presidential election. All respondents, regardless of citizenship, were questioned about their engagement in nonelectoral activities. In addition to reporting whether they

86   *The Politics of Race in Latino Communities*

tried to get government officials to pay attention to something of concern by calling, writing a letter, or going to a meeting, they are also asked whether they participate in the activities of one or more social, cultural, civic, or political groups.

Although Latino citizens from each racial group report high rates of registration, Black Latinos report the highest rate of registration (91 percent), followed by multiracial Latinos (87percent), White Latinos (85 percent), and other race Latinos (80 percent).[2] The registration rate for Latinos who self-identify as other race increases only slightly (81 percent) when this racial category is disaggregated. Whereas Black Latinos are most likely to be registered, White and multiracial Latinos are more likely to vote. Seventy percent of White and multiracial Latinos reported voting in the 2004 presidential election compared to 69 percent of Black Latinos and 64 percent of other race Latinos. It is worth noting that the turnout rate among other race Latinos who conceptualize that identity as a distinct racial identity is higher than that for respondents who also self-identify as other. Whereas 64 percent of other race Latinos and other race Latinos who self-identify as Latino/Hispanic (SOR_Latino) voted, 68 percent of other race Latinos who self- identified as Latino/Hispanic and believe Latinos are a distinct racial group reported voting during the presidential election.

Focus group participants were asked to talk about the way they participate in politics. The intentionally broad wording was meant to allow participants to define their activism and what it means to participate in their own terms. The answers given were fairly similar in that most participants defined participation as voting. Yet, the responses also capture a greater degree of ambivalence about the value of voting. For example:

> I always vote. . . . I have asthma and I still go out and vote. It is very important. (Puerto Rican woman, first Chicago group)

> No, I don't vote. I don't like politics. I stay as far away from that as possible. They [politicians] don't identify with us so how are we supposed to identify with them? They don't make you feel part of the system so how can you identify with the political system—so that is why I say as little as possible. (Ecuadorian man, second Chicago group)

> I vote and we all should vote. Not so much to help us but when you need someone who will think of us when making decisions later? We don't want to be coddled but someone to think and consider the impact on us–on those who can't afford certain things. (Puerto Rican woman, first New York group)

> Don't vote and don't bother to get involved. I think the world is dirty and politics is just making it dirtier. All these things people are doing

... nothing's fair when it comes to the running of the country. Everyone is looking out for themselves, their families ... they jump from one party to the next using their position to make money, you know what I mean? (Dominican man, second New York group)

I educate myself about candidates and try to know something about their careers. Then I vote. (Mexican man, third Chicago group)

The responses range from feelings of optimism and hope to feelings of disempowerment. Clearly, some respondents express positive feelings about participating in politics, believing that voting in particular has great value in its ability to make positive changes in the lives of people. Others are less efficacious, expressing frustration and distrust of politics and elected officials. There is a strong sense among these participants that voting does not matter because it is not a credible or effective accountability mechanism through which to ensure that the political system is providing benefits for everyone.

Turning to the questions measuring nonvoting political activity, crosstabulations reveal that respondents are much less likely to engage in these activities than in voting. This is inconsistent with extant research that finds Latinos to be more likely to participate in nonelectoral activities than in voting and other formal political activities (e.g. Verba et al. 1993; Hero and Campbell 1996; Wrinkle et al. 1996). Comparatively, the focus group participants expressed greater interest in nonelectoral activities. For instance, several said they participated in marches and petition drives. A number of respondents, mostly in the New York focus groups, also reported participating in the activities of social, cultural, civic, and religious groups. A young female participant explained:

Well, I recently got involved in this program working with low-income kids who live around the ghetto—they have been abused or have a disability ... so they have people my age to be a mentor for them so they know someone cares about them. (Puerto Rican woman, second New York group)

A Puerto Rican male in the second New York group also noted that he participated "in the LBGT Latin community and several Asian awareness groups—groups that work to let people know about health benefits. . . . I do a lot of work in Chinatown." Other examples included working with the elderly and religious groups (evangelical Christians, Jehovah's Witnesses). Yet, even among the focus group participants, there was greater support for formal political activities, particularly voting. The response of one participant nicely illustrates this broader pattern. When asked about the ways in which participants get involved in politics, this woman responded, "In my family, we express our rights through voting. That is best" (Mexican woman, first Chicago group).

When exploring racial differences in nonelectoral participation, we see that Black Latinos are most likely to contact elected official (41 percent) compared to multiracial Latinos (39 percent), White Latinos (34 percent), and other race Latinos (33 percent). Most respondents report little to no participation in groups. In fact, there is no statistical difference in participation among the Latino racial groups—79 percent of White and Black Latinos, 77 percent of multiracial Latinos, and 80 percent of other race Latinos do not participate in any groups. Approximately 13 percent of all Latinos, regardless of race, participate in the activities of one group, and there are small differences in participation among respondents who participate in two or more groups. Multiracial Latinos are most likely to participate in multiple groups (9 percent), followed by Black Latinos (8 percent) and White and other race Latinos (7 percent). As was the case with registration and voting, there are noticeable differences in the rate of participation among racialized other race respondents and the remaining other race respondents. Whereas 33 percent and 7 percent of all other race Latinos reported contacting an elected official and participating in two or more groups, respectively, 37 percent and 10 percent of racialized other race respondents engaged in these forms of political action.

Respondents were also asked to how they might address an issue or problem. Responses were coded so that 0 equals "nothing," 1 equals "get together informally," 2 equals "use existing groups," and 3 equals "getting together informally and using existing groups."[3] Approximately one-quarter of all respondents said they would do nothing to solve or address an issue, whereas 11 percent said they would use both methods. The remaining respondents were slightly more likely to use informal methods (35 percent) than existing groups (32 percent). Once again, there is no statistical difference in engagement among the racial groups ($p = .54$) or in the rate of participation among other race respondents. There are, however, slight differences among those willing to use both methods. Sixteen percent of Black Latinos supported the use of both methods, as compared to 12 percent of multiracial Latinos and 10 percent of White and other race Latinos.

In summary, the bivariate results suggest that racial identity influences political participation, particularly electoral activities. Black identity is positively associated with high registration and contacting elected officials but White and multiracial identity is associated with voting. In what follows, I outline how additional theoretically relevant variables are also expected to influence Latino political participation and then discuss the results of multivariate models that explore the extent to which racial identity affects Latino political activism.

Nationality, Phenotype, and Other Demographic Factors

When examining national origin groups, extant research has found significant differences in terms of participation among Latinos. For instance,

The Impact of Race on Latino Political Participation   89

Cubans vote at a higher rate than Mexicans and Puerto Ricans, and Dominicans are more likely to report voting than Mexicans and Puerto Ricans (DeSipio et al. 2003). Given that skin tone has a marked impact of individuals' life chances and identities, it may also affect political behavior (e.g. Hochschild et al. 2004). If lighter skin is analogous to high socioeconomic status (e.g. Relethford et al. 1983; Mason 2004), then light-skinned Latinos might be expected to register, vote, and participate in nonelectoral activities at a higher rate than darker-skinned Latinos. Gender and age are also typically raised as key explanatory variables of Latino political participation, with older Latinos participating at a higher rate than younger Latinos (DeSipio 1996). Latinas differ from Latino males in various aspects of political participation (Hardy-Fanta 1993; Montoya et al. 2000; Garcia, 2000), with men participating in more Latino-specific activities than women (Sanchez 2006).

Socioeconomic Status

Early models of political participation established that socioeconomic variables such as education and income are positively linked to the propensity to vote in elections and participate in politics (Verba and Nie 1972; Wolfinger and Rosenstone 1980; Uhlaner 2002; DeSipio et al. 2003; Hritzuk and Park 2000). Thus, those with higher levels of education and income are expected to be political involved, engaging in a wide range of political activities.

Discrimination, Linked Fate, and Commonality

Linked fate, discrimination, and commonality, as measures of group consciousness, have been found to be positively correlated with Latino political behavior (Stokes 2003; Sanchez 2006; Valdez 2011). Experiences with discrimination may lead individuals to become active in politics in order to challenge inequality (e.g. Uhlaner 1991). Using the 1999 Kaiser/Washington Post National Survey of Latinos, Sanchez (2006) found that perceived discrimination increasing voting. Yet it is possible that experiencing discrimination might make Latinos turn away from the political system because they feel isolated and alienated from the process (e.g. Valdez 2011).

Acculturation/Assimilation

Language proficiency and generational status are also expected to influence Latino participation, as Latinos who are more integrated into the American political system participate at greater levels than do those who are not (e.g. Verba et al. 1995; DeSipio 1996; DeSipio et al. 2003). Language has been consistently identified as a dominant influencing factor of Latino political participation, as English-speaking Latinos are likely to have greater access to the resources necessary to participate (de la Garza and DeSipio, 1997; Uhlaner 1989). Yet some studies have found that measures of assimilation and acculturation do not significantly impact Latino voting (e.g. Sanchez 2006; Barreto and Munoz 2003).

In addition to including key variables from the noted theoretical frameworks, the multivariate models also include measures of political interest and partisanship, given that Latinos who are interested in politics and are strongly committed to a political party are more likely to be politically active (Hritzuk and Park 2000).[4]

WHAT FACTORS PREDICT LATINO POLITICAL PARTICIPATION?

The results from logistic and ordered probit regressions presented in Table 6.1 show that racial group identity encourages some forms of participation. Latinos who self-identify as Black and other race are significantly more likely to register. That these racial identities play a distinct role in mobilizing Latinos to register deserves special attention. The act of voting requires first that citizens are registered, making this a critical first step toward political incorporation. This finding suggests that a heightened awareness of their non-White status may encourage these Latinos to place greater value on this political act. Yet here we see that for Black Latinos in particular, higher registration does not translate into higher levels of voting. Whereas there is no significant difference in voting among White and Black Latinos, other race Latinos and multiracial Latinos are more likely to vote than White Latinos.

Figure 6.1 shows the probability of registering and voting for each group. When compared to the predicted probability of voting, we see that the predicted probability of registering is higher for all racial groups. Yet the registration/voting gap is most pronounced for Black Latinos. It may be that having come to understand how identifying with Blackness can create social problems (Duany 1998), Black Latinos ultimately see themselves as disenfranchised from the electoral process, which deters them from voting. As we saw in Chapter Four, Black Latinos are more likely to feel frustration toward and alienated from the political system. It is possible that this sense of alienation and dissatisfaction with politics keeps them from exercising their right to vote.[5]

Although it is true that not having citizenship is a critical roadblock on the path to political participation, citizenship is not required to participate in nonelectoral activities. Yet, when we turn to the measures of nonelectoral participation, here we see few differences in political action across the different racial subgroups. Black Latinos are more likely to use multiple methods to solve an issue or problem yet Latinos of different races are not markedly different in their willingness to contact an elected official or participate in groups.

Table 6.1 Latino Racial Identity and Political Participation

	Register to vote	Vote in 2004	Contact elected official	Participate in groups	Work with others
Demographic Characteristics					
Black	2.03 (1.05)*	.30 (.52)	.36 (.37)	.06 (.24)	.31 (.18)*
Multiracial	.94 (.65)	.88 (.50)*	-.05 (.27)	-.05 (.16)	.01 (.14)
Some other race	.40 (.15)**	.31 (.12)*	.07 (.08)	.06 (.05)	-.04 (.05)
Mexican	-.01 (.17)	-.03 (.14)	.16 (.09)*	.02 (.05)	.02 (.04)
Cuban	.25 (.34)	.21 (.27)	.11 (.17)	.09 (.10)	-.25 (.09)**
Puerto Rican	.28 (.30)	-.06 (.22)	-.02 (.17)	-.09 (.11)	.00 (.09)
Dominican	-.02 (.34)	.14 (.28)	.15 (.18)	.13 (.12)	.02 (.08)
Ties to Afro-Latino country	.33 (.38)	-.06 (.29)	-.10 (.17)	.07 (.11)	-.07 (.09)
Skin color (dark to light)	.11 (.06)*	.04 (.05)	-.02 (.03)	-.01 (.02)	-.03 (.02)*
Female	.15 (.13)	.19 (.10)*	.23 (.07)***	.06 (.04)	.13 (.03)***
Age	.05 (.00)***	.05 (.00)***	.02 (.00)***	.01 (.00)***	-.02 (.00)**
Socioeconomic Status					
Income	.13 (.03)***	.19 (.03)***	.16 (.02)***	.06 (.01)***	.02 (.01)*
Education	.27 (.01)***	.30 (.03)***	.21 (.02)***	.17 (.01)***	.06 (.01)***

Table 6.1 (continued)

	Register to vote	Vote in 2004	Contact elected official	Participate in groups	Work with others
Commonality/Linked Fate/Discrimination					
Socioeconomic commonality with Blacks	.03 (.07)	.03 (.06)	.08 (.04)*	-.03 (.02)	.01 (.02)
Socioeconomic commonality with Whites	-.00 (.07)	.14 (.06)	.00 (.04)	.10 (.02)**	.01 (.03)
Political commonality with Blacks	.03 (.08)	.08 (.06)	.13 (.04)***	.02 (.03)	.05 (.02)**
Political commonality with Whites	.03 (.09)	-.05 (.06)	.04 (.05)	-.00 (.03)	.04 (.02)*
Linked fate with Latinos	.01 (.06)	.00 (.05)	.11 (.04)**	.00 (.02)	.03 (.02)*
Linked fate with Blacks	.00 (.06)	-.06 (.05)	-.07 (.03)*	.01 (.02)	-.01 (.02)
Discrimination (scale)	.01 (.08)	.04 (.06)	.27 (.04)***	.15 (.03)***	-.00(.02)
Discrimination—R is Latino	-.09 (.21)	.03 (.17)	.09 (.12)	-.06 (.07)	.24 (.06)***
Discrimination—skin color	.37 (.31)	.34 (.23)	.14 (.18)	.00 (.10)	.27 (.09)**
Acculturation/Assimilation					
Generation	.21 (.09)*	.18 (.08)**	.07 (.05)	.00 (.04)	-.08 (.03)**
English interview	.29 (.15)*	.19 (.13)	.11 (.09)	.36 (.05)***	-.32(.04)***
Keep Spanish language	.07 (.11)	-.05 (.09)	.04 (.06)	.06 (.04)	.08 (.03)*
Republican	.01 (.20)	.03 (.16)	.04 (.11)	.09 (.07)	-.01 (.05)
Independent	-.12 (.18)	-.23 (.14)	-.12 (.09)	-.08 (.06)	-.04 (.05)
Nonpartisan	-1.11(.15)***	-.92 (.13)***	-.35 (.09)***	-.08 (.06)	-.03 (.05)
Political interest	.54 (.09)***	.61 (.08)***	.65 (.05)***	.36 (.03)***	.19(.03)***
Constant/Cut 1	-3.39(.68)***	-4.28(.56)***	-3.99(.38)***	2.78 (.25)	-.26(.19)
Cut 2	–	–	–	3.54 (.25)	.82 (.19)
Cut 3	–	–	–	–	1.99 (.19)
N	2334	2333	4340	4331	4026
Log Likelihood	-844.49	-1128.47	-2428.72	-2527.59	-5010.49
Pseudo R2	.18	.21	.14	.13	.02

Note: Estimates are logit and ordered probit coefficients. Standard errors are in parentheses.
*Significant at p<.05, **Significant at p<.01, ***Significant at p<.001

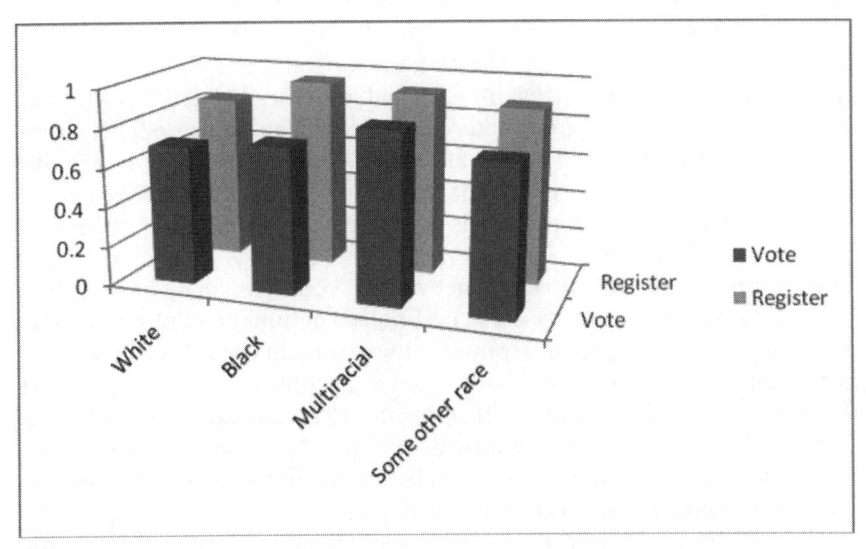

Figure 6.1 Predicted probability—Latino voter registration and turnout.

All other conditions being equal, national origin, phenotype, gender, age, socioeconomic status, measures of acculturation/assimilation, political interest, and partisanship are significantly associated with political activism. Political interest, age, and traditional measures of socioeconomic status are highly predictive across all measures of participation—being interested in politics, older, having more income, and higher levels of education are consistently associated with registering to vote, voting, contacting an elected official, participating in groups, and working with people in numerous ways to solve a problem or issue. Interestingly, whereas the relationship between political interest, income, education, and the last nonelectoral participation variable (work with others) is positive and significant, being older is negatively associated with using both formal and informal groups. Given the generational shift in norms of what it means to be engaged and participate in politics more broadly (e.g. Dalton 2009), a greater willingness among younger Latinos to be involved in a wider range of activities (both formal and informal) may not be very surprising. Whereas being Mexican is associated with greater nonelectoral participation (specifically contacting an elected official), Cubans are less likely to work with others in a group and to solve problems informally. Phenotype is also a significant predictor of some forms of participation. Why might skin color matter? If lighter-skinned Latinos have greater interactions with non-Hispanic Whites and greater social status, darker-skinned Latino immigrants may ultimately feel more alienated from the polity and that alienation may encourage them to retreat from politics and problem solving more broadly.

There are significant gender differences in participation, as being a woman is positively associated with both forms of participation, specifically voting, contacting an elected official, and working with others to solve problems. Latinos farthest removed from the immigrant experience are more likely to engage in electoral activities but are less likely to work with others in a group and to solve problems informally. Interestingly, English-dominant Latinos are more likely to register but are just as likely to vote as Spanish-dominant Latinos. These findings are consistent with extant research that finds that poor English proficiency hinders registration (Parkin and Zlotnick 2011) and findings that suggest that English proficiency has little impact on the vote (e.g. Shaw et al. 2000; but see Parkin and Zlotinick 2011). English-dominant Latinos are also more likely to participate in groups, but whereas they are less likely to use both formal and informal methods to solve a problem, Latinos who desire to maintain Spanish are more likely to use these methods. As expected, partisanship also influences political participation. Latinos who are not attached to political parties are much less likely to register to vote, to vote, and to contact an elected official.

Previous research has shown that perceptions of commonality and linked fate and of discrimination, as measures of group consciousness, influence participation (Stokes 2003; Sanchez 2006; Valdez 2011). Here we see that Latinos who feel greater socioeconomic commonality with Whites are more likely to vote and participate in groups, whereas Latinos who feel socioeconomic and political commonality with Blacks are more likely to contact their elected official. Political commonality with both Blacks and Whites positively predicts Latinos' likelihood of working with others in groups and to solve problems informally. Linked fate and discrimination are also more predictive of nonelectoral participation. Latinos who share a sense of linked fate with other Latinos are more likely to contact elected officials and work with others to solve problems, but a sense of linked fate with African Americans decreases the likelihood that Latinos will contact elected officials. Experiencing discrimination is also predictive, as Latinos who have numerous experiences with discrimination are much more likely to contact elected officials and participate in groups than those who experience no discrimination. We also see that Latinos who believe that skin color or being Latino is the reason for experiencing discrimination are more likely to work with others in formal and informal ways to address issues and problems.

When we disaggregate the Latino population that racially self identifies as "other," once again there are important differences among the groups. As one moves along the scale and this identity becomes racialized, we see an increased propensity to participate. Latinos who hold a racialized conceptualization of other race identity are more likely to register, vote, and participate in a wide number of groups. Thus, for these Latinos, conceptualizing their identity as a shared racialized group identity mobilizes them to participate in both electoral and nonelectoral activities.

Table 6.2 Other Race Identity and Political Participation

	Some other race	SOR_Latino	Latino
Register to vote	.40 (.15)**	.39 (.15)**	.42 (.18)**
Vote in 2004	.31 (.12)*	.30 (.13)*	.40 (.14)**
Contact elected official	.07 (.08)	.04 (.09)	.11 (.10)
Participate in groups	.06 (.05)	.05 (.06)	.11 (.06)*
Work with others	-.04 (.05)	-.05 (.04)	-.06 (.05)

Note: Each column represents coefficients from logit and ordered probit regression models that include the independent variables listed in Table 6.1. Standard errors are in parentheses. *Significant at p<.05, **Significant at p<.01, ***Significant at p<.001

RACIAL IDENTITY AND POLITICAL PARTICIPATION AMONG IMMIGRANT LATINOS

An examination of the predictors of political participation among immigrants, as the results in Table 6.3 show, demonstrates that racial identity remains a significant predictor of political activism. Immigrants who self-identify as Black, multiracial, and other are more likely to register to vote than White Latinos, whereas only multiracial and other race Latinos are more likely to vote. Yet among immigrants racial identity also facilitates nonpolitical participation, as multiracial Latinos are more likely to participate in social, cultural, civic, or political groups.

Here we also see that there are meaningful differences in participation among Latino national origin groups, as Mexicans, Cubans, and Dominicans are more likely to contact an elected official and those from countries with substantial Afro-Latino populations are more likely to register to vote. Cubans are also less likely to work with others in groups and to solve problems informally. In addition, phenotype influences political participation among immigrants, as lighter-skinned Latinos are more likely than darker-skinned Latinos to register and to vote.

As one might expect, political interest, age, and socioeconomic status drive participation, as politically interested, older, wealthier, and highly educated Latinos are more likely to register, vote, participate in groups, and use existing and informal groups to help solve problems. Latinos with higher incomes and education are also more likely to contact an elected official than are their less affluent, less educated counterparts. Gender is also significant, as Latinas are more likely to use both formal and informal methods to solve problems. Perceptions of commonality, linked fate, and discrimination also condition political action. Latinos who feel a sense of political and socioeconomic commonality with Blacks and feel their fate is linked to other Latinos are more likely to contact an elected official, whereas those who feel a sense of commonality with Whites are more likely

Table 6.3 Latino Racial Identity and Political Participation among Immigrants

	Register to vote	Vote in 2004	Contact elected official	Participate in groups	Work with others
Demographic Characteristics					
Black	1.03 (.05)*	1.13 (.92)	.05 (.50)	-.09 (.33)	.24 (.23)
Multiracial	1.90 (1.08)*	1.36 (.72)*	.19 (.34)	.33 (.20)*	.15 (.16)
Some other race	.39 (.19)*	.29 (.16)*	.09 (.10)	.06 (.07)	-.04 (.05)
Mexican	-.02 (.21)	-.13 (.19)	.17 (.11)	.03 (.07)	-.00 (.05)
Cuban	.22 (.37)	.11 (.31)	.15 (.19)	.04 (.12)	-.24 (.09)**
Dominican	-.07 (.38)	.21 (.32)	.28 (.19)	.09 (.12)	.03 (.09)
Ties to Afro-Latino country	.75 (.42)*	.32 (.34)	.10 (.19)	.03 (.11)	-.06 (.09)
Skin color (dark to light)	.15 (.08)*	.14 (.07)*	-.02 (.04)	-.04 (.03)	-.01 (.02)
Female	.09 (.17)	.17 (.15)	.13 (.09)	.06 (.08)	.11 (.04)**
Age	.03 (.01)***	.03 (.00)***	.00 (.01)	.00 (.01)	-.00 (.02)
Naturalized citizen	—	—	-.44 (.10)***	-.17 (.06)*	.04 (.05)
Time in U.S.	.04 (.01)***	.05 (.00)***	.02 (.00)***	.00 (.01)	.00 (.01)
Socioeconomic Status					
Income	.11 (.05)*	.14 (.04)***	.12 (.03)***	.03 (.02)	.02 (.01)*
Education	.17 (.05)***	.20 (.04)***	.13 (.02)***	.15 (.02)***	.05 (.00)***

(continued)

The Impact of Race on Latino Political Participation   97

Commonality/Linked Fate/Discrimination				
Socioeconomic commonality with Blacks	.05 (.09)	.10 (.08)	.10 (.05)*	-.03 (.04)	.01 (.02)
Socioeconomic commonality with Whites	-.09 (.10)	-.03 (.09)	-.00 (.05)	.09 (.04)**	.01 (.03)
Political commonality with Blacks	.00 (.10)	-.01 (.09)	.13 (.05)***	-.01 (.03)	.03 (.02)
Political commonality with Whites	-.03 (.10)	-.05 (.09)	-.06 (.05)	-.02 (.04)	.05 (.02)*
Linked fate with Latinos	.00 (.09)	-.02 (.08)	.10 (.05)*	-.04 (.03)	.00 (.02)
Linked fate with Blacks	.09 (.08)	.07 (.08)	-.02 (.04)	.03 (.05)	-.02 (.03)
Discrimination (scale)	-.14 (.11)	-.11 (.10)	.25 (.06)***	.09 (.04)**	-.01 (.03)
Discrimination—R is Latino	.01 (.29)	-.01 (.26)	-.06 (.15)	-.04 (.10)	.28 (.07)***
Discrimination—skin color	.07 (.49)	.68 (.46)	-.12 (.28)	-.00 (.17)	.18 (.14)
Acculturation/Assimilation				
English interview	.17 (.20)	-.39 (.18)*	-.12 (.11)	.41 (.07)***	-.42 (.06)***
Keep Spanish language	-.02 (.22)	-.04 (.19)	.08 (.12)	.03 (.07)	.04 (.05)
Republican	.00 (.26)	-.23 (.22)	.06 (.15)	.19 (.09)*	-.00 (.07)
Independent	-.01 (.23)	-.32 (.20)	.03 (.12)	-.06 (.07)	-.03 (.05)
Nonpartisan	-.86 (.20)***	-.82 (.19)***	-.17 (.11)	.05 (.07)	-.04 (.05)
Political interest	.46 (.12)***	.59 (.11)***	.53 (.06)***	.31 (.04)***	.18 (.03)***
Constant/Cut 1	-2.94 (1.10)**	-4.13 (.97)***	-2.97 (.60)***	2.12 (.38)	-.46 (.28)
Cut 2	-	-	-	2.91 (.39)	.66 (.28)
Cut 3	-	-	-	-	1.79 (.29)
N	1151	1159	3062	3061	2848
Log Likelihood	-481.85	-579.40	-1652.50	-1566.48	-3555.48
Pseudo R2	.17	.22	.12	.13	.02

Note: Estimates are logit and ordered probit coefficients. Standard errors are in parentheses.
*Significant at p<.05, **Significant at p<.01, ***Significant at p<.001

to participate in groups (socioeconomic commonality), work with others in a group, and solve problems informally (political commonality). Latinos who have experienced discrimination are more likely to participate in nonelectoral activities by contacting an elected official and participating in groups. Similarly, Latinos who believe that being Latino explains why they were discriminated against are more likely to work with others in a group and to solve problems informally. English proficiency has a significant effect on Latino participation, increasing the likelihood of some forms of nonelectoral participation, yet it has a negative effect on formal and informal collaboration to solve problems and on voting. The result for voting supports Johnson et al.'s finding that Spanish-speaking residents were more likely to vote than their English-speaking counterparts (2003). However, it should be noted that they find this to be true for Latinos living in four majority Latino counties in southern Texas. That this finding also holds when using a nationally representative sample suggests that additional attention should be given to the relationship between language abilities and social context.

It is also the case that one's tenure in the U.S. is positively correlated with increased electoral and nonelectoral participation. This is consistent with previous findings that show that the odds of being a frequent voter are greater as the length of time an individual lives in the U.S. increases (Sanchez 2006). Yet, we also see that naturalized immigrants are less likely than other Latino immigrants to engage in nonelectoral activities. As expected, partisan attachments promote participation, as Independents and those not attached to political parties are less likely to vote. Those not attached to political parties are also much less likely to register and contact an elected official, whereas Republican partisanship is positively correlated with some forms of nonelectoral participation.

Turning to the three groups on the scale of "other" identity, once again I find distinct differences in participation. As was the case with the total sample, there is an increased propensity for immigrants to participate in both nonelectoral and electoral activities as other race identity becomes more racialized.

CONCLUSION

Although Latinos are often called the "sleeping giant" of American politics, it still remains to be seen whether the visibility and size of the Latino population will result in a degree of political influence commensurate with their numbers. Participation plays an important role in political incorporation, as it is the primary method through which groups are represented by candidates of their choice and group interests can be addressed in the policies crafted by decision-making bodies. Consistent with the findings from extant research on the link between Latino racial identity and political participation, racial group identity influences Latinos' political action.

The Impact of Race on Latino Political Participation 99

Specifically, I find that Black and other race Latinos are more likely to register to vote, and multiracial and other race Latinos are more likely than White Latinos to vote. Black Latinos are also more likely to use multiple methods to solve an issue or problem, yet Latinos of different races are not markedly different in their willingness to contact an elected official or participate in groups. Among immigrants, multiracial Latinos are more likely to participate in social, cultural, civic, or political groups. Interestingly, disaggregating the other race category shows that a racialized other race identity is a positive predictor of both electoral and nonelectoral participation. This finding is consistent with extant research that finds that a racialized group identity can mobilize Latinos to participate in politics (Masouka 2008; but see Valdez 2011). Yet the findings presented in this chapter also show that the central issue when studying the link between Latino racial identity and participation is not how much racial identity informs political action (e.g. Masouka 2008), but *which* racial identity facilitates participation. With respect to racial identity, Latinos appear to be markedly different from one another in their electoral and nonelectoral activities. Thus, the findings for both electoral and nonelectoral activity suggest that as scholars continue to explore the connection between Latino identity and participation, further examination of the personal and social construction of racial identity will be necessary to better understand under what conditions Latinos will engage in the political system.

7 Latino Racial Identity and the Dynamics of Public Opinion

Public opinion, the collective beliefs of the people in a society, measures attitudes toward various issues facing the country. How does the nation's citizenry feel about health care? Government spending? Education reform? Often, the answers to these and other questions are sought through public opinion surveys designed to inform policy makers and citizens more broadly of our perceptions. Therefore, public opinion plays an important role in American society, measuring thoughts and feelings on important political and social issues that affect everyday life. The practice of measuring public opinion also allows citizens to play a role in the political process, thus facilitating representation. Through polling, citizens have an opportunity to voice their opinions about public policy, increasing the chances that they can influence government and public discourse.

A number of studies have suggested that race is an important variable in the explanation of public opinion. Racial differences in public opinion are well documented, as non-Hispanic Blacks and Whites differ systematically in their outlook on politics and public policy (see Kinder and Sanders 1996; see also Combs and Welch 1982; Kluegel and Smith 1986; Hall and Ferree 1986; Schuman et al. 1997; Sigelman and Welch 1991; Tate 1994). This racial divide is most pronounced over overt and covert racial issues. Whereas Whites' political attitudes are generally influenced by individual self-interests and other social group identities such as class (Verba and Nie 1972; Verba et al. 1995), Black political attitudes tend to be much more uniform in nature. Perceiving race as a central barrier to individual social advancement, African Americans tend to use group-based interests to determine individual interests (Dawson 1994; Tate 1994). Thus, African American public opinion on general and race salient issues is strongly connected to racial identity.

Although our knowledge of Latino public opinion is much less developed than that of White and African American public opinion, we do know that for Latinos, ethnicity is a significant determinant of political choices (Alvarez and Garcia Bedolla 2003; de la Garza et al. 1992; DeSipio 1996). Latinos are diverse and differences exist between Latinos of different ancestry, yet characteristics such as shared language and a shared Latin American heritage can help to unite them, promoting a shared political perspective. Indeed, research shows that Latinos often express opinions that are distinctive from those of other groups. Latinos tend to support the death penalty and favor more liberal immigration policies than Whites and African Americans (e.g. Cain and Kiewiet 1986; Miller et al. 1984; Uhlaner and Garcia 2002). Similarly, Latinos have distinctly different attitudes about bilingualism and amnesty for illegal immigrants (Cain and Kiewiet 1987). Although this provides some indication of how Latinos orient themselves toward various issues, we know very little about racial identity and its influence as an individual-level determinant of Latino policy positions.

In this chapter, I seek to understand Latino public opinion, using the lens of race to illuminate Latino views on a range of social and public policy issues. Recent demographic shifts have made understanding Latino attitudes salient, yet the tremendous diversity of the population calls for careful analysis that recognizes this heterogeneity. According to social group theorists, group identification should lead to support for public policies that in some way benefit the in-group and opposition to policies that benefit the out-group (e.g. Conover 1984, 1987). Given the social and economic differences among Latino racial groups, the racial identity of Latinos is likely to influence their attitudes about various policies. Thus, by exploring the distinctiveness of racial identity, we further acknowledge intragroup differences, which helps us understand to what degree we can really speak of an aggregate Latino opinion (e.g. Leal 2007).

RESEARCH ON LATINO PUBLIC OPINION

Much of the research on Latino public opinion centers largely on Latino attitudes toward immigration. Although the American public holds a variety of opinions about immigration and the effects of immigration policy, this issue is particularly salient for the Latino population. As a result of legislation and ballot initiatives passed in the 1990s, several states with significant Latino populations made English the official state language, denied noncitizens access to public services, and implemented punitive measures against undocumented immigrants. Given the size of the foreign-born population, it is not surprising that immigration policy and attitudes toward immigrants has been a central focus in Latino politics research. Several studies have examined the impact of acculturation on Latino attitudes toward immigration and found that more recent immigrants and individuals with stronger cultural ties to their country of origin are more supportive of policies that benefit immigrants (de la Garza et al. 1993; Miller et al. 1984). Latinos more acculturated into U.S. society are more likely to support restrictive immigration policies (Hood et al. 1997; Binder et al. 1997) and are less likely to support policies that provide benefits to immigrants and refugees (de la Garza et al. 1993; Branton 2007). Wealthier, more educated, and older Latinos tend to be more supportive of restrictive immigration policies (Hood et al. 1997; Binder et al. 1997). There are also significant differences in opinion among Latinos of different national origins. Although Cubans are more likely to support increased legal immigration (Sanchez 2006), they tend to be most concerned about illegal immigration, and Mexican Americans are more likely to believe that the government is already doing too much to stop illegal immigration (Michelson 2001). Central Americans also tend to be much more open to increasing levels of legal immigration into the U.S. (Hood et al. 1997). Latinos of Caribbean origin are less likely to believe that legal immigration should remain unchanged rather than being decreased (Sanchez 2006).

Immigration is a salient issue confronting the Latino population, but not unlike members of other groups, Latinos are concerned about other issues. A handful of studies have examined Latino attitudes about abortion and vouchers. Again, although the American public holds a variety of opinions about abortion, there are several reasons to be particularly interested in Latinos' views. Core beliefs such as religious affiliation and religiosity influence attitudes toward abortion (e.g. Hertel and Hughes 1987; Cook et al. 1992; Welch et al. 1995), and Catholics and conservative (i.e. fundamentalist, evangelical, and charismatic) Protestants are most likely to oppose abortion. Latinos tend to be Catholic and very religious, and ideologically conservative (de la Garza et al. 1992) and are more likely than Anglos to oppose abortion (Leal 2004b).[1] Committed Catholic Latinos and Protestants, and Latinos who have received a great deal of guidance from their faith, tend to express greater opposition to abortion rights than others, whereas less devout Catholics exhibit greater acceptance of legalized abortion (Bolks et al. 2000; see also Ellison et al. 2005). Cubans tend to be much more pro-choice than Mexicans and Puerto Ricans (Bolks et al. 2000; Leal 2004b; Ellison et al. 2005; Sanchez 2006). Central/South Americans are also more likely to believe that abortion should be legal in all or most cases (Sanchez 2006). Latinas and English-dominant Latinos are also more likely to hold a pro-choice attitude about abortion than are Latino males and Spanish-dominant Latinos (Leal 2004b). Turning to the issue of vouchers, we also know from extant research that Latinos (and African Americans) are more likely than Whites to support vouchers (Moe 2001). However, this support is largely explained by Latinos' Catholic affiliation (Leal 2004b). There are also significant differences in support among Latino national origin groups, as Puerto Ricans uniquely support vouchers (Leal 2004).

A considerably smaller body of research has explored Latino attitudes across other policy issues. Focusing on the relationship between acculturation and attitudes toward immigration, government spending, services for people in need, affirmative action, and education policy (No Child Left Behind), Branton (2007) finds that less acculturated Latinos are more likely to support policy positions that distribute benefits to the needy and

Latino Racial Identity and the Dynamics of Public Opinion 103

minority groups in general than are more acculturated Latinos. In his study of Latino public opinion toward Latino salient issues (immigration, bilingual education) and issues not directly tied to Latinos (abortion, the death penalty), Sanchez (2006) finds that perceived discrimination influences Latino attitudes on Latino salient issues.

The body of research exploring the relationship between racial identity and Latino public opinion is even smaller. Using the 1999 Harvard Kennedy School/Kaiser Family Foundation/Washington Post Latino Survey, Nicholson et al. (2005) find clear differences in Latino opinion by race on implicitly racial policies and issues concerning social welfare that generally tend to polarize non-Hispanic Whites and Blacks. Black Latinos are more likely to be more supportive of government-sponsored health care and less supportive of the death penalty than White Latinos. This chapter revisits and expands this study which included two implicitly racial policies. We know from previous research that differences between Whites and Blacks are less apparent for non-race-related issues because perspectives on racial inequality play less of a role in determining one's position on these issues. It remains unclear whether differences in opinion between Latino racial groups will also follow this trend or whether variability in attitudes among Latinos as a function of race exists across a wide range of policy items, including Latino salient issues (i.e. immigration).

RACE AND LATINO PUBLIC OPINION

Using the LNS data, I examine three different issue groups. The first set of questions deals with a Latino salient issue: immigration. Respondents were asked to identify their preferred policy on illegal immigration: sealing/closing off the border; a guest worker program designed for temporary entrance; a guest worker program leading to legalization; or immediate legalization. The second grouping contains questions about implicitly racial/social welfare policies: government spending and health care. Respondents were asked whether they strongly oppose, oppose, support, or strongly support governmental income support for those who need it and governmental intervention to reform health care. The remaining set of policy issues are not directly tied to the Latino community but are high-profile political issues. Two education policy questions asked respondents to state their level of support for the use of standardized tests to determine whether a child is promoted to the next grade or graduates from high school and for vouchers that pay a portion of the cost to send children to private schools.[2] Respondents were also asked whether same-sex couples should receive no legal recognition, be permitted to enter into civil union, or be permitted to legally marry, and whether abortion should be illegal in all circumstances, legal only to save the life of the mother, legal in most circumstances, or legal in all circumstances.

A preliminary review of the data suggests that Latino attitudes toward various policy items vary somewhat by racial identity, yet the differences are generally modest. The most popular response for most Latino racial groups is immediate legalization (approximately 42–46 percent), followed by a guest worker program leading to legalization (approximately 32–36 percent). This pattern, however, is reversed for other race Latinos who believe Latinos are a distinct racial group: 44 percent prefer a guest worker program and 38 percent prefer immediate legalization. Although few respondents chose the most punitive measure, multiracial, Black, and White Latinos (8 percent each) are more likely to prefer that the borders be sealed or closed off than other race Latinos (5 percent). In the first New York focus group, the issue of illegal immigration was raised as part of a broader discussion about how Latino/a identity shapes respondents' political identity. Two participants commented about the impact of Arizona immigration law SB1070 on families and the need for illegal immigrants to have a path to citizenship:

> Kids are being ripped apart from their parents because they are the ones that are citizens not their parents and it's a disgrace. (Mixed Latina)

> It's like my nail lady—she had to leave her little 4 year old kid and then she gets deported. . . . People have no criminal record, given them a chance. Give them a working visa, give them a chance to earn their citizenship. (Puerto Rican woman)

> So now these kids are being put in the foster care system and being institutionalized and raised like that and become the stereotypical criminals, drug dealers, gang members, gang bangers, etc (Mixed Latina)

Turning to the next set of policies, it appears that Latino attitudes toward various implicitly racial/social welfare policies also vary by racial identity. Previous studies suggest that all Latinos, regardless of national origin group, support government health care and other social insurance programs (Martinez-Ebers et al. 2000; Leal 2007). Although it is the case that most of the respondents support some form of government income support, Black Latinos are most likely to express some form of support (91 percent), followed by other race Latinos (87 percent), White Latinos (85 percent), and multiracial Latinos (84 percent). Racial identity is also positively correlated with Latino attitudes toward health care. Black Latinos (60 percent) and other race Latinos (62 percent) are more likely to voice strong support for government intervention to improve access to health care and reduce costs than are White Latinos (59 percent) and multiracial Latinos (57 percent). Interestingly, this level of support among other race Latinos increases slightly as this identity becomes racialized.

Unlike the other policy areas, it appears that attitudes about education policy, same-sex marriage, and abortion are not strongly associated with racial identification. The distribution of support for standardized tests is similar across most groups, with a majority of Latinos from each racial group expressing some degree of support. Black Latinos (21 percent) are somewhat less likely to strongly support these tests than are other race Latinos (34 percent), White Latinos (33 percent), and multiracial Latinos (30 percent). Latinos also express similar levels of support for vouchers, with approximately half of the respondents in each racial group supporting them and half of the respondents expressing opposition. There is some variation among those who express the greatest level of support—32 percent of multiracial Latinos strongly support vouchers compared to 28 percent of White Latinos and other race Latinos, and 27 percent of Black Latinos. There is also little variation across the racial groups for the remaining two policy items. A majority of respondents believe that same-sex marriage should receive no legal recognition, whereas the remaining respondents favor legal marriage or civil unions. The distribution of opinions concerning abortion is fairly stable across the Latino racial groups—most Latinos favor making abortion legal only to save the life of the mother and in cases of rape and/or incest, with 55 percent of other race Latinos, 53 percent of White Latinos, 49 percent of multiracial Latinos, and 41 percent of Black Latinos expressing support. However, it should be noted that Black Latinos (21 percent) are somewhat more likely to believe that abortion should be legal in all circumstances compared to White Latinos and other race Latinos (12 percent) and multiracial Latinos (13 percent).

Overall, the bivariate results suggest that racial identity has the greatest impact on Latino political attitudes when the issues are salient to the Latino community and when the issues are implicitly racial. Racial identity has a weaker relationship with Latino attitudes on more general policy issues. The remainder of the chapter is dedicated to developing and testing multivariate regression models to predict the degree to which racial identity influences Latino policy attitudes, while controlling for the effects of theoretically relevant variables expected to be predictive of Latino opinions.

Nationality, Phenotype, and Other Demographic Factors

There is considerable diversity of opinion by national origin group on a wide range of policy issues (e.g. Uhlaner and Garcia 2002), including immigration policy (e.g. Michelson 2001; Martinez 2000; Leal 2007). Given that skin color can have a direct and immediate effect on the lives of Latinos, it may also be the case that phenotype operates as a critical linkage between respondents and society, influencing policy positions. Extant literature also shows that many individual-level characteristics explain Latino political attitudes (e.g. Branton 2007; Sanchez 2006, Jones-Correa 1998).

For example, older Latinos tend to be less supportive of liberal immigration reforms (Binder et al. 2007). Age and gender, particularly being a woman, have also been shown to increase the likelihood of holding a pro-life stance about abortion (e.g. Bolks et al. 2000; Sanchez 2006).

Socioeconomic Status

Latino political attitudes are also likely to be influenced by one's level of educational attainment and income. Policy preferences are often reflective of individual social and economic circumstances. Thus, the higher a Latino's socioeconomic status, the less likely he or she is to favor government support for social welfare and the more likely he or she is to support greater protection for business interests (Ulhaner and Garcia 2002: 86). Similarly, Bolks et al. (2000) find socioeconomic status to be a significant predictor of attitudes about abortion, as respondents with higher education and income levels are more likely to adopt a pro-life stance. Several studies also show that Latino public opinion varies by educational attainment. Highly educated Latinos are much more likely to express support for restricting immigration (Suro 2005; Hood et al. 1997). It is also the case that Latinos with higher levels of income are more likely to believe that immigration policies should remain the same relative to immigration being decreased (Sanchez 2006).

Discrimination, Linked Fate, and Commonality

It is well documented that the perception that race-based inequalities can motivate identity, which then leads to group interests dominating policy preferences (e.g. Dawson 1994; Tate 1993). Latinos who believe that discrimination against Latinos in society is a problem are more likely to favor increasing immigration and more likely to support bilingual education than those who believe that discrimination is not a problem (Sanchez 2006). Similarly, we might also expect Latinos who feel a sense of commonality and linked fate with a specific racial group to develop attitudes closer to the group they feel attached to.

Acculturation/Assimilation

Several extant works note the significant relationship between acculturation and Latino policy attitudes (e.g. Miller et al. 1984; Polinard et al. 1984; Branton 2007). Native and foreign-born Latinos differ significantly in their public policy attitudes. This is indeed the case with immigration policy, as native-born Latinos tend to favor more restrictive policies than foreign-born Latinos (Binder et al. 1997). English-language-dominant Latinos farthest removed from the immigrant experience tend to be less supportive of increased government spending, are less likely to believe that the

Latino Racial Identity and the Dynamics of Public Opinion 107

government is doing the best job of providing services to the needy, are less likely to support affirmative action, and are less likely to think that parents' top priority is to help a failing school when compared to less acculturated Latinos (Branton 2007: 298). Thus, one might expect to find that language competence is highly predictive of Latino public opinion. Finally, in addition to including key variables from the noted theoretical frameworks, the multivariate models also include measures of political partisanship, given its influence on political attitudes and beliefs (e.g. Campbell et al. 1960).[4]

WHAT FACTORS PREDICT LATINO PUBLIC OPINION?

Table 7.1 presents estimates for ordered probit regression models exploring attitudes toward illegal immigration, government spending, health care, vouchers, same-sex marriage, and abortion. Here we see that racial identity influences Latino policy attitudes yet this influence is not consistent across all measures of public opinion. Other race Latinos are significantly more likely to prefer immediate legalization for illegal immigrants. This provides some evidence that differences in opinion exist beyond issues on which White-Black attitudes have long been bifurcated and that there are clear racial differences in opinion on Latino salient issues. Other race Latinos are also more likely to believe that government should provide income support and believe that the health care system needs government intervention. Multiracial Latinos, however, are more likely to oppose governmental intervention to reform health care. This is consistent with previous research that has found clear racial differences in Latino opinion on implicitly racial policies (Nicholson et al. 2005). This finding is rather intriguing, given the high-profile debate over health care reform in 2009. On March 23, 2010, President Obama signed into law the Affordable Care Act, designed to expand health coverage within the health care system. Polls show that although a strong majority (61 percent) of Latinos believed that the federal government should ensure that all people have health insurance, partisanship strongly influenced support for the expansion of coverage. Seventy-two percent of Latino Democrats supported expansion compared with 31 percent of Republicans and 35 percent of Independents (Sanchez and Medeiros 2009). We saw in Chapter Five that multiracial Latinos are more likely to be Republicans than Democrats. Yet here we see that even when controlling for partisanship (Republicans are less likely to support government intervention), multiracial identity exerts its own independent effect. Thus, this finding highlights the value of efforts to study Latino opinion in a comparative manner to understand more fully the orientations of Latinos.

The results also demonstrate that variability in attitudes among Latinos as a function of race exists across a range of policy issues. Respondents' attitudes about vouchers and abortion are significantly related to racial identity. Other race Latinos are more likely to support vouchers. This

Table 7.1 Latino Racial Identity and Public Opinion

	Illegal immigration	Gov. spending	Health care	Std. Tests	Vouchers	Same-sex marriage	Abortion
Demographic Characteristics							
Black	-.10 (.20)	-.10(.19)	-.13 (.19)	-.31(.29)	-.32 (.27)	.61(.38)*	.05(.27)
Multiracial	-.03 (.15)	-.12 (.14)	-.21 (.15)*	-.01(.19)	.14 (.19)	-.09 (.25)	-.03 (.20)
Some other race	.09 (.05)*	.13 (.04)**	.12 (.04)**	-.00 (.06)	.15 (.06)*	-.10 (.07)	-.09 (.06)
Mexican	.06 (.04)	-.07 (.04)	-.04 (.05)	-.09(.07)	-.07 (.06)	.00 (.09)	.04 (.07)
Cuban	-.02 (.09)	-.00 (.09)	.18 (.10)*	-.24(.13)*	-.05 (.09)	.10 (.16)	.20 (.13)
Puerto Rican	-.14 (.09)	.31 (.10)***	.05 (.10)	-.04(.12)	-.11 (.12)	.12 (.17)	.35 (.14)**
Dominican	-.03 (.09)	.04 (.09)	.08 (.10)	-.03 (.13)	.14 (.12)	.09 (.18)	-.08 (.14)
Ties to Afro-Latino country	.07 (.09)	-.02 (.03)	.11 (.10)	-.12(.13)	.01 (.13)	.12 (.16)	.15 (.13)
Skin color (dark to light)	-.04 (.02)**	.02 (.03)	-.04 (.02)*	-.02(.03)	.06(.02)*	.04 (.03)	-.03 (.02)
Female	.12 (.04)***	-.02 (.04)	.09 (.04)*	-.13(.05)**	-.06(.03)**	.17 (.07)**	.02 (.05)
Age	-.01(.00)***	-.00 (.01)	.01 (.00)**	.01(.01)***	-.00(.01)	-.01 (.00)***	-.00 (.01)
Socioeconomic Status							
Income	-.03 (.01)**	-.08 (.01)***	-.00 (.01)	-.02(.01)*	-.03 (.01)*	-.00 (.01)	.05 (.01)***
Education	-.04 (.01)***	-.03 (.01)***	.02 (.01)*	-.02(.01)	-.02 (.01)	.04 (.02)*	.09 (.02)***

(continued)

Latino Racial Identity and the Dynamics of Public Opinion 109

Commonality/Linked Fate/Discrimination							
SES commonality w/Blacks	.03 (.02)	.05 (.02)**	-.01 (.02)	-.01 (.03)	-.02 (.03)	.11 (.04)**	.06 (.03)*
SES commonality w/Whites	-.01 (.03)	-.05 (.02)**	-.00 (.02)	.07 (.03)*	.03 (.04)	-.07 (.04)*	.03 (.04)
Political commonality w/Blacks	-.00 (.02)	.02 (.03)	.05 (.02)*	-.03(.04)	-.05 (.03)	.06 (.04)	.02 (.03)
Political commonality w/Whites	-.03 (.04)	.00 (.03)	-.06 (.02)**	-.05(.03)	.09 (.03)**	.01 (.04)	-.04 (.03)
Linked fate w/Latinos	.04 (.02)*	.06 (.02)**	.08 (.02)***	.01 (.03)	.03 (.04)	.01 (.04)	-.01 (.02)
Linked fate w/Blacks	.05 (.02)**	.07 (.02)***	.07 (.02)***	-.01(.02)	.04 (.02)	-.03 (.04)	-.07 (.02)**
Discrimination (scale)	.00(.02)	-.01 (.02)	.08 (.02)***	-.05 (.03)*	-.01(.03)	.09(.04)*	.03 (.04)
Discrimination—R is Latino	.06 (.07)	.08 (.06)	.00 (.06)	-.06 (.08)	-.08(.09)	-.23 (.11)*	-.04 (.09)
Discrimination—skin color	-.00 (.09)	.06 (.09)	-.09 (.10)	-.05 (.13)	.09(.14)	-.11 (.17)	.05 (.14)
Acculturation/Assimilation							
Generation	-.11 (.02)***	.03 (.04)	-.00 (.02)	-.09 (.04)**	.04 (.03)	.10 (.05)*	.02 (.04)
English interview	-.69 (.05)***	-.14 (.05)**	-.25(.05)***	.33 (.06)***	-.70(.06)***	.24 (.08)**	.32 (.07)***
Keep Spanish language	.12 (.03)***	.11 (.03)***	.05 (.03)	.04 (.05)	.04 (.05)	-.00 (.06)	-.13 (.05)**
Republican	-.26 (.06)***	.13 (.06)*	-.17 (.06)**	.41 (.08)***	.29 (.08)***	-.41 (.11)***	-.34(.08)***
Independent	-.03 (.05)	.00 (.05)	.01 (.05)	.03 (.07)	.06 (.07)	.23 (.09)**	-.03 (.07)
Nonidentifier	-.02 (.05)	-.02 (.04)	-.14 (.05)**	-.02 (.06)	.07 (.06)	.13 (.08)	-.19 (.06)**
Cut 1	-2.04 (.20)	-1.17 (.19)	-1.14 (.20)	-.97 (.28)	-.59 (.28)	.34 (.36)	-1.13 (.28)
Cut 2	-1.22 (.20)	-.65 (.19)	-.74 (.20)	-.44 (.28)	.14 (.28)	.74 (.36)	.59 (.28)
Cut 3	-.06 (.20)	.52 (.19)	.30 (.20)	.45 (.29)	.92 (.28)	-	1.03 (.28)
N	4218	4272	4296	2041	2056	1437	2003
Log Likelihood	-4394.62	-4501.60	-3889.31	-2660.50	-2673.73	-1299.95	-2123.26
Pseudo R2	.09	.03	.02	.02	.06	.05	.07

Note: Estimates are ordered probit coefficients. Standard errors are in parentheses.
*Significant at p<.05, **Significant at p<.01, ***Significant at p<.001

finding for vouchers is intriguing because although it is often assumed that African American and Latino educational interests are closely related or even identical because they share similar objective circumstances, Latinos tend to be more supportive than African Americans of voucher programs and standards-based education reforms such as high-stakes testing (Leal 2004a; Moe 2001; Lay and Stokes-Brown 2009). The fact that most Latinos self-identify as other race, coupled with the finding that they are more supportive of this reform than other Latino racial groups, may help us better understand why we see differences between African American and Latino opinion on this issue. There are also significant racial differences in Latino opinion about same-sex marriage. Black Latinos are more supportive of same-sex marriage than are White Latinos. Predicted probabilities reveal that Black Latinos express the highest levels of support for legalizing same-sex marriage (.58), followed by White Latinos (.31), multiracial Latinos (.30), and other race Latinos (.29). It is also the case that although the opinions of other race and White Latinos are much more similar, other race Latinos (.59) are somewhat more likely than White Latinos (.51) to believe that same-sex marriage should receive no legal recognition.

Additionally, the models show that national origin and phenotype are also significantly related to Latino policy attitudes. Puerto Ricans are significantly more supportive of government spending for income support and hold more pro-choice attitudes, yet contrary to other research, they are no more likely than other Latino national origin groups to support vouchers (see Leal 2004). Cubans are more likely to support government invention to reform health care but are less likely to support the use of standardized tests. Interestingly, we also see that skin color influences public opinion, as Latinos with lighter skin tones are less supportive of immigration efforts and government intervention to improve health care but are significantly more likely to support the use of vouchers to send children to private schools. Latinas tend to hold more liberal attitudes than Latino males—women are significantly more likely to favor legalization for illegal immigrants and government spending for health care. Being a woman is also associated with greater support for same-sex marriage but with less support for standardized tests. Older Latinos are much more likely to oppose policies that favor legalization for illegal immigrants and same-sex marriage but are more likely than younger Latinos to support government intervention for health care and standardized tests.

There is also evidence to suggest that predictions of Latino policy attitudes should take into account socioeconomic factors. Affluent and highly educated Latinos are less likely to support liberal immigration policies and are more likely to oppose government spending. Yet these respondents tend to have more liberal, pro-choice attitudes about abortion, and highly educated Latinos are more likely to support government intervention for health care. Interestingly, the results also show that income negatively predicts support for standardized tests and vouchers. Affluent Latinos are more likely to oppose the use of standardized tests to determine promotion or graduation and the use of vouchers to send children to private schools. This finding is consistent with Lay and Stokes-Brown's finding (2009) that Latinos with higher levels of income are less supportive of high-stakes standardized tests than their poorer counterparts.

It is also the case that intergroup perceptions, experiences with discrimination, and feelings of linked fate are important contributing factors to Latino policy attitudes. Latinos who perceive socioeconomic commonality with Blacks are more likely to favor governmental income support and have more liberal attitudes about same-sex marriage and abortion. Perceived socioeconomic commonality with Whites negatively predicts governmental income support and same-sex marriage but is a positive predictor of support for standardized tests. Political commonality is also predictive of Latino attitudes—Latinos who express political commonality with Blacks are more supportive of government intervention to improve health care, whereas those who feel political commonality with Whites are less likely to support this type of reform. Political commonality with Whites is also a significant and positive predictor of support for vouchers.

The linked fate variables are also significant for some policy issues. A sense of linked fate with African Americans negatively predicts support for abortion. Latinos who believe that the success of their national origin group is tied to other national origin groups and Latinos who feel a sense of linked fate with African Americans are more likely to support more liberal immigration policies. Also noteworthy is that a sense of linked fate with both other Latinos and African Americans positively predicts support for both implicitly racial policies—governmental income support and health care. Perceived discrimination is also significant, as Latinos who have experienced some level of discrimination are more likely to support government intervention to improve health care, have more liberal attitudes toward same-sex marriage, and are less likely to support standardized tests. We also see that Latinos who believe that being Latino was the reason for a discriminatory experience are less likely to support same-sex marriage.

Consistent with extant research (e.g. Branton 2007), measures of acculturation have a significant impact on Latino attitudes. Whereas extant research finds that generational status impacts Latino opinions toward Latino salient issues like immigration (e.g. Branton 2007; Garcia Bedolla 2005; Hood et al. 1997), generational status is also predictive of Latino attitudes about implicitly racial issues. Later-generation Latinos are less likely to support standardized tests but are more likely to support same-sex marriage. Preferring to be interviewed in English (commonly noted as a measure of language proficiency) is highly predictive across almost every policy item. These respondents are less likely to favor liberal immigration policies. They are also less likely to favor government spending and government intervention for health care reform. Most of these attitudes are the opposite of those who are attached to Spanish language use. These respondents favor liberal immigration policies and are supportive of government spending. English-dominant speakers also have distinct opinions about education, as they are more likely to favor standardized tests but oppose vouchers. Language preference also divides Latino opinion on abortion. Respondents who prefer to be interviewed in English are more likely to adopt pro-choice attitudes and support same-sex marriage, whereas respondents who are concerned about maintaining the ability to speak Spanish are more likely to be pro-life. It is also the case that generational status is highly predictive of Latino public opinion, as Latinos farthest away from the immigrant experience support more liberal immigration policies and same-sex marriage but are less likely to support standardized tests.

Lastly, as we might expect, partisanship is highly correlated with political attitudes. Here we see major differences in opinion among those attached to mainstream political parties. Republicans are less likely than Democrats to support more liberal immigration policies and are less likely to favor income support, governmental intervention to reform health care, same-sex marriage, and abortion. Conversely, they are more likely than Democrats to support education reforms such as standardized tests and vouchers. There are also some differences in opinion among those who shy away from mainstream parties. Independents are more likely than Democrats to express support for same-sex marriage, whereas nonidentifiers are less likely than Democrats to support government intervention to reform health care and abortion.

Recognizing the diversity among Latinos who self-identify as some other race, the multivariate analyses in Table 7.2 explore the pattern of difference in Latino public opinion among three groups. Included in the table is the coefficient for the variables of interest (racial identity) from regression analyses predicting levels of support for each public policy. Each regression model includes the independent variables listed in Table 7.1.

Table 7.2 Other Race Identity and Public Opinion

	Some other race	SOR_Latino	Latino
Illegal immigration	.09(.05)*	.08 (.04)*	.02 (.05)
Gov. spending	.13 (.04)**	.06 (.04)	.07 (.05)
Health care	.12 (.04)**	.13 (.04)**	.14 (.05)**
Std. tests	-.00 (.06)	.01 (.06)	.06 (.07)
Vouchers	.15 (.06)**	.15 (.06)**	.17 (.07)**
Same-sex marriage	-.10 (.07)	-.10 (.08)	-.10 (.09)
Abortion	-.09 (.06)	-.09 (.06)	-.08 (.07)

Note: Each column represents coefficients from ordered probit regression models that include the independent variables listed in Table 7.1. Standard errors are in parentheses. *Significant at p<.05, **Significant at p<.01, ***Significant at p<.001

Here we see some degree of similarity in opinion among these groups. Much like respondents in the first column, other race Latinos who conceptualize this identity as a panethnic or non-White racial identity are significantly more likely to favor government intervention to improve health care and support the use of vouchers. However, there are some important differences. Whereas other race Latinos in the first two categories are more likely to be more supportive of more liberal immigration policies, the opinion of other race Latinos in the third category (where a racialized conceptualization of Latino identity is most evident) is not statistically different from that of White Latinos. It is also worth noting that some groups have uniquely different perspectives. Although all other race Latinos generally support government spending to provide income support, the opinion of other race Latinos who hold panethnic and racialized conceptualizations of that identity is not statistically different from that of White Latinos.

RACIAL IDENTITY AND PUBLIC OPINION AMONG IMMIGRANT LATINOS

Thus far, the results suggest that racial identity has political meaning for Latinos. However, given immigration's important role in shaping the Latino population, I look to understand whether racial identity influences Latino public opinion among non-native Latinos. The multivariate analyses in Table 7.3 show once again that variability in attitudes among Latinos as a function of race exists across a range of policy issues. Immigrants who self-identify as other race are more likely to support government intervention to reform health care than are their White immigrant counterparts. It is worth noting that although other race Latinos in the full sample support more liberal immigration policies, favor income support for those in need, and are more likely to support vouchers, there is no significant difference in opinion on these issues among Latino racial groups in the immigrant sample. Turning to the remaining variables, we see again that national origin and phenotype are significantly related to Latino policy attitudes. Mexicans are less supportive of government spending for income support and standardized tests. Cubans are also less supportive of standardized tests but unlike other respondents from countries with significant Afro-Latino populations, they are supportive of government intervention to reform health care. Phenotype is predictive of Latino public opinion, as lighter-skinned immigrants are less likely to support health care reform and favor the use of vouchers. Latina immigrants hold more liberal attitudes than Latino males, as they are more likely to favor legalization for illegal immigrants and same-sex marriage. Older Latino immigrants are much more likely to oppose policies that favor same-sex marriage but are more likely than younger Latinos to support government intervention for health care.

Socioeconomic status, particularly education, also influences Latino policy attitudes. Affluent and highly educated Latinos are more likely to oppose government spending but have more liberal attitudes about abortion. Affluent immigrants are also less likely to support vouchers. Highly educated Latinos also hold more conservative positions on illegal immigration but are more supportive of government intervention for health care and same-sex marriage.

It is also the case that many of the commonality/linked fate variables are strong predictors of opinions among immigrants. Respondents who feel socioeconomic commonality with African Americans favor income support for those in need, whereas feelings of socioeconomic commonality with Whites is negatively correlated with income support and positively correlated with support for standardized tests. Similarly, whereas feelings of political commonality with Blacks predict opposition to vouchers (but support for government assistance for the poor), White political commonality has the opposite impact for vouchers (and predicts opposition to government invention to reform health care and the use of standardized tests). The results also suggest that sharing a sense of linked fate with other Latinos has a liberalizing effect, as these respondents are more likely to favor income support for the poor and government intervention to reform health care. Linked fate with African Americans has the same effect for the implicitly racial/social welfare variables and immigration, but leads to more conservative positions on abortion and same-sex marriage. Perceived discrimination is also significant, as Latinos who have experienced some level of discrimination are more likely to support government intervention to improve health care, and Latinos who believe that being Latino was the reason for a discriminatory experience are more likely to favor income support for the poor but are less likely to support same-sex marriage.

As we saw in models using the full data, preferring to be interviewed in English is highly predictive across every policy item. A desire to maintain Spanish is also predictive of policy attitudes, as these immigrants are more likely to favor liberal immigration policies, income support, and health care reform and hold conservative, pro-life views on abortion. Naturalized citizens hold more liberal views than immigrants who have not been naturalized, favoring more liberal immigration and marriage policies and conservative abortion policies. Immigrants who have been in the country for many years are also more likely to favor the use of standardized tests than those who are new to the country. Lastly, partisanship is highly correlated with immigrant political attitudes. Republicans are less likely than Democrats to support more liberal immigration policies and are less likely to favor same-sex marriage and abortion. Conversely, they are more likely than Democrats to support the use of standardized tests and vouchers. Those less attached to political parties also hold unique views. Independents are more likely than Democrats to express support for same-sex marriage, whereas nonidentifiers are less likely than Democrats to support government intervention to reform health care and abortion. Nonidentifiers are also more likely to support same-sex marriage.

Table 7.3 Latino Racial Identity and Public Opinion among Immigrants

	Illegal immigration	Gov. spending	Health care	Std. tests	Vouchers	Same-sex marriage	Abortion
Demographic Characteristics							
Black	-.01 (.27)	-.08(.24)	.00 (.25)	-.47 (.45)	-.10 (.39)	-.35 (.51)	-.15 (.33)
Multiracial	-.08 (.17)	-.18 (.17)	-.08 (.18)	.08 (.23)	-.05 (.22)	-.15 (.33)	.24 (.26)
Some other race	.02 (.05)	.02 (.05)	.12 (.05)**	-.01 (.07)	.09 (.07)*	-.09 (.10)	-.07 (.08)
Mexican	.07 (.05)	-.11 (.05)*	.02 (.05)	-.17 (.08)*	-.04 (.08)	.07 (.09)	.08 (.09)
Cuban	-.13 (.10)	-.02 (.10)	.20 (.11)*	-.32 (.14)*	-.13 (.14)	.12 (.19)	.22 (.14)
Dominican	-.11 (.10)	.03 (.11)	.08 (.11)	-.08 (.13)	.14 (.15)	.15 (.20)	-.13 (.15)
Ties to Afro-Latino country	-.02 (.09)	.00 (.09)	.15 (.10)	-.20 (.13)	-.04 (.13)	.18 (.17)	.16 (.13)
Skin color (dark to light)	-.02 (.03)	-.00 (.02)	-.05 (.02)*	-.04 (.03)	.07 (.03)*	.06 (.05)	-.02 (.03)
Female	.17 (.04)***	-.02 (.04)	.02 (.04)	-.08 (.06)	.03 (.06)	.17 (.08)**	.05 (.06)
Age	.00 (.01)	-.00 (.01)	.01 (.00)**	.01 (.00)	-.00 (.01)	-.01 (.00)**	-.00 (.01)
Naturalized citizen	.11 (.05)*	-.05 (.06)	-.01 (.05)	.03 (.09)	.15 (.08)*	.21 (.10)*	-.20 (.08)**
Time in U.S.	-.00 (.01)	.00 (.01)	-.00 (.01)	.01 (.00)*	.00 (.01)	-.01 (.00)	-.00 (.01)
Socioeconomic Status							
Income	-.02 (.03)	-.08 (.01)***	-.00 (.01)	-.03(.02)	-.03 (.01)*	-.02 (.03)	.07 (.02)***
Education	-.04 (.01)***	-.04 (.01)**	.02 (.01)*	-.02(.01)	-.02 (.03)	.05 (.02)*	.08 (.02)***

(*continued*)

Table 7.3 (continued)

	Illegal immigration	Gov. spending	Health care	Std. tests	Vouchers	Same-sex marriage	Abortion
Commonality/Linked Fate/Discrimination							
SES commonality w/Blacks	.03 (.02)	.05 (.02)**	-.03 (.02)	-.02(.03)	.01 (.03)	.06 (.05)	-.00 (.03)
SES commonality w/Whites	-.04 (.03)	-.05 (.02)**	-.00 (.02)	.08 (.03)*	.02 (.03)	-.07 (.04)	.04 (.05)
Political commonality w/Blacks	.00 (.03)	-.02 (.03)	.04 (.03)	-.01 (.04)	-.08 (.03)*	.00 (.04)	.03 (.05)
Political commonality w/Whites	-.02 (.03)	.02 (.03)	-.05 (.03)*	-.07(.03)**	.10 (.03)**	.07 (.05)	-.01 (.04)
Linked fate w/Latinos	.02 (.04)	.06 (.02)***	.08 (.02)***	.02 (.03)	.03 (.04)	.07 (.04)	.02 (.03)
Linked fate w/Blacks	.04 (.02)*	.07 (.02)**	.06 (.02)**	.02 (.04)	.02 (.03)	-.08 (.04)*	-.07 (.03)*
Discrimination (scale)	.01 (.03)	-.02 (.03)	.09 (.02)***	-.05 (.04)	-.03 (.04)	.08 (.06)	.03 (.04)
Discrimination—R is Latino	.04 (.08)	.16 (.08)*	.05 (.09)	-.04 (.11)	-.12 (.11)	-.25 (.15)*	.10 (.11)
Discrimination—skin color	-.09 (.15)	.07 (.14)	-.14 (.15)	.14 (.22)	.16 (.22)	.07 (.23)	.02 (.20)
Acculturation/Assimilation							
English interview	-.52 (.06)***	-.18 (.06)**	-.25(.06)**	.32 (.08)***	-.59(.08)***	.29 (.10)**	.25 (.09)***
Keep Spanish language	.19 (.05)***	.15 (.05)***	.10 (.05)*	.10 (.07)	.05 (.08)	.03 (.09)	-.13 (.07)*
Republican	-.19 (.07)**	.02 (.07)	-.11 (.08)	.31 (.11)**	.09 (.11)	-.26 (.15)*	-.26(.11)**
Independent	-.05 (.06)	.07 (.05)	.01 (.06)	.04 (.08)	.00 (.08)	.29 (.11)*	-.07 (.08)
Nonidentifier	-.04 (.05)	.03 (.05)	-.16 (.06)**	-.03 (.07)	-.01 (.07)	.18 (.10)*	-.14 (.08)*
Cut 1	-1.38 (.29)	-1.23 (.28)	-.92 (.30)	-.57 (.42)	-.35 (.42)	1.05 (.53)	-1.35 (.40)
Cut 2	-.40 (.29)	-.74 (.28)	-.49 (.30)	-.03 (.42)	.34 (.42)	1.43 (.53)	.50 (.40)
Cut 3	.62 (.29)	.41 (.28)	.61 (.29)	.82 (.42)	1.20 (.42)	-	.92 (.40)
N	3018	3027	3052	1386	1409	985	1429
Log Likelihood	-2935.02	-3128.65	-2635.28	-1816.66	-1813.35	-863.29	-1412.55
Pseudo R2	.05	.03	.02	.02	.04	.05	.05

Note: Estimates are ordered probit coefficients. Standard errors are in parentheses.
*Significant at p<.05, **Significant at p<.01, ***Significant at p<.001

Although many of the patterns found in data with the full sample are present when examining immigrants only, there are some interesting differences. Whereas phenotype is a significant predictor of Latino attitudes about immigration policy, with lighter-skinned Latinos rejecting more liberal policies, lighter-skinned immigrants are no more likely to support more conservative efforts than are other immigrants. It is also the case that Republican partisanship is negatively correlated with income support when observing all Latino respondents. Yet this variable is statistically insignificant in the immigrant model. Once again, this highlights the value of examining this subgroup within the Latino population to better capture the immigrant experience. Among immigrants, there is, however, much less difference in opinion among other race Latinos. The only exception is vouchers—whereas the opinions of other race Latinos in the first two groups (some other race, SOR_Latino) are not statistically different than those of White Latinos, other race Latinos who conceptualize that identity as a non-White racial identity are much more likely to favor vouchers.

CONCLUSION

With respect to the influence of racial identity on Latino policy attitudes, the results presented here show that the personal and social construction of one's identity has implications for Latino public opinion, as race is a significant determinant of Latino attitudes about Latino salient, racially implicit, and high-profile political issues. Other race Latinos are significantly more likely to support liberal immigration policies, governmental income support for the poor, government invention to reform health care, and vouchers. They are less likely to support same-sex marriage. Multiracial Latinos are more likely to oppose governmental intervention to reform health care, whereas Black Latinos are more likely to support same-sex marriage. Among immigrants, there are significant differences among White and other race Latinos, as other race Latinos are significantly more likely to support health care reform than are their White immigrant counterparts.

As David Leal notes in his seminal study of Latino public opinion (2007: 41), the growth of the Latino population makes it impractical to study public opinion more broadly without referencing this group. Yet, as this chapter suggests, when we reject the homogenization of Latino opinion, it is clear that racial identity shapes political attitudes. The political reality for Latinos in the U.S. is one in which they must negotiate the political system while facing a racial context framed by the experiences of non-Hispanic Whites and Blacks. Despite evidence that Latinos conceptualize race differently than do other Americans (e.g. Rodriguez 2000), Latinos are in fact making racial choices by framing their racial identity within or, most commonly, outside the bounds of this context. If identity and changes in identity are fundamental to how Latinos incorporate themselves into politics, then the research presented here shows that the political consequences of Latino racial identity must be explored to improve the understanding of Latinos' incorporation into political life. Identity (and therefore identification choice) may indeed be situational (e.g. Padilla 1985) and race may be one of many collective identities to which Latinos can subscribe. Yet, as we see here, Latino racial group identities shape political behavior. In answering the call to ask more probing questions about Latino identity and its relationship to political attitudes and actions (Marquez 2007: 25), we may now begin to consider the implications of this research for our understanding of Latino politics, and American politics more broadly.

8 Conclusion

What role, if any, does race play in Latino communities? How do the constraints of the American system of racial classification affect this rapidly growing ethnic immigrant population? Recognizing the pervasiveness of racialization and persistent power of race as a dynamic social force, this book examines how Latinos construct their identities in light of the racial categorizations prevalent in America and how those identities shape political behavior. Although it is true that racial categories and labels imposed by the state do not correspond to the forms of self identification that most Latinos hold, Latinos' lived experiences are framed by the categories and labels imposed by the government and by others in society. When forced to self-identify within this framework, most Latinos self-identify as other race. But contrary to the belief that this category is simply a residual category (e.g. Rodriguez 2000), we see here that this label has meaning. For some this choice serves as a collective panethnic identity, whereas for others it is a racialized panethnic identification. Whereas the first choice signals a willingness to transcend traditional national origin boundaries to forge a collective and distinct group identification yet denotes a degree of racial ambiguity, the second signals the adoption of an affirmative non-White identity that acknowledges and challenges the White-Black paradigm. Thus, Latinos' understanding of race and the process of racialization in the U.S. are working concurrently to produce new racial categorizations (e.g. Golash-Boza and Darity 2008).

It is also clear that these labels are important for politics. The process of racialization in the U.S. is indeed of consequence for Latinos, as Latino racial identity structures political attitudes and behaviors. Latino racial identity has a significant effect on individuals' orientations toward politics, including levels of political interest, internal and external efficacy, and political trust. Latino racial identity is also linked to political participation, influencing the degree to which Latinos participate in electoral and nonelectoral activities. Racial identities also matter in Latinos' attitudes toward a wide range of public policy issues. Not only do we see significant differences in political orientations and behavior among Latinos who self-identify as White, Black, multiracial, and other race, there are notable differences among other race Latinos who hold conceptually different interpretations of that identity. Thus, other race Latinos not only hold views about politics distinctly different from the views of those who choose to identify with established and sanctioned racial categories, but also hold different views among themselves based on what that identification means to them.

This study of the politics of race in Latino communities raises a number of questions, including questions about how best to measure race as American society changes and questions about the future of the U.S. racial color line. Arguments against and in favor of the current practice of separating Hispanic ethnic identity from race categories abound. Advocating a social psychological approach to understanding self identification, those against the current practice argue that existing racial categories do not adequately represent Latinos' self conceptions (e.g. Brown et al. 2007; Hitlin et al. 2007). Yet a severe consequence of this approach, which stresses the social construction of race, is an undercount of Latinos in the U.S. A lower count has significant political implications, as the size of a population (as recorded by census) is directly connected to distribution of government resources, political representation, and the creation of public policy to address inequality. Thus, the prevailing argument in favor of the current practice of using two different questions to measure Hispanic origin and race is that it maximizes Latino identification (see Campbell and Rogalin 2006; Rodriguez 2000).

The survey design employed in the LNS is ideal in that it maximizes the advantages inherent in both of these approaches. A maximum count of Latinos is maintained, yet by probing respondents who choose to self-identify as other race, the LNS provides a better understanding of how Latinos process their group membership and how Latinos draw boundaries between themselves and other non-Hispanic groups, and between one another. This last point is especially useful and something that self-administered questionnaires like the census are bound to miss, regardless of the format of the question.[1] In the case of the combined question, we are likely to collect less racial data, as Latinos are likely to choose a Latino or Hispanic racial label. That Latinos would gravitate to a Latino or Hispanic label in the combined question is not the issue; rather, the issue is the meaning of that label. Presumably, the label would further exacerbate the homogenization of Latinos, as we are likely to assume that everyone who selects that category has the same understanding of that identity—all Latinos reporting a Latino or Hispanic identity is tantamount to claiming an African American or Asian identity in the American context. As we saw from the disaggregation of the other race category in both the focus group interviews and the LNS data, although some may truly conceptualize that choice as a racialized non-White identity, it is also likely that many will not. If 1) the principle purpose of the census, as some have argued, is solely enumeration, and 2) the count is a key determinant of political power, then the current format would seem ideal. But the census is not just about numbers, and the size of a group, although an important source of potential political power, is not always converted into actual power (Barker et al. 1999). The census is also a place of self-expression where individuals should have the freedom to describe themselves as they see fit. In its current state, the census plays a central role in the construction of racial categories, and in the case of Latinos, this construction occurs without much regard for how the lived experience of race influences self identification. The adoption of a combined race/ethnicity question would provide the opportunity to assert a racialized non-White identity in a way that the current census format does not. However, one would be remiss not to acknowledge that even this format fails to fully capture the diversity of identity that exists within Latino communities.

The study of Latino racial identity has also been shaped by larger questions regarding the shifting nature of race categorization and race relations. W. E. B. Du Bois once argued that the color line would be the central problem of the twentieth century ([1903] 1997: 45) and with the growth of the Latino population, some have argued that the color line as we know it will transform in part because Latinos do not subscribe to a racial identity that corresponds to either of the two U.S. polar categories of White and Black. This study's findings offer preliminary support for a tri-racial color line model where Latinos may *eventually* be an intermediate race category between Whites and Blacks. Clearly, racial self identification is fluid, and as a result of their experiences, some Latinos do come to believe that they occupy a unique position in the U.S. racial hierarchy and their self identification reflects this. Yet the findings suggest a cautionary view, given that many other race Latinos do not hold an affirmative non-White Latino racial identity. Most Latinos who reject White and Black racial categories are ultimately pulled in two seemingly similar but distinct directions when asked to think about their collective identity. On one hand, some Latinos have adopted a collective ethnic other race identity that stresses commonality based on mutable characteristics and traits like language and religion. For others, that collective identity is formed on the basis that Latinos are racialized, subject to the same treatment as other non-White racial group as a result of the existing racial hierarchy (e.g. Haney Lopez 1994). When most Latinos self-identify as other race, only a sizable minority is actually claiming a non-White racial group identity that is often socially imposed on Latinos. Latinos, as a whole, are not strongly assimilating as racialized minorities who see their experiences with race as akin to those of other non-White racial minorities. It is possible that as Latinos achieve increased socioeconomic status and continue to experience treatment by society as racialized minorities (e.g. Rodriguez 2000), more Latinos may adopt that identity. Education has been shown to increase one's knowledge about the social world and structural inequalities. Other race respondents in the LNS who hold a racialized conceptualization of that identity (Latino) tend to have slightly higher levels of education, and as we saw in Chapter Three, education does not have the same "whitening" effect for racialized other race Latinos that it has for the remaining other race respondents. Latinos, although constrained by the U.S. system of racial classification, are challenging that system but have yet to fundamentally change it. Thus, it is not yet clear that Latino racial choices will lead to a deconstruction of that enduring color line.

With regard to the identity-to-politics link (e.g. Lee 2008), my findings show that Latinos' self understanding of their racial identity influences political attitudes and opinions, and facilitates different types of political engagement. Latinos are members of multiple social groups. This fact has, for some, called into question the political significance of race over other socially relevant identities. Here we see that racial group identity does play a role in shaping orientations toward politics and political behavior. Ultimately, this suggests that the process of incorporation into a racialized society leads to substantial political variation among those who claim Latino ancestry. Race, therefore, has important implications for our understanding of how and why Latinos become incorporated into the American political system.

This study also strengthens the call for additional research on the multiracial and Black Latino populations. As Masuoka (2008) notes, the political consequences of multiracial identity formation will take years to mature, but as this study shows, multiracial Latinos hold distinct political attitudes and behave differently from other Latino racial groups. Similarly, Black Latinos have distinctly different attitudes and behaviors. This group is particularly interesting, given that Black Latinos in particular embark on a unique journey in which they must come to understand how identifying with Blackness can create social problems and must confront a fundamental tension of self-identity—being both Latino and Black (Duany 1998). The relatively small sample of Black Latinos in the LNS data, coupled with the absence of focus group participants who self-identified as Black, provided little opportunity to explore in great depth the process by which Latinos reject or accept a Black identity. Extant research has done so, looking primarily at Dominicans in specific parts of the country (e.g. Itzigsohn 2009; Aparicio 2006). Understanding this population becomes particularly important when one considers the attention given to the role of Black Latinos in the formation and maintenance of inter-minority political coalitions. It has been suggested that Black Latinos serve as a critical bridge between the African American and Latino communities (Affigne 2007: 10; see also Logan 2003). This is fueled in part by reports of commonality between African Americans and Black Latinos (e.g. Nicholson et al. 2005; see also Chapter Four). The relatively small size of the Black Latino population and the results presented in Chapter Three, showing that phenotype, gender, and discrimination predict the adoption of a Black identity but linked fate and commonality with African Americans do not, call into question the extent to which this group (which is severely constrained in its ability to grow over time, given these predictors) can play a significant role in forging sustained political alliances.[2]

This research also raises interesting questions about the evolving nature of Latino politics. Although a significant portion of the Latino population are noncitizen adults and are thus ineligible to vote, the responses from both focus group participants and LNS respondents suggest that most Latinos are far more comfortable with electoral politics than with nonelectoral forms of participation, including participation in voluntary groups. Scholars have noted that it is in the nonelectoral political arena that individuals develop the social capital that is so necessary to prepare and motivate individuals to participate in politics (e.g. Putnam 2000). As a theoretical framework, social capital argues that individual and social connectedness yield answers as to how and why people choose to participate in politics. Voluntary associations help to develop and maintain one's skills, networks, and political inclinations at a level that will encourage long-term participation over one's lifetime (Putnam 2000). Sustained evidence of low levels of nonelectoral participation among Latinos would have significant consequences for Latino participation more broadly, given that higher levels of social capital yield increased Latino political activity (Manzano 2007). If Latinos are increasingly shying away from these forms of engagement, the group may become limited in its ability to achieve and retain political power.

Finally, although this study shows that race matters, additional questions about how race matters need to be addressed. Given that identity is situational and fluid, there are times in which one might expect Latino racial identity to be more or less salient depending on the social context. Additional research exploring whether the salience of Latino racial identity is subject to short-term contextual influences would enhance our understanding of the role of racial identity in Latino politics. For example, extant research has found that Latinos are likely to vote for Latino candidates when given the opportunity (e.g. Barreto 2004; Hill et al. 2001; Barreto et al. 2005; DeFrancesco 2004). But if race plays a plays a significant role in determining the life chances and social positions of groups in the U.S., there are times in which racial self identification within the Latino community may influence Latinos' decision to cast a ballot for a coethnic candidate over a non-Latino candidate (e.g. Stokes-Brown 2006). The growth and rapid dispersement of the Latino population has presented several opportunities to observe elections in which Latinos are running against other people of color (African Americans, Asians) and non-Hispanic Whites. This was the case in 2007 in California's 37th congressional district's special election to replace the late Rep. Juanita Millender-McDonald. The Democratic primary contest in this once-majority African American district pitted Laura Richardson, who is African American, against Jenny Oropeza, who is Latina, in a district where Latinos and African Americans make up 43 percent and 25 percent of the population, respectively.[3] Comparative studies of this and other elections and the use of experimental surveys would further illuminate under what conditions the personal and social construction of Latino racial identity is made relevant to political behavior.

In sum, this study and the findings presented highlight the meanings Latinos attach to their group membership and acknowledges race as an overarching concept that structures Latino political life. Drawing attention to the role of racial identities in Latino politics, I suggest that exploring Latinos' incorporation into a racialized society and recognizing race as a dynamic social force is critical to the study of Latino politics. Ultimately, to understand the dynamics of Latinos' political incorporation, we need to understand how Latinos use self-ascribed racial identities to engage the political system.

Appendix A
Select Variables from LNS Questionnaire

Racial Identification

RACE What is your race? Are you White, Black, American Indian, Asian, Native Hawaiian/Pacific Islander, some other race or more than one?
(Open ended question; interviewer will probe if respondent says some other race and will check one or more races to indicate what this respondent considers himself/herself to be).

LATRACE In the US, we use a number of categories to describe ourselves racially. Do you feel that Latinos/Hispanics make up a distinctive racial group in America?

National Origin

ANCESTRY Families of Latino/Hispanic origin or background in the United States come from many different countries. From which country do you trace your Latino heritage?
Mexican, Puerto Rican, Cuban, Dominican, and *Ties to Afro-Latino country* (Columbia, Costa Rica, Nicaragua, Panama, or Venezuela) were coded from this variable.

Phenotype

SKNCOLOR Latinos/Hispanics can be described based on skin tone or complexion shades. Using a scale from 1 to 5 where 1 represents very dark and 5 represents being very light, where would you place yourself on that scale?

Gender

GENDER *(Ask only if necessary)* Are you male or female?

Age

BIRDATE What year were you born?
Age was calculated by subtracting the respondent's birth year from the year the survey was conducted (2006).

Income

HHINC Which of the following best describes the total income earned by all members of your household?

Education

REDUC What is your highest level of formal education completed?

Socioeconomic Commonality with Blacks

AFCOMM Thinking about issues like job opportunities, educational attainment or income, how much do Latinos/Hispanics have in common with other racial groups in the United States today? Would you say Latinos/Hispanics have a lot in common, some in common, little in common, or nothing at all in common with African Americans?

Socioeconomic Commonality with Whites

WHICOMM Thinking about issues like job opportunities, educational attainment or income, how much do Latinos/Hispanics have in common with other racial groups in the United States today? Would you say Latinos/Hispanics have a lot in common, some in common, little in common, or nothing at all in common with whites?

Political Commonality with Blacks

AAPOLCOM Now I'd like you to think about the political situation of Latinos/Hispanics in society. Thinking about things like government services and employment, political power and representation, how much do Latinos/Hispanics have in common with OTHER RACIAL GROUPS IN THE UNITED STATES TODAY? Would you say Latinos/Hispanics have a lot in common, some in common, little in common, or nothing at all in common with African Americans?

Political Commonality with Whites

WHPOLCOM Now I'd like you to think about the political situation of Latinos/Hispanics in society. Thinking about things like government services and employment, political power and representation, how much do Latinos/Hispanics have in common with other racial groups in the United States today? Would you say Latinos/Hispanics have a lot in common, some in common, little in common, or nothing at all in common with whites?

Linked Fate with Latinos

LATFATE How much does [respondent's ethnic subgroup] "doing well" depend on how other Hispanics or Latinos also doing well? A lot, some, a little, or not at all?

Linked Fate with Blacks

AAFATE How much does Latinos/Hispanics "doing well" depend on African Americans also doing well? A lot, some, a little, or not at all?

Discrimination (Scale)

In the following questions we are interested in your beliefs about the way other people have treated you in the U.S. Have you ever . . .

DFIRED Been unfairly fired or denied a job or promotion?

DBADPOLC Been unfairly treated by the police?

DHOUSING Been unfairly prevented from moving into a neighborhood (vecindario o barrio) because the landlord or a realtor refused to sell or rent you a house or apartment?

DRESTAUR Been treated unfairly or badly at restaurants or stores?

Discrimination (scale) represents "yes" responses for each question that were combined into an additive scale (0–4).

Discrimination b/c R Is Latino

WHYDISC There are lots of possible reasons why people might be treated unfairly, what do you think was the main reason for your experience(s)? Would you say being Latino?

Discrimination b/c of Skin Color

WHYDISC There are lots of possible reasons why people might be treated unfairly, what do you think was the main reason for your experience(s)? Would you say your skin color?

Generation

BORNUS Were you born in the mainland United States, Puerto Rico or some other country?

PARBORN Where your parents were born, were they both born in the US, was one born in the US, and were both born in another country?

Generation was calculated by combining these variables so that first-generation Latinos are those Latinos born outside the United States or on the island of Puerto Rico; second-generation Latinos are those born in the United States to at least one foreign born parent; and third or higher-generation Latinos are those born in the United States to U.S. born parents.

English Interview

LANGPREF Would you prefer that I speak in English or Spanish?

Keep Spanish Language

KEEPSPAN How important do you think it is for you or your family to maintain the ability to speak Spanish?

Partisanship

PARTYID Generally speaking, do you usually consider yourself a Democrat, a Republican, an Independent, some other party, or what?

If Democrat or Republican:
STRDEMO Would you consider yourself a strong (Democrat or Republican), or a not very strong (Democrat or Republican)?

If Independent:
INDPARTY Do you think of yourself as closer to the Republican or Democratic Party?

Political Ideology

IDEOLOGY Generally speaking, in politics do you consider yourself to be conservative, liberal, middle-of-the-road, or don't you think of yourself in these terms?

STRCONSV Do you consider yourself a strong or not very strong conservative?

STRLIBL Do you consider yourself a strong or not very strong liberal?

LEANIDEO Do you consider yourself more like a liberal, or more like a conservative, or truly middle-of-the road?

Political Interest

POLINTERE How interested are you in politics and public affairs? Would you say you are very interested, somewhat interested, or not at all interested?

Political Knowledge

WATCHNEW How frequently would you say you watch television news? Would it be daily, most days, only once or twice a week, or almost never?

For Immigrant Models

NATUSCIT Are you a naturalized American citizen? (Yes/No)

ARRIVEUS When did you first arrive to live in the US?
 Time in U.S. was calculated by subtracting the respondent's year of arrival from the year the survey was conducted (2006).

Appendix B
Focus Group Questionnaire

For each focus group, the research team used a common protocol to guide discussion. The interviews were semi-structured and the questions were always asked in the same order.

1. What race do you consider yourself?
2. Of the races specified on the census list [shown to participants after answering question #1] which best describes you?
3. Do you feel you are generally conscious or made aware of your race/racial identity? Under what circumstances?
4. How do you think most people in the U.S. perceive you/see you?
5. Do you think Latinos make up a distinct racial group in the U.S, like non-Hispanic Whites or Blacks?
6. There are many ways people can participate in politics. Can you tell me how you define your political participation?
7. Thinking about your political identity, how important is being Latino when it comes to your political ideas? When (if ever) has your racial identity influenced your political behavior (i.e. voting, political attitudes and opinions, partisanship, etc.)?
8. Thinking about issues like job opportunities, educational attainment and income, how much do you think you have in common with other racial groups (Whites/Blacks/Asians)?
9. Do you participate in the activities of social, cultural, civic and/or political groups?
10. (Extra question if time permits) Do you think your race has helped you or hindered you in general?

Notes

NOTES TO CHAPTER 1

1. Throughout the book, I use the terms "Latino" and "Hispanic" interchangeably, as both are widely used to refer to individuals in the U.S. who trace their ancestry to Spanish-speaking regions of the Caribbean and Latin America. The term Hispanic is used exclusively by the U.S. government.
2. To be clear, entry to this intermediate category will likely be based on class and skin color, making the intermediate racial category an "honorary White" category.
3. Latinos and African Americans combined represent more than one-fourth of the U.S. population and a plurality in several cities (Garcia and Sanchez 2008: 155).
4. Fraga, Luis R., John A. Garcia, Rodney Hero, Michael Jones-Correa, Valerie Martinez-Ebers, and Gary M. Segura. Latino National Survey (LNS), 2006 [Computer file]. ICPSR20862-v4. Ann Arbor, MI: Inter-university Consortium for Political and Social Research [distributor], 2010-05-26. doi:10.3886/ICPSR20862.
5. Hu-Dehart, Evelyn, Matthew Garcia, Cynthia Garcia Coll, Jose Itzigsohn, Marion Orr, Tony Affigne, and Jorge Elorza. Latino National Survey (LNS)—New England, 2006 [Computer file]. ICPSR24502-v1. Ann Arbor, MI: Inter-university Consortium for Political and Social Research [distributor], 2009-06-04. doi:10.3886/ICPSR24502.
6. New York ranks first and Chicago ranks third, following Los Angeles (U.S. Census Bureau 2001).
7. Understanding groups' political attitudes and behavior is essential to engagement in coalition politics, a key pathway to political incorporation (Geron 2005). Other pathways include: 1) demand/protest, 2) nonconfrontational political evolution, and 3) challenges to structural barriers (see Geron 2005 for a fuller discussion).

NOTES TO CHAPTER 2

1. More than a third of the respondents to the 2004 National Survey of Latinos: Politics and Civic Participation (Pew Hispanic Center/Kaiser Family Foundation) self-identified as Latino or Hispanic. Approximately 47 percent of the respondents to the 2002 National Survey of Latinos (Pew Hispanic Center/Kaiser Family Foundation) volunteered their race as "Latino/Hispanic" and 9 percent indicated that they would prefer to identify their race as "Latino" or "Hispanic."

2. According to Guzman (2001), the question was only asked of a 5 percent sample of households. This question's wording was problematic, as hundreds of thousands of people living in southern and central regions of the country were mistakenly included in the Central or South American category (Passel 2010).
3. The previously problematic "Central or South American" category did not appear in the Hispanic origin question, and the Hispanic origin question followed the race, age, and marital status questions (Passel 2010).
4. The fourth proposal was the addition of a special category for Middle Easterners/Arab Americans (Rodriguez 2000).
5. In 2000, a significantly higher percentage of respondents who self-identified as other race did so without specifying a specific country of origin (Passel 2010).
6. To be clear, Latinos, like other respondents, would then have the opportunity to choose more than one category. So Latinos could theoretically choose only the Latino label or could choose the Latino label and a standard racial label (i.e. White, Black, etc.).
7. This category can therefore be viewed as the expression of racialized ethnic label that is applied in a similar way to other racial labels in the U.S. (e.g. Golash-Boza and Darity 2008).

NOTES TO CHAPTER 3

1. Percentages were calculated using three crosstabulations. The first tabulation of the selected factor included a race variable with four categories: White, Black, multiracial, and some other race. The second and third tabulations of the selected factor included a race variable with three racial categories (White, Black, multiracial) and a distinct version of the other race category (SOR_Latino or Latino). These crosstabulations were run separately because all three other race categories share a primary racial identification, making it impossible compare the relationships between the independent variables and all the some other race identification choices in one model.
2. The question wording is "There are lots of possible reasons why people might be treated unfairly. What do you think was the main reason for your experience(s)? Would you say . . ." In addition to being Latino and skin color, the list also included being an immigrant, national origin, language or accent, gender, age, and other.
3. The categories here differ from the SOR_Latino and Latino categories introduced in Chapter Two. Recall that the total number of other race respondents is 6486. 6486 (all respondents who said other race)—1161 (respondents who said other race *only*) = 4875 (*SOR_Latino*; all the respondents who self-identified as Hispanic/Latino after initially self-identifying as other race). 4875 (*SOR_Latino*; all the respondents who self-identified as Hispanic/Latino after initially self-identifying as other race)—2308 (respondents who self-identified as Hispanic/Latino after initially self-identifying as other race *but do not believe Latinos are a distinct racial group*) = 2567 (*Latino*; respondents who self-identified as Hispanic/Latino after initially self-identifying as other race *and believe that Latinos are a distinct racial group*).
4. The measure of phenotype in the LNS is based on self-ratings only, making it impossible to gauge how interviewer ratings of phenotype compare to self-assessments. Thus, we have no way of assessing with this data whether

respondents may self-identify as "whiter" than their phenotype might suggest because of the social benefits whiteness offers (see Jones-Correa 1998; Rodriguez 2000; Forman et al. 2002).

NOTES TO CHAPTER 4

1. Data from the 2002 Pew National Hispanic Survey found that whereas approximately 15 percent of Latinos always trust the government, only 9 percent of African Americans, 13 percent of Whites, and 6 percent of Asians expressed similar levels of trust.
2. Specifically, Michelson (2003) finds that the longer Latinos live in the U.S., the more cynical and disaffected they become.

NOTES TO CHAPTER 5

1. See for example the 1993–1994 Multi-City Study of Urban Inequality (MCSUI) (Hajnal and Lee 2006) and the 1989 Latino National Political Survey (Wong 2000).
2. Independents who identified themselves as closer to either major party were coded as leaning partisans.

NOTES TO CHAPTER 6

1. A key difference in measurement exists between these studies and my research. Both Masuoka (2008) and Valdez (2011) use multidimensional conceptualization of group consciousness that includes group identity as a central component. It should also be noted that Valdez (2011), using the 2006 LNS, utilizes the PRIMEID variable, not the RACE variable, to establish Latino racial identity. So in her study, respondents who indicated that Latino/Hispanic best describes them (i.e. their primary identification) where further classified racially if they responded yes or maybe to the question asking whether Latinos make up a distinct race in the U.S. (LATRACE).
2. As registering and voting are socially desirable acts, people often overreport them, claiming to have engaged in these activities when they did not. However, the design of the survey and the analysis is comparable to previous surveys (e.g. Stokes 2003; Sanchez 2006).
3. The question wording is "When an issue or problem needs to be addressed, would you work through existing groups or organizations to bring people together, would you get together informally, or would you do nothing to deal with this matter?"
4. Although extant research has paid attention to additional factors, including mobilization (e.g. Leighley 2001; Shaw et al. 2000), social connectedness from organization membership (e.g. Hritzuk and Park 2000; Highton and Burris 2002), and other political attitudes (e.g. Sanchez 2006; Verba et al. 1995), they are excluded here because the more predictive variables included in the model, the larger the variance, the wider the confidence intervals, and the less precise the estimates (Hy and Wollscheid 2007: 795).
5. The addition of the efficacy and trust variables from Chapter Four significantly lowers the number of observations but does not change the results for the race variables.

NOTES TO CHAPTER 7

1. Although the vast majority of Latinos continue to identify with Catholicism, several studies show that that the numbers of Hispanics belonging to Protestant churches, and those with no religious affiliation, have increased markedly since the 1970s (Hunt 1999).
2. It can be argued that the issue of school vouchers may be perceived by some as an implicitly racial issue by those who believe that vouchers may further exacerbate racial segregation in schools.
3. It should be noted that the education policy questions (*standardized tests, vouchers*) and social issue questions (*same-sex marriage, abortion*) were asked of only half the respondents. It is not clear from the survey materials why this was done. In an effort to make sure that the results are not an artifact of which respondents were chosen to respond to these questions, multivariate models were also run, using only those respondents who were asked about their opinion about illegal immigration policy. The use of this restricted sample did not cause the regression results to change; thus, we can be confident that the survey's randomization process was successful.
4. Attempts to control for political ideology in addition to political partisanship significantly reduced the number of cases because 46 percent of the respondents (4832) failed to report this information. Specifically, 31 percent (3059) said they do not think of themselves in these terms, and 16 percent (1574) gave a "don't know" response. A control for religion (Catholic) was also tested in the model. The variable was significant for one issue area (abortion) and did not substantively change the results for any issue. Thus, this variable is not included in the tables presented in the chapter.

NOTES TO CHAPTER 8

1. Beginning in 1960, a majority of people in the U.S. were enumerated in the census by a self-administered questionnaire mailed to their place of residence (Cork and Voss 2006).
2. According to census figures, the Afro-Latino population is 1.9 million. Although the number of Black Latinos has increased since 1980, Black Latinos remain about 3 percent of the Latino population (Logan 2003).
3. Richardson won the primary, garnering 38 percent of the vote compared to Oropeza's 31 percent of the vote.

Bibliography

Aberbach, J. D. and J. L. Walker. 1970. "Political Trust and Racial Ideology." *American Political Science Review* 64: 1199–1219.
Abrajano, Marissa A. and R. Michael Alvarez. 2007."Why Are Latinos More Politically Trusting Than Other Americans?" Retrieved February 23, 2008, from http://ssrn.com/abstract=1017861.
Abrajano, Marissa A. and R. Michael Alvarez. 2010. "Assessing the Causes and Effects of Political Trust Among U.S. Latinos." *American Political Research* 38:110–141.
Abramson, Paul R. 1977. *The Political Socialization of Black Americans: A Critical Evaluation of Research on Efficacy and Trust.* New York: Free Press.
Abramson, Paul R. 1983. *Political Attitudes in America.* San Francisco: Freeman and Co.
Abramson, Paul R., and John H. Aldrich. 1982. "The Decline of Electoral Participation in America." *American Political Science Review* 76:502–21.
Affigne, Tony. 2007. "Negrura en Política: The Politics of Blackness in Latino Communities." Paper presented at the annual meeting of the American Political Science Association, Chicago, August 30–September 2.
Agius Vallejo, Jody and Jennifer Lee. 2009. "Brown Picket Fences: The Immigrant Narrative and 'Giving Back' among the Mexican-Origin Middle Class." *Ethnicities* 9: 5–31.
Aguirre, Benigno E. and Eduardo Bonilla Silva. 2002. "Does Race Matter among Cuban Immigrants? An Analysis of the Racial Characteristics of Recent Cuban Immigrants." *Journal of Latin American Studies* 34: 311–324.
Alba, Richard and Islam Tariqul. 2009. "The Case of the Disappearing Mexican Americans: An Ethnic-Identity Mystery." *Population Research and Policy Review* 28: 109–121.
Alba, Richard and Victor Nee. 2003. *Remaking the American Mainstream; Assimilation and Contemporary Immigration.* Cambridge: Harvard University Press.
Aldrich, John H. and Forrest D. Nelson. 1984. *Linear Probability, Logit, and Probit Models.* Beverly Hills: Sage.
Alesina, Alberto and Eliana La Ferrara. 2002. "Who Trusts Others?" *Journal of Public Economics* 85: 207–34.
Almond, Gabriel and Sidney Verba. 1963. *The Civic Culture: Political Attitudes and Democracy in Five Nations.* Princeton, NJ: Princeton University Press.
Alvarez, R. Michael and Lisa García Bedolla. 2003. "The Foundation of Latino Voter Participation: Evidence from the 2000 Election." *Journal of Politics* 65:31–49.
Anderson, Margo. 1988. *The American Census: A Social History.* New Haven, CT: Yale University Press.
Antunes, George and Charles M. Gaitz. 1975. "Ethnicity and Participation: A Study of Mexican-Americans, Blacks and Whites." *American Journal of Sociology* 80:1192-1211.

Aparicio, Ana. 2006. *Dominican-Americans and the Politics of Empowerment.* Gainesville, FL: University Press of Florida.
Aparicio, Frances. 1993. "From Ethnicity to Multiculturalism: An Historical Overview of Puerto Rican Literature in the United States" in Francisco Lomeli (ed). *Handbook of Hispanic Cultures: Literature and Art.* Houston: Arte Público.
Arce, Carlos, Edward Mueguia, and W. Parker Frisbie. 1987. "Phenotype and Life Chances among Chicanos." *Hispanic Journal of Behavioral Sciences* 9: 19–32.
Arvizu, John R. and F. Chris Garcia. 1996. "Latino Voting Participation: Explaining and Differentiating Latino Voter Turnout." *Hispanic Journal of Behavioral Sciences* 18: 104–28.
Bailey, Benjamin. 2001. "Dominican-American Ethnic/Racial Identities and United States Social Categories." *International Migration Review* 35: 677–708.
Barker, Lucius J., Mack H. Jones, and Katherine Tate. 1999. *African Americans and the American Political System, 4th edition.* Upper Saddle River, NJ: Prentice Hall.
Barreto, Matt A. 2004. "Ethnic Cues: The Role of Shared Ethnicity in Latino Vote Choice." Paper presented at the annual meeting of the American Political Science Association, Chicago, September 2–5.
Barreto, Matt A. 2007. "Si Se Puede! Latino Candidates and the Mobilization of Latino Voters." *American Political Science Review* 101: 425–441.
Barreto, Matt A. and Jose A. Munoz. 2003. "Reexamining the "Politics of In-Between": Political Participation Among Mexican Immigrants in the United States." *Hispanic Journal of Behavioral Sciences* 25: 427–447.
Barreto, Matt A. and Francisco I. Pedraza. 2009. "The Renewal and Persistence of Group Identification in American Politics." *Electoral Studies* 28: 595–605.
Barreto, Matt A., Gary M. Segura, and Nathan D. Woods. 2004. "The Mobilizing Effect of Majority-Minority Districts on Latino Turnout." *American Political Science Review* 98: 65–75.
Barreto, Matt A. and Nathan D. Woods. 2005. "The Anti-Latino Political Context and its Impact of GOP Detachment and Increasing Latino Voter Turnout in Los Angeles County" in Gary Segura and Shaun Bowler (eds). *Diversity in Democracy: Minority Representation in the United States.* Charlottsville, VA: University of Virginia Press.
Bashi, V. and A. McDaniel. 1997. "A Theory of Immigration and Racial Stratification." *Journal of Black Studies* 27: 668–682.
Basler, Carleen. 2008. "White Dreams and Red Votes: Mexican Americans and the Lure of Inclusion in the Republican Party." *Ethnic and Racial Studies* 31: 123–166.
Bates, Nancy A., Manuel de la Puente, Theresa K. De Maio, and Elizabeth A. Martin. 1994. "Research on Race and Ethnicity: Results from Questionnaire Design Tests." Paper presented at the U.S. Census Bureau's annual research conference, Rosslyn, VA, March 20–23.
Bean, Frank D. and G. Stevens. 2003. *America's Newcomers and the Dynamics of Diversity.* New York: Russell Sage Foundation.
Bean, Frank D. and Marta Tienda. 1987. *The Hispanic Population of the United States.* New York: Russell Sage.
Beck, Paul and M. Jennings. 1991. "Family Traditions, Political Periods, and the Development of Partisan Orientations." *Journal of Politics* 53: 742–763.
Berelson, B. R., P. F. Lazarsfeld, and W. N. McPhee. 1954. *Voting.* Chicago: University of Chicago Press.
Bernal, Martha and Phylis Martinelli. 1993. *Mexican American Identity.* Encino, CA: Floricanto.
Binder, Norman E., J. L. Polinard, and Robert D. Wrinkle. 1997. "Mexican American and Anglo Attitudes toward Immigration Reform: A View from the Border." *Social Science Quarterly* 78: 324–337.

Binshin, Benjamin G., Karen M. Kaufmann, and Dan P. Stevens. 2005. Turf Wars: How Local Power Struggles Influence Latino Political Socialization and Voting Behavior. Paper presented at the annual meeting of the American Politics Workshop, Department of Government and Politics, University of Maryland. Retrieved July 1, 2006, www.bsos.umd.edu/gvpt/apworkshop/kaufmann05.pdf
Bobo, Lawrence and Franklin D. Gilliam. 1990. "Race, Sociopolitical Participation, and Black Empowerment." *American Political Science Review* 84: 377–393.
Bobo, Lawrence. 2000. "Race and Beliefs about Affirmative Action" in D. O. Sears, J. Sidanius, and L. Bobo (eds). *Racialized Politics: Values, Ideology, and Prejudice in American Public Opinion.* Chicago, IL: University of Chicago Press.
Bobo, Lawrence, Michael. C. Dawson, and D. Johnson. 2001. "Enduring Twoness: Through the Eyes of Black America." *Public Perspectives* 12: 13–16.
Bohara, Alok K. and Alberto Davila. 1992. "A Reassessment of the Phenotypic Discrimination and Income Differences among Mexican Americans." *Social Science Quarterly* 73: 114–119.
Bolks, Sean M., Diana Evans, J. L. Polinard, and Robert D. Wrinkle. 2000. "Core Beliefs and Abortion Attitudes: A Look at Latinos." *Social Science Quarterly* 81: 253–260.
Bonilla-Silva, Eduardo. 1997. "Rethinking Racism: Towards a Structural Interpretation." *American Sociological Review* 62: 465–480.
Bonilla-Silva, Eduardo. 1999. "The Essential Social Fact of Race." *American Sociological Review* 64:899–906.
Bonilla-Silva, Eduardo. 2003. *Racism with Racists.* Lanham, MD: Rowman and Littlefield.
Bonilla-Silva, Eduardo. 2004. "From Bi-racial to Tri-racial: Towards a New System of Racial Stratification in the USA." *Ethnic and Racial Studies* 27: 931–950.
Bonilla-Silva, Eduardo and David G. Embrick. 2006. "Black, Honorary White, White: The Future of Race in the United States? in David L. Brunsma (ed.) Mixed Messages: Multiracial Identities in the "Color-Blind" Era. Boulder, CO: Lynne Rienner Publishers.
Bonilla-Silva, Eduardo, T. Forman, A. Lewis, and David. Embrick. 2003. "It Wasn't Me: How Will Race and Racism Work in 21st Century America." *Research in Political Sociology* 12: 111–134.
Bonilla-Silva, Eduardo and Karen S. Glover. 2004. "We are all Americans: The Latin Americanization of Race Relations in the U.S." In Amanda E. Lewis and Maria Kryson (eds). *The Changing Terrain of Race and Ethnicity: Theory, Methods, and Public Policy.* New York: Russell Sage Foundation.
Branton, Regina. 2007. "Latino Attitudes toward Various Areas of Public Policy." *Political Research Quarterly* 60: 293–303.
Brown, J. Scott, Steven Hitlin, and Glen H. Elder, Jr. 2006. "The Greater Complexity of Lived Race: An Extension of Harris and Sim." *Social Science Quarterly* 87: 412–431.
Brown, J. Scott, Steven Hitlin, and Glen H. Elder, Jr. 2007. "The Importance of Being Other: A Natural Experiment about Lived Race over Time." *Social Science Research* 36: 159–174.
Brown, T.D., F.C. Dane, and M.D. Durham. 1998. "Perception of Race and Ethnicity." *Journal of Social Behavior and Personality* 13: 295–306.
Browning, Rufus P., Dale Rogers Marshall, and David H. Tabb. 2003. *Racial Politics in American Cities, 3rd edition.* New York: Longman Press.
Brubaker, Rogers and Frederick Cooper. 2000. "Beyond 'Identity.'" *Theory and Society* 29: 1–47.
Burns, Nancy, Kay Lehman Schlozman and Sidney Verba. 2001. *The Private Roots of Public Action: Gender, Equality, and Political Participation.* Cambridge: Harvard University Press.

Cain, B. E., D. Kiewiet, and C. Uhlaner. 1991. "The Acquisition of Partisanship by Latinos and Asian Americans." *American Journal of Political Science* 35: 390–422.
Cain, Bruce and D. Roderick Kiewiet. 1987. "Latinos and the 1984 Election: A Comparative Perspective" in Rodolfo de la Garza (ed). *Ignored Voices: Public Opinion Polls and the Latino Community*. Austin: Center for Mexican American Studies.
Cain, Bruce and D. Roderick Kiewiet. 1986. "California's Coming Minority Majority." *Public Opinion* 9: 50–52.
Calvo, M. A. and S. J. Rosenstone. 1989. *Hispanic Political Participation*. San Antonio, TX: Southwest Voter Research Institute.
Campbell, Andrea L., Cara Wong, and Jack Citrin. 2006. "Racial Threat, Partisan Climate and Direct Democracy: Contextual Effects in Three California Initiatives." *Political Behavior* 28: 128–150.
Campbell, A., P. Converse, W. Miller, and D. Stokes. 1960. *The American Voter*. Ann Arbor, MI: University of Michigan Press.
Campbell, M.E. and C. L. Rogalin. 2006. "Categorical Imperatives: The Interaction of Latino and Racial Identification." *Social Science Quarterly* 87: 1030–1052.
Coffin, Michael. 2003. "The Latino Vote: Shaping America's Future." *Political Quarterly* 74: 214–222.
Cornell, Stephen and Douglass Hartmann. 1998. *Ethnicity and Race: Making Identities in a Changing World*. Thousand Oaks, CA: Pine Forge Press.
Combs, Michael and Susan Welch. 1982. "Blacks, Whites, and Attitudes toward Abortion." *Public Opinion Quarterly* 46: 510–520.
Conover, Pamela Johnston. 1984. "The Influence of Group Identifications on Political Perception and Evaluation." *Journal of Politics* 46: 760–785.
Conover, Pamela Johnston and Stanley Feldman. 1984. "How People Organize the Political World: A Schematic Model." *American Journal of Political Science* 28: 95–126.
Converse, Philip E. 1969. "Of Time and Partisan Stability." *Comparative Political Studies* 2:139–171.
Converse, Philip E. 1976. *The Dynamics of Party Support: Cohort Analyzing Party Identification*. Beverly Hills, CA: Sage.
Cook, Elizabeth Adell, Ted G. Jelen, and Clyde Wilcox. 1992. *Between Two Absolutes: Public Opinion and the Politics of Abortion*. Boulder, CO: Westview Press.
Conway, M. Margaret. 2000. *Political participation in the United States*. Washington, 3rd edition. Washington DC: Congressional Quarterly Press
Conway, M. Margaret. 1991. *Political Participation in the* United States, 2nd edition. Washington, DC: Congressional Quarterly Press.
Cork, Daniel L. and Paul R. Voss, eds. 2006. *Once, Only Once, and in the Right Place: Residence Rules in the Decennial Census*. Washington, DC: The National Academies Press.
Cornell, Stephen and Douglas Hartmann. 1998. *Ethnicity and Race: Making Identities in a Changing World*. Thousand Oaks, CA: Pine Forge Press.
Craig, S.C., R.G. Niemi, and G.E. Silver. 1990. "Political Efficacy and Trust: A Report on the NES Pilot Study Items," *Political Behavior* 12: 289-314.
Crenshaw, Kimberle. 1998. "Race, Reform, and Retrenchment: Transformation and Legitimation in Antidiscrimination Law." *Harvard Law Review* 101: 1331–1387.
Dalton, Russell J. 2009. *The Good Citizen: How a Younger Generation Is Reshaping American Politics*. Washington, DC: CQ Press.
Dahl, Robert A. 1961. *Who Governs? Democracy and Power in an American City*, New Haven/London: Yale University Press.
Daniel, G. R. 1999. "Either Black or White: Race Relations in Contemporary Brazil" in G. Verona-Lacey and J. Lopez-Arias (eds). *Latin America: An Interdisciplinary Approach*. New York: P. Lang.

Dawson, Michael. 1994. *Behind the Mule: Race and Class in African-American Politics*. Princeton, NJ: Princeton University Press.

De la Garza, Rodolfo O., Angelo Falcon, and F. Chris Garcia. 1996. "Will the Real Americans Please Stand Up? Anglo and Mexican-American Support of Core American Political Values." *American Journal of Political Science* 40: 335–351.

De la Garza, Rodolfo, Angelo Falcon, F. Chris Garcia, and John Garcia. 1993. "Attitudes toward U.S. Immigration Policy." *Migration World Magazine* 21:13–16.

De la Garza, Rodolfo and Louis DeSipio. 1992. *From Rhetoric to Reality: Latino Politics in the 1988 Elections*. Boulder, CO: Westview.

De la Garza, Rodolfo O., Louis DeSipio, F. Chris Garcia, John Garcia, and Angelo Falcon. 1992. *Latino Voices: Mexican, Puerto Rican, and Cuban Perspectives on American Politics*. Boulder, CO: Westview Press.

De la Garza, Rodolfo O., J. L. Polinard, Robert D. Wrinkle, and Tomas Longoria. 1991. "Understanding Intra-Ethnic Attitude Variations: Mexican-Origin Population Views of Immigration." *Social Science Quarterly* 72: 379–387.

De la Garza, Rodolfo and David Vaughan. 1984. "The Political Socialization of Chicano Elites: A Generational Approach." *Social Science Quarterly* 65: 290–307.

DeFrancesco, Victoria M. 2004. "Identity Fluidity in the Voting Booth: Social Group Identification and Latino Vote Choice." Paper presented at the annual meeting of the American Political Science Association, Chicago, September 2–5.

Delgado, Richard. *Critical Race Theory: The Cutting Edge*. Philadelphia: Temple University Press, 1995.

Denton, Nancy A., and Douglass S. Massey. 1989. "Racial Identity Among Caribbean Hispanics: The Effect of Double Minority Status on Residential Segregation." *American Sociological Review* 54: 790–808.

DeSipio, Louis. 1996. *Counting on the Latino Vote: Latinos as a New Electorate*. Charlottesville, VA: University of Virginia Press.

DeSipio, Louis, and James Richard Henson. 1997. "Cuban Americans, Latinos, and the Print Media: Shaping Ethnic Identities." *Press/Politics* 2: 52-70.

DeSipio, Louis, Harry Pachon, Rodolfo O. de la Garza, and Jongho Lee. 2003. *Immigrant Politics at Home and Abroad: How Latino Immigrants Engage the Politics of Their Home Communities and the United States*. Claremont, CA: The Tomás Rivera Policy Institute.

Downs, Anthony. 1957. *An Economic Theory of Democracy*. New York: Harper & Row.

Du Bois, W. E. B. [1903] 1997. *The Souls of Black Folk*. David W. Blight and Robert Gooding-Williams (eds). Boston, MA: Bedford Books.

Duany, Jorge. 1998. "Reconstructing Racial Identity: Ethnicity, Color, and Class among Dominicans in the United States and Puerto Rico." *Latin American Perspectives* 25: 147–172.

Duany, Jorge. 2005. "Neither White nor Black: The Representation of Racial Identity among Puerto Ricans on the Island and in the U.S. Mainland" in Anani Dzidzienyo and Suzanne Oboler (eds). *Neither Enemies nor Friends: Latinos, Blacks, Afro-Latinos*. New York: Palgrave Macmillan.

Edmonston, B., S. M. Lee, and J. S. Passel. 2002. "Recent Trends in Intermarriage and Immigration and Their Effects on the Future Racial Composition of the U.S. Population" in J. Perlmann and M. C. Waters (eds). *The New Race Question: How the Census Counts Multiracial Individuals*. New York: Russell Sage Foundation and the Levy Economics Institute of Bard College.

Ellison, Christopher, Samuel Echevarría, and Brad Smith. 2005. "Religion and Abortion Attitudes among U.S. Hispanics: Findings from the 1990 Latino National Political Survey." *Social Science Quarterly* 86:192–208.

Emerson, Michael O. 1996. "Through Tinted Glasses: Religion, Worldviews, and Abortion Attitudes." *Journal for the Scientific Study of Religion* 35: 41–55.

Ennis, Sharon R., Merarys Ríos-Vargas, and Nora G. Albert. 2011. *The Hispanic Population: 2010*. Washington, DC: U.S. Census Bureau.
Entwistle, Doris R. and Nan Marie Astone. 1994. "Some Practical Guidelines for Measuring Youth's Race/Ethnicity and Socioeconomic Status." *Child Development* 65: 1521–1540.
Espino, Rodolfo and Michael M. Franz. 2002. "Latino Phenotypic Discrimination Revisited: The Impact of Skin Color on Occupational Status." *Social Science Quarterly* 83: 612–623.
Farley, Reynolds. 2000. "Counting on the Census? Race, Group Identity, and the Evasion of Politics." *Population and Development Review* 26: 606–609.
Feagin, Joe. R. 2006. *Systemic racism: A Theory of Oppression*. New York: Routledge.
Ferdman, Bernardo M. and Placida I. Gallegos. 2001. "Latinos and Racial Identity Development" in C. L. Wijeyesinghe and B. W. Jackson III (eds). *New Perspectives on Racial Identity Development: A Theoretical and Practical Anthology*. New York: New York University Press.
Fergus, Edward. 2004. *Skin Color and Identity Formation*. New York: Routledge.
Fiorina, Morris. 1981. *Retrospective Voting in American National Elections*. New Haven, CT: Yale University Press.
Forman, Tyrone, Carla Goar, and Amanda E. Lewis. 2002. "Neither Black nor White? An Empirical Test of the Latin Americanization Thesis." *Race & Society* 5: 65–84.
Fraga, Luis Ricardo, John A. Garcia, Rodney E. Hero, Michael Jones-Correa, Valerie Martinez-Ebers, and Gary M. Segura. 2010. *Latino Lives in America: Making it Home*. Philadelphia, PA: Temple University Press.
Fraga, Luis Ricardo and David Leal. 2004. "Playing the 'Latino Card': Race, Ethnicity, and National Party Politics." *Du Bois Review* 1: 297–317.
Fraga, Luis Ricardo, Ali Adam Valenzaula, and Danielle Harlen. 2009. "Patterns of Latino Partisanship: Foundations and the Prospects for Change." Prepared for delivery at the annual meeting of the Western Political Science Association, Vancouver, BC, Canada, March 19–21.
Frank, Reanne, Ilana Redstone Akresh, and Bo Lu. 2010. "Latino Immigrants and the U.S. Racial Order: How and Where Do They Fit In?" *American Sociological Review* 75: 378–401.
Fry, Richard. 2008. *Latino Settlement in the New Century*. Washington, DC: Pew Hispanic Center.
Fuchs, Lawrence. 1990. *The American Kaleidoscope*. Middletown, CT: Wesleyan University Press.
Gans, Herbert J. 1999. "The Possibility of a New Racial Hierarchy in the Twenty-First Century United States" in Michele Lamont (ed). *The Cultural Territories of Race*. Chicago, IL: University of Chicago Press and Russell Sage Foundation.
Garcia, Chris and Gabriel Sanchez. 2008. *Hispanics and the U.S. Political System: Moving into the Mainstream*. Upper Saddle River, NJ: Pearson Prentice Hall.
Garcia, John A. 1987. "The Political Integration of Mexican Immigrants: An Examination of Political Orientations." *International Migration Review* 21: 372–389.
Garcia, John A. 2003. *Latino Politics in America: Community, Culture, and Interests*. Lanham, MD: Rowman and Littlefield.
Garcia, John A. 2006. "Pan Ethnicity: Politically Relevant For Latino Political Engagement?" in William T. Nelson and Jessica Perez-Monforti (eds). *Black and Latina/o Politics: Issues in Political Development in the United States*. Miami, FL: Barnhardt and Ashe Publishing.
Garcia, John and Gabriel Sanchez. 2004. "With the Spotlight on Latinos, Examining Their Political Participation in the United States" in S. Navarro and A. Mejia (eds). *Latino Political Participation in the Next Millennium*. Santa Barbara, CA: ABC-CLIO Publishers.

Garcia, Jorge J. 1999. *Hispanic/Latino Identity*. Malden, MA: Blackwell Publishers.
Garcia Bedolla, Lisa. 2003. "The Identity Paradox: Latino Language, Politics and Selective Dissociation. *Latino Studies* 1: 264–283.
Garcia Bedolla, Lisa. 2005. *Fluid Borders: Latino Power, Identity and Politics in Los Angeles*. Berkeley, CA: University of California Press.
Garcia Bedolla, Lisa. 2009. *Latino Politics*. Cambridge, UK: Polity.
Garcia Bedolla, Lisa, Michael Alvarez, and Jonathan Nagler. 2006. "Anglo and Latino Vote Choice in the 2004 Election." Paper presented at the annual meeting of the Western Political Science Association, Albuquerque, NM, March 11–13.
Geron, Kim. 2005. *Latino Political Power*. Boulder, CO: Lynne Rienner Publishers.
Golash-Boza, T. and W. Darity, Jr. 2008. "Latino Racial Choices: The Effects of Skin Colour and Discrimination on Latinos' and Latinas' Racial Self Identifications." *Ethnic and Racial Studies* 31: 899–934.
Gomez, Christina. 1998. "The Racialization of Latinos in the United States: Racial Options in a Changing Society." Unpublished doctoral dissertation. Cambridge, MA: Harvard University.
Gomez, Christina. 2000. "The Continual Significance of Skin Color: An Exploratory Study of Latinos in the Northeast." *Hispanic Journal of Behavioral Sciences* 22: 94–103.
Gomez, Christina. 2008. "We Are Not Like Them: Social Distancing and Realignment in the Racial Hierarchy" in Andrew Grant-Thomas and Gary Orfield (eds). *21st Century Color Lines: Multiracial Change in Contemporary America*. Philadelphia, PA: Temple University Press.
Gordon, Milton. 1964. *Assimilation in American Life*. New York: Oxford University Press.
Greene, William H. 2003. *Economic Analysis*, 5th ed. Saddle River, N.J.: Prentice-Hall.
Grieco, Elizabeth M. and Rachel C. Cassidy. 2001. "Overview of Race and Hispanic Origin." Census 2000 Brief (March). Washington, DC: U.S. Bureau of the Census.
Gurin, P., A. H. Miller, and G. Gurin. 1980. "Stratum Identification and Consciousness." *Social Psychology Quarterly* 43: 30–47.
Guzman, B. 2001. *The Hispanic Population: Census 2000*. US Census Bureau. Washington, DC: Government Printing Office.
Hacker, Andrew. 1992. *Two Nations: Black and White, Separate, Hostile, Unequal*. Scribner.
Hakken, K. 1979. "Discrimination and Chicanos in the Dallas Rental Housing Market: An Experimental Extension of the Housing Market Practices Survey." Washington, DC: Office of Policy Development and Research, U.S. Department of Housing and Urban Development.
Hall, Ronald E. 1994. "The 'Bleaching Syndrome': Implication of Light Skin for Hispanic American Assimilation." *Hispanic Journal of Behavioral Sciences* 16: 307–314.
Hajnal, Zoltan L. and Mark Baldassare. 2001. *Finding Common Ground: Racial and Ethnic Attitudes in California*. San Francisco, Public Policy Institute of California.
Hall, Ronald E. 1998. "Skin Color Bias: A New Perspective on an Old Social Problem." *Journal of Psychology* 138: 238–240.
Hall, Elaine and Myra Marx Ferree. 1986. "Race Differences in Abortion Attitudes." *Public Opinion Quarterly* 50: 193–207.
Hajnal, Zoltan and Taeku Lee. 2004. "Latino Independents and Identity Formation Under Uncertainty." Paper prepared for presentation at The Center for Comparative Immigration Studies Research Seminar. Working Paper 89. San Diego, CA. January 1.

144 Bibliography

Hajnal, Zoltan and Taeku Lee. 2006. "Out of Line: Immigration and Party Identification among Latinos and Asian Americans" in Taeku Lee, S. Karthick Ramakrishnan, and Ricardo Ramirez (eds). *Transforming Politics, Transforming America: The Political and Civic Incorporation of Immigrants in the United States.* Charlottesville, VA: University of Virginia Press.

Hajnal, Zoltan and Taeku Lee. 2011. *Why Americans Don't Join the Party: Race, Immigration, and the Failure of Political Parties to Engage the Electorate.* Princeton,NJ: Princeton University Press.

Haney- Lopez, Ian. 1996. *White by Law.* New York: New York University Press.

Hernandez, Ramona. 2002. *The Mobility of Workers under Advanced Capitalism: Dominican Migration to the United States.* New York: Columbia University Press.

Hero, Rodney E. and Anne G. Campbell. 1996. "Understanding Latino Political Participation: Exploring the Evidence from the Latino National Political Survey." *Hispanic Journal of Behavioral Sciences* 18: 129–141.

Hertel, Bradley and Michael Hughes. 1987. "Social and Political Attitudes among Religious Groups: Convergence and Divergence over Time." *Journal for the Scientific Study of Religion* 36: 52–70.

Hetherington, Marc J. 1998. "The Political Relevance of Political Trust." *American Political Science Review* 92: 791–808.

Highton, Benjamin and Arthur L. Burris. 2002. "New Perspectives on Voter Turnout in the United States." *American Politics Research* 30: 285–306.

Hill, Kevin A., Dario V. Moreno, and Lourdes Cue. 2001. "Racial and Partisan Voting in a Tri-Ethnic City: The 1996 Dade County Mayoral Election." *Journal of Urban Affairs* 23: 291–307.

Hirschman, Charles. 2004. "The Origins and Demise of the Concept of Race." *Population and Development Review* 30: 385–415.

Hirschman, Charles, Richard Alba, and Reynolds Farley. 2000. "The Meaning and Measurement of Race in the United States Census: Glimpses into the Future." *Demography* 37: 381–394.

Hitlin, Steven, J.Scott Brown, and Glen H. Elder, Jr. 2007. "Measuring Latinos: Racial vs. Ethnic Classification and Self-Understandings." *Social Forces* 86: 587–600.

Hood, M. V., Irwin Morris, and Kurt Shirkey. 1997. "Quedate o Vente: Uncovering the Determinants of Hispanic Public Opinion toward Immigration." *Political Research Quarterly* 50: 627–647.

Hochschild, Jennifer, Traci Burch, and Vesla Weaver. 2004. Effects of Skin Color Bias in SES on Political Activities and Attitudes. Paper presented at the Annual Meeting of the American Political Science Association, September 2–5.

Hochschild, Jennifer L. and Brenna Marea Powell. 2008. "Racial Reorganization and the United States Census 1850–1930: Mulattoes, Half-Breeds, Mixed Parentage, Hindoos, and the Mexican Race." *Studies in American Political Development* 22: 59–96.

Hritzuk, Natasha, and David K. Park. 2000. "The Question of Latino Participation: From an SES to a Social Structural Explanation." *Social Science Quarterly* 81:151–165.

Humes, Karen, Nicholas A. Jones, and Roberto R. Ramirez. 2011. "Overview of Race and Hispanic Origin: 2010." Census 2010 Brief (March). Washington, DC: U.S. Bureau of the Census.

Hunt, Larry L. 1999. "Hispanic Protestantism in the United States: Trends by Decade and Generation." *Social Forces* 77: 1601–1623.

Hy, Ronald John and Jim R. Wollscheid. 2007. "Economic Modeling" in Yang Kaifeng and Gerald J. Miller (ed). *Handbook of Research Methods in Public Administration.* New York: Taylor and Francis.

Itzigsohn, Jose. 2009. *Encountering American Faultlines: Race, Class, and the Dominican Experience in Providence*. New York: Russell Sage Foundation.

Itzigsohn, Jose and Carlos Dore-Cabral. 2000. "Competing identities? Race, Ethnicity and Panethnicity among Dominicans in the United States." *Sociological Forum* 15: 225-247.

Itzigsohn, Jose, S. Giorguli , and O. Vasquez. 2005. "Immigrant Incorporation and Racial Identity: Racial Self-Identification among Dominican Immigrants." *Ethnic and Racial Studies* 28: 50-78.

Jackman, Mary R. 1994. *The Velvet Glove: Paternalism and Conflict in Gender, Class, and Race Relations*. Berkeley, CA: University of California Press.

Jackson, Robert A. 2009. "Latino Political Connectedness and Electoral Participation." *Journal of Political Marketing* 8: 233-262.

Jennings, J. T. 1993. *Voting and registration in the election of November 1992* (U.S. Census Bureau, Current Population Reports, pp. 20-466). Washington, DC: Government Printing Office.

Jimenez, Thomas R. 2008. "Mexican-Immigrant Replenishment and the Continuing Significance of Ethnicity and Race." *American Journal of Sociology* 113: 1527-1567.

Johnson, Martin, Robert M. Stein, and Robert Winkle. 2003. "Language Choice, Residential Stability, and Voting among Latino Americans." *Social Science Quarterly* 84: 412-424.

Jones-Correa, Michael. 1998. *Between Two Nations: The Political Predicament of Latinos in New York City*. Ithaca, NY: Cornell University Press.

Jones-Correa, Michael and David Leal. 1996. "Becoming 'Hispanic': Secondary Pan-Ethnic Identification among Latin American-Origin Populations in the United States." *Hispanic Journal of Behavioral Sciences* 18: 214-255.

Kam, Cindy D. and Anna Maria Ortiz. 1998. "Who's Asking Whom? Race, Recruitment and Political Participation." Paper presented at the annual meeting of the American Political Science Association, Boston, September 3-6.

Kaufmann, Karen. 2003. "Cracks in the Rainbow: Group Commonality as a Basis for Latino and African-American Political Coalitions." *Political Research Quarterly* 56: 199-210.

Kaufmann, Karen. 2004. *The Urban Voter*. Ann Arbor, MI: University of Michigan Press.

Kennedy, Peter. 1992. *A Guide to Econometrics*, 3rd ed. Cambridge, MA: MIT Press.

Kelly, Nathan J. and Jana Morgan Kelly. 2005. "Religion and Latino Partisanship in the United States." *Political Research Quarterly* 58: 87-95.

Kertzer, David I. and Dominique Arel. 2002. "Censuses, Identity Formation and the Struggle for Political Power" in David I. Kertzer and Dominique Arel (eds). *Census and Identity: The Politics of Race, Ethnicity and Language in National Censuses*. Cambridge: Cambridge University Press.

Kinder, Donald and Lynn Sanders. 1996. *Divided By Color: Racial Politics and the Democratic Ideal*. Chicago,IL: University of Chicago Press.

Kissam, Edward, Enrigue Herrera, and Jorge M. Nakamoto. 1993. "Hispanic Response to Census Enumeration Forms and Procedures." Task order no. 46-YABC-2-0001, contract no. 50-YABC-2-66027, submitted by Aguirre International, 411 Borel Avenue, Suite 402, San Mateo, CA, to U.S. Bureau of the Census, Center for Survey Methods Research, March.

Kluegel, James R. and Elliot R. Smith. 1986. *Beliefs about Inequality: Americans' Views about What Is and What Ought to Be*. New York: Aldine de Gruyter.

Korgen, K. O. 1998. *From Black to Biracial: Transforming Racial Identity among Americans*. Westport, CT: Praeger.

Landale, N. S. and Ralph Salvatore Oropesa. 2002. "White, Black, or Puerto Rican? Racial Self Identification among Mainland and Island Puerto Ricans." *Social Forces* 81: 231–254.
Lane, Robert E. 1959. *Political Life.* New York: Free Press.
Lavariega-Monforti, Jessica and Gabriel R. Sanchez. 2010. "The Politics of Perception: An Investigation of the Presence and Source of Perceived Discrimination Toward and Among Latinos." *Social Science Quarterly* 90: 245–265.
Lay, J. Celeste and Atiya Kai Stokes-Brown. 2009. "Put to the Test: Racial and Socioeconomic Differences in Support for High-Stakes Testing." *American Politics Research* 37: 429–448.
Lazarsfeld, Paul F., Bernard Berelson, and Hazel Gaudet. 1944. *The People's Choice: How the Voter Makes up his Mind in a Presidential Campaign.* New York: Columbia University Press.
Leal, David L. 2002. "Political Participation by Latino Non-Citizens in the United States." *British Journal of Political Science* 32: 353–370.
Leal, David L. 2004a. "Latinos and School Vouchers: Testing the 'Minority Support' Hypothesis." *Social Science Quarterly* 85: 1227–1237.
Leal, David L. 2004b. "Latino Public Opinion?" Paper presented at the Latino Politics: The State of the Discipline conference sponsored by Texas A&M University and the University of Texas at Austin, College Station, TX, April 30–May 1.
Leal, David L. 2007. "Latino Public Opinion: Does It Exist?" in Rodolfo Espino, David L. Leal, and Kenneth J. Meier (eds). *Latino Politics: Identity, Mobilization, and Representation.* Charlottesville, VA: University of Virginia Press.
Leal, David L. and Luis Ricardo Fraga. 2004. "Playing the Latino Card: Race, Ethnicity, and National Party Politics." *Du Bois Review* 1: 297–317.
Lee, Jennifer and Frank D. Bean. 2007. "Reinventing the Color Line: Immigration and America's New Racial/Ethnic Divide." *Social Forces* 86: 561–586.
Lee, Jennifer and Frank D. Bean. 2004. "America's Changing Color Lines." *Annual Review of Sociology* 30: 221–242.
Leighley, A. V., and Vedlitz, A. 1999. "Race, Ethnicity, and Political Participation: Competing Models and Contrasting Explanations." *Journal of Politics* 61:1092- 114.
Lien, Pei-te. 1994. "Ethnicity and Political Participation: A Comparison between Asian and Mexican Americans." *Political Behavior* 16: 237–264.
Lien, Pei-te, Margaret Conway, and Janelle Wong. 2004. *The Politics of Asian Americans: Diversity and Community.* New York: Routledge.
Lewis-Beck, M. S., W. G. Jacoby, H. Norpoth, and H. F. Weisberg. 2008. *The American Voter Revisited.* Ann Arbor, MI: University of Michigan Press.
Logan, John R. 2003. *How Race Counts for Hispanic Americans.* Accessed February 1, 2005, from http://mumford1.dyndns.org/cen2000/BlackLatinoReport/BlackLatino01.htm
Long, J. S. and J. Freese. 2001. *Regression Models for Categorical Dependent Variables Using Stata.* College Station, TX: Stata Press.
Lopez, Mark. 2008. *The Hispanic Vote in 2008.* Washington, DC: Pew Hispanic Center.
Lopez, Mark Hugo and Paul Taylor. 2009. *Dissecting the 2008 Electorate: Most Diverse in U.S. History.* Pew Hispanic Center. Accessed April 10, 2010, from http://www.pewhispanic.org/2009/04/30/dissecting-the-2008-electorate-most-diverse-in-us-history/
Malone, N., K. F. Baluja, J. M. Costanzo, and C. J. Davis. 2003. "The Foreign-Born Population: 2000." Census 2000 Brief. Washington, DC: U.S. Census Bureau.
Manzano, Sylvia. 2007. "Bonding and Bridging: Latinos and Social Capital" in Rodolfo Espino, David Leal, and Kenneth J. Meier (eds). *Latino Politics: State of the Discipline.* Charlottesville, VA: University of Virginia Press.

Marable, Manning. 1985. *Black American Politics: From Washington Marches to Jackson*. London: Verso.
Markus, Gregory B. and Philip E. Converse. 1979. "A Dynamic Simultaneous Equation Model of Electoral Choice." *American Political Science Review* 73: 1055–1070.
Marquez, Benjamin. 2007. "Latino Identity Politics Research: Problems and Opportunities." in Rodolfo Espino, David Leal, and Kenneth J. Meier (eds). *Latino Politics: State of the Discipline*. Charlottesville,VA: University of Virginia Press.
Marquez, Benjamin and James Jennings. 2000. "Representation by Other Means: Mexican American and Puerto Rican Social Movement Organizations." *PS: Political Science and Politics* 33: 541–546.
Marrow, Helen B. 2003. "To Be or Not to Be (Hispanic or Latino): Brazilian Racial and Ethnic Identity in the United States." *Ethnicities* 3: 427–464.
Marrow, Helen. 2005. "New Destinations and Immigrant Incorporation." *Perspectives on Politics* 3: 781–799.
Martinez, Anne. 2000. "Established Latinos More Likely to Support Curbing Immigration." San Jose Mercury News, p. 19A, October 15.
Martinez-Ebers, Valerie, Luis Fraga, Linda Lopez, and Arturo Vega. 2000. "Latino Interests in Education, Health, and Criminal Justice Policy." *PS: Political Science & Politics* 33: 547–554.
Marx, Anthony. 1998. *Making Race and Nation: A Comparison of South Africa, the United States and Brazil*. New York: Cambridge University Press.
Mason, Patrick L. 2004. "Annual Income, Hourly Wages, and Identity among Mexican Americans and Other Latinos." *Industrial Relations* 43: 817–834.
Massey, Douglas S. 2007. *Categorically Unequal: The American Stratification System*. New York: Russell Sage.
Masuoka, Natalie. 2008. "Political Attitudes and Ideologies of Multiracial Americans: The Implications of Mixed Race in the United States." *Political Research Quarterly* 61: 253–267.
Masuoka, Natalie. 2011. "The Multiracial Option: Social Group Identity and Changing Patterns of Racial Categorization." *American Politics Research* 39: 176–204.
McClain, Paula D. 1993. "The Changing Dynamics of Urban Politics: Black and Hispanic Municipal Employment—Is There Competition?" *Journal of Politics* 55: 399–414.
McClain, Paula D. and A. J. Karnig. 1990. "Black and Hispanic Socioeconomic and Political Competition." *American Political Science Review* 84: 535–545.
McClain, Paula D., and Joseph Stewart Jr. 1995. *Can We All Get Along? Racial and Ethnic Minorities in American politics*. Boulder, CO: Westview.
McDaniel, Eric and Christopher G. Ellison. 2008. "God's Party? Race, Religion, and Partisanship over Time." *Political Research Quarterly* 61: 180–191.
McKuen, Michael B., Robert S. Erikson, and James A. Stimson. 1989. "Macropartisanship." *American Political Science Review* 73(4): 1125–1142.
McLemore, S. D., & Romo, R. 1985. The Origins and Development of the Mexican American people. In R. O. de la Garza, F. D. Bean, C. M. Bonjean, R. Romo, & R. Alvarez (eds.), *The Mexican American Experience: An Interdisciplinary Anthology*. Austin: University of Texas Press.
Meier, Kenneth J. and Joseph Stewart, Jr. 1991. *The Politics of Hispanic Education*. Albany: SUNY Press.
Menchaca, Martha. 2001. *Recovering History, Constructing Race: The Indian, Black, and White Roots of Mexican Americans*. Austin, TX: University of Texas Press.
Merton, R. K. and P.L. Kendall. 1946. "The Focused Interview." *American Journal of Sociology* 51: 541–557.

Michael, Joseph and Jeffrey M. Timberlake. "Are Latinos Becoming White? Determinants of Latinos' Racial Self-Identification in the U.S." in C. A. Gallagher (Ed.), *Racism in Post-Race America: New Theories, New Directions*. Chapel Hill, NC: Social Forces, 107–122.

Michelson, Melissa R. 2000. "Political Efficacy and Electoral Participation of Chicago Latinos." *Social Science Quarterly* 81: 136–150.

Michelson, Melissa R. 2001. "Political Trust among Chicago Latinos." *Journal of Urban Affairs* 23: 323–334.

Michelson, Melissa R. 2003. "Getting Out the Latino Vote: How Door-to-Door Canvassing Influences Voter Turnout in Rural Central California." *Political Behavior* 25: 247–263.

Michelson, Melissa R. 2006. "Mobilizing the Latino Youth Vote: Some Experimental Results." *Social Science Quarterly* 87: 1188–1206.

Miller, Lawrence, Jerry Polinard, and Robert Wrinkle. 1984. "Attitudes toward Undocumented Workers: The Mexican American Perspective. *Social Science Quarterly* 65:482–494.

Miller, Arthur H., Patricia Gurin, Gerald Gurin, and Oksana Malanchuk. 1981. "Group Consciousness and Political Participation." *American Journal of Political Science* 25(3):494–511.

Moe, T. 2001. *Schools, Vouchers and the American Public*. Washington, DC: Brookings Institution.

Montalvo, Frank F. and G. Edward Codina. 2001. "Skin Color and Latinos in the United States." *Ethnicities* 1: 321–341.

Morgan, David L. 1997. *Focus Groups as Qualitative Research*. Thousand Oaks, CA: Sage Publications.

Montoya, Lisa, Carol Hardy-Fanta, and Sonia Garcia. 2000. "Latina Politics: Gender, Participation, and Leadership." *PS: Political Science and Politics* 33: 555–561.

Murguia, Edward and Edward E. Telles. 1996. "Phenotype and Schooling among Mexican Americans." *Sociology of Education* 59: 276–269.

Mutua, Athena D. 1999. "Shifting Bottoms and Rotating Centers: Reflections on LatCrit III and the Black/White Paradigm." *Miami Law Review* 53: 1177–1217.

Nagel, Joane. 1994. "Constructing Ethnicity: Creating and Recreating Ethnic Identity and Culture." *Social Problems* 41:152–168.

Nagel, Joane. 1995. "American Indian Ethnic Renewal: Politics and the Resurgence of Identity." *American Sociological Review* 60: 947–965.

Nicholson, S. P., A. D. Pantoja, and G. M. Segura. 2005. "Race Matters: Latino Racial Identities and Political Beliefs." Paper presented at the annual meeting of the American Political Science Association, Washington, DC, September 1–4.

Nelson, Candace and Marta Tienda. 1985. "The Structuring of Hispanic Ethnicity: Historical and Contemporary Perspectives." *Ethnic and Racial Studies* 8:49–74.

Neuman, Russell W. 1986. *Paradox of Mass Politics: Knowledge and Opinion in the American Electorate*. Cambridge, MA: Harvard University Press.

Nicholson, Stephen P., Adrian Pantoja, and Gary M. Segura. 2006. "Political Knowledge and Issue Voting among the Latino Electorate." *Political Research Quarterly* 59: 259–271.

Nobles, Melissa. 2000. *Shades of Citizenship: Race and the Census in Modern Politics*. Stanford,CA: Stanford University Press.

Nobles, Melissa. 2001. "Racial Categorization and Censuses" in David I. Kertzer and Dominique Arel (eds). *Census and Identity: The Politics of Race, Ethnicity, and Language in National Censuses*. Cambridge, U.K.: Cambridge University Press.

Nutini, Hugo G. 1997. "Class and Ethnicity in Mexico: Somatic and Racial Considerations." *Ethnology* 36: 227–38.
Oboler, Suzanne. 1995. *Ethnic Labels, Latino Lives: Identity and the Politics of (Re)presentation in the United States*. Minneapolis: University of Minnesota Press.
Oboler, Suzanne. 1992. "The Politics of Labeling: Latino/a Cultural Identities of Self and Others." *Latin American Perspectives* 19: 18–36.
Omi, M. and H. Winant. 1994. *Racial Formation in the United States: From the 1960s to the1990s*, 2nd edition. New York: Routledge.
Padgett, Tim. 2010. "Still Black and White: How the Census Misreads Hispanic and Arab Americans." *Time Magazine*, Mar. 29, 2010. Accessed April 1, 2010, from http://www.time.com/time/nation/article/0,8599,1975883,00.html
Padilla, Felix M. 1982. "What is a Latino? Interpretations of an Ethnic Identity in an Urban Context." Paper presented at the annual meeting of the Midwest Sociological Society, Des Moines, April 7–9.
Padilla, Felix M. 1984. "On the Nature of Latino Ethnicity." *Social Science Quarterly* 65: 651–664.
Padilla, Felix. 1986. "Latino Ethnicity in the City of Chicago" in Susan Olzak and Joane Nagel (eds). *Competitive Ethnic Relations*. New York: Academic Press.
Pantoja, Adrian D., Ricardo Ramirez, and Gary Segura. 2001. "Citizens by Choice, Voters by Necessity: Patterns in Political Mobilization by Naturalized Latinos." *Political Research Quarterly* 54: 729–750.
Parkin, Michael and Frances Zlotnick. 2011. "English Proficiency and Latino Participation in U.S. Elections." *Politics and Policy* 39: 515–537.
Passel, Jeffrey S. 2006. *The Size and Characteristics of the Unauthorized Migrant Population in the U.S.: Estimates Based on the March 2005 Current Population Survey*. Washington, DC: Pew Hispanic Center.
Passel, Jeffrey S. 2010. *Census History: Counting Hispanics*. Washington, DC: Pew Research Center. Accessed July 8, 2011, from http://pewsocialtrends.org/2010/03/03/census-history-counting-hispanics-2/
Passel, Jeffrey and D'Vera Cohn. 2008. *US Population Projections 2005–2050*. Washington, DC: Pew Hispanic Center.
Patton, M. Q. 1990. *Qualitative Evaluation and Research Methods*, 2nd ed. Newbury Park, CA: Sage Publications.
Perez, Anthony Daniel and Charles Hirschman. 2009. "An Historical Perspective on the Racial and Ethnic Composition of the American Population at the Turn of the Millennium." *Population and Development Review* 35: 1–51.
Pew Hispanic Center. 2009. *Statistical Portrait of Hispanics in the United States, 2007*. Accessed August 1, 2010 from http://pewhispanic.org/factsheets/factsheet.php?FactsheetID=46.
Pew Hispanic Center. 2010. *The Latino Vote in the 2010 Elections*. Accessed December 1, 2010 from http://pewresearch.org/pubs/1790/2010-midterm-elections-exit-poll-hispanic-vote.
Philpot, Tasha S. 2007. *Race, Republicans, and the Return to the Party of Lincoln*. Ann Arbor, MI: University of Michigan Press.
Polinard, Jerry, Robert D. Wrinkle, and Rodolfo de la Garza. 1984. "Attitudes of Mexican Americans toward Irregular Mexican Immigration." *International Migration Review* 18: 782–799.
Portes, Alejandro. 1984. "The Rise of Ethnicity: Determinants of Ethnic Perceptions among Cuban Exiles in Miami." *American Sociological Review* 49: 387–397.
Portes, Alejandro and Ruben G. Rumbaut. 1996. *Immigrant America: A Portrait*. Berkeley, CA: University of California Press.

Portes, Alejandro and Ruben G. Rumbaut. 2001. *Legacies: The Story of the Second Generation*. Berkeley, CA: University of California Press.
Portes, Alejandro and Cynthia Truelove. 1987. "Making Sense of Diversity: Recent Research on Hispanic Minorities in the United States." *Annual Review of Sociology* 13: 359–385.
Portes, Alejandro and Min Zhou. 1993. "The New Second Generation: Segmented Assimilation and Its Variants among Post-1965 Immigrant Youth," *Annals of the American Academy of Political and Social Science* 530:74–98.
Putnam, Robert D. 2000. *Bowling Alone: The Collapse and Revival of American Community*. New York: Simon & Schuster.
Rabinowitz, George and Stewart Elaine Macdonald. 1989. "A Directional Theory of Issue Voting." *American Journal of Political Science* 83: 93–121.
Relethford, John H., Michael P. Stern, Sharon P. Gaskill, and Helen P. Hazuda. 1983. "Social Class, Admixture, and Skin Color Variation in Mexican-Americans and Anglo-Americans Living in San Antonio, Texas." *American Journal of Physical Anthropology* 61: 97–102.
Rodriguez, Clara. 2000. *Changing Race: Latinos, the Census, and the History of Ethnicity in the United States*. New York: New York University Press.
Rodriguez, Clara. 1992. "Race, Culture, and Latino 'Othernesss' in the 1980 Census." *Social Science Quarterly* 73: 931–937.
Rodriguez, Clara and Hector Cordero-Guzman. 1992. "Placing Race in Context." *Ethnic and Racial Studies* 15: 523–542.
Rosales, Arturo. 1993. "Mexican Immigrant Nationalism as an Origin of Identity for Mexican Americans: Exploring the Sources" in Marta E. Bernal and Phylis C. Martinelli (eds). *Mexican American Identity*. Encino, CA: Floricanto Press.
Rosenstone, Steven and John M. Hansen. 1993. *Mobilization, Participation, and Democracy in America*. New York: Macmillan Press.
Sanchez, Gabriel R. 2006. "The Role of Group Consciousness in Latino Public Opinion." *Political Research Quarterly* 59: 435–446.
Sanchez, Gabriel and Jillian Mederios. 2009. "Latinos' Views on Health Care Reform in the Midst of the Historic Congressional Debates of 2009." Policy Brief of the Robert Wood Johnson Foundation Center for Health Policy of the University of New Mexico, Albuquerque, NM.
Sanchez, Gabriel R. and Jessica Lavariega Monforti. 2007. "Is Perception Reality? An Investigation of the Presence and Source of Perceived Discrimination toward and among Latinos." Paper presented at the annual meeting of the American Political Science Association, Chicago, August 30-September 2.
Schermerhorn, Richard A. 1978. *Comparative Racial and Ethnic Relations: A Framework for Theory and Research*. Chicago: University of Chicago Press.
Schildkraut, Deborah. 2005. Press *"One" for English: Language Policy, Public Opinion, and American Identity*. Princeton: Princeton University Press.
Schuman, Howard, Charlotte Steeh, Lawrence Bobo, and Maria Krysan. 1997. *Racial Attitudes in America: Trends and Interpretations*. Cambridge, MA: Harvard University Press.
Shaw, Darren, Rodolfo O. de la Garza and Jongho Lee. 2000. "Explaining Latino Turnout in 1966: A Three-State, Validated Survey Approach." *American Journal of Political Science* 44:332–340.
Shingles, Richard D. 1981. "Black Consciousness and Political Participation: The Missing Link." *American Political Science Review* 75:76–91.
Sidanius, James, P. Singh, J. J. Hetts, and C. Federico. 2000. "It's Not Affirmative Action, It's the Blacks: The Continuing Relevance of Race in American Politics" in David O. Sears, James Sidanius, and Lawrence Bobo (eds). *Racialized Politics: Values, Ideology, and Prejudice in American Public Opinion*. Chicago, IL: University of Chicago Press.

Sigelman, Lee and Susan Welch. 1991. *Black Americans' Views of Racial Inequality: The Dream Deferred.* Cambridge, MA: Harvard University Press.
Skrentny, John D. 2002. *The Minority Rights Revolution.* Cambridge, MA: Harvard University Press.
Smith, James P. and Barry Edmonston. 1997. *The New Americans.* Washington, DC: National Academy Press.
Sniderman, Paul M. and Thomas Piazza. 1993. *The Scar of Race.* Cambridge, MA: Harvard University Press.
Stewart, David W. and Prem Shamdasani. 1990. *Focus Groups: Theory and Practice.* Sage Publications, Beverley Hills.
Stokes, Donald E. 1962. "Popular Evaluations of Government: An Empirical Assessment." In Harlan Cleveland and Harold D. Lasswell (eds) *Ethics and Bigness: Scientific, Academic, Religious, Political, and Military.* New York: Harper and Brothers.
Stokes-Brown, Atiya Kai. 2006. "Racial Identity and Latino Vote Choice." *American Politics Research* 34: 627–652.
Stokes-Brown, Atiya Kai. 2009. "The Hidden Politics of Identity: Racial Self Identification and Latino Political Engagement." *Politics and Policy* 37: 1281–1305.
Stokes, Atiya Kai. 2003. "Latino Group Consciousness and Political Participation." *American Politics Research* 31: 361–378.
Sullins, D. Paul. 1999. "Catholic/Protestant Trends on Abortion: Convergence and Polarity." *Journal for the Scientific Study of Religion* 38:354–369.
Suarez, Ray. 2010. "2010 Census: Who's a Latino?" PBS NewsHour, April 13, 2010. Accessed April 20, 2010, from http://www.pbs.org/newshour/rundown/2010/04/ray-suarez-whos-a-latino.html
Suro, Roberto. 2005. *Attitudes toward Immigrants and Immigration Policy: Surveys among Latinos in the U.S. and in Mexico.* Washington, DC: Pew Hispanic Center.
Suro, Roberto and J. S. Passel. 2003. *The Rise of the Second Generation: Changing Patterns in Hispanic Population Growth.* Washington, DC: Pew Hispanic Center.
Tafoya, Sonya M. 2004. *Shades of Belonging: Latinos and Racial Identity.* Washington, DC: Pew Hispanic Center.
Tajfel, Henri. 1981. *Human Groups and Social Categories Studies in Social Psychology.* Cambridge, MA: Cambridge University Press.
Tajfel, Henri. 1978. "The Psychological Structure of Intergroup Relations" in Henri Tajfel (ed). *Differentiation between Social Groups: Studies in the Social Psychology of Intergroup Relations.* London: Academic Press.
Tajfel, Henri, and John Turner. 1986. "The Social Identity Theory of Intergroup Behavior" in Stephen Worchel and William Austin (eds). *Psychology of Intergroup Relations.* Chicago, IL: Nelson Hall.
Tate, Katherine. 1994. *From Protest to Politics: The New Black Voters in American Elections.* New York: Russell Sage.
Telles, Edward. 1992. "The Continuing Significance of Phenotype Among Mexican Americans." *Social Science Quarterly* 73: 120–132.
Telles, Edward E. and Vilma Ortiz. 2008. *Generations of Exclusion: Mexican Americans, Assimilation, and Race.* New York: Russell Sage Foundation.
Telles, Edward E. and Edward Murguia. 1990. "Phenotypic Discrimination and Income Differences among Mexican Americans." *Social Science Quarterly* 71: 682–696.
Tienda, Marta and F. Mitchell, eds. 2006. *Multiple Origins, Uncertain Destinies.* Washington, DC: National Academies Press.
Tienda, Marta and Vilma Ortiz. 1986. "'Hispanicity' in the 1980 Census." *Social Science Quarterly* 67: 3–20.

Tomz, Michael, Jason Wattenberg, and Gary King. 2003. *CLARIFY: Software for Interpreting and Presenting Statistical Results* (version 2.1). Cambridge, MA: Harvard University. Available at http://gking.harvard.edu

Torres-Saillant, Silvo.1998. "The Tribulations of Blackness: Stages in Dominican Racial Identity." *Latin American Perspectives* 25: 126–146.

Trucios-Haynes, Enid. 2000. "Why 'Race Matters': LatCrit Theory and Latina/o Racial Identity." *Berkeley La Raza Law Review* 12: 1–42.

Trueba, Enrique. 1999. *Latinos Unidos: From Cultural Diversity to the Politics of Solidarity*. Lanham, MD: Rowman & Littlefield.

Uhlaner, Carole. 1991. "Perceived Prejudice and Coalitional Prospects among Black, Latinos, and Asian Americans" in Byron Jackson and Michael Preston (eds). *Ethnic and Racial Politics in California*. Berkeley, CA: Institute for Governmental Studies.

Uhlaner, Carole. 1996. "Latinos and Ethnic Politics in California: Participation and Preference" in Anibal Yaiez-Chavez (ed). *Latino Politics in California*. San Diego, CA: University of California Press.

Uhlaner, Carole Jean and F. Chris Garcia. 2001. "Learning Which Party Fits: Experience, Ethnic Identity, and the Demographic Foundations of Latino Party Identification." Paper presented at the Minority Representation: Institutions, Behavior, and Identity conference, Claremont, CA, February 2–3.

Uhlaner, Carole Jean, and F. Chris Garcia. 2002. "Latino Public Opinion" in Barbara Norrander and Clyde Wilcox (eds). *Understanding Public Opinion*. Washington, DC: CQ Press.

Uhlaner, Carole Jean, Mark M. Gray, and F. Chris Garcia. 2000. "Ideology, Issues, and Partisanship Among Latinos." Paper presented at the annual meeting of the Western Political Science Association, San Jose, CA, March 24–26.

U.S. Census Bureau. 2001. *The Hispanic Population*. Census 2000 Brief (May).

Valdez, Zulema. 2011. "Political Participation Among Latinos in the United States: The Effect of Group Identity and Consciousness." *Social Science Quarterly* 92: 466–482.

Vaquera, Elizabeth and Grace Kao. 2006. "The Implications of Choosing 'No Race' on the Salience of Hispanic Identity: How Racial and Ethnic Backgrounds Intersect among Hispanic Adolescents." *The Sociological Quarterly* 47: 375–396.

Verba, Sidney, Kay Lehman Schlozman, and Henry Brady. 1995. *Voice and Equality: Civic Voluntarism in American Politics*. Cambridge, MA: Harvard University Press.

Verba, Sidney, and Norman Nie. 1972. *Participation in America: Political Democracy and Social Equality*. Chicago: University of Chicago Press.

Warren, Johnathan W. and Frances Winddance Twine. 1997. "White Americans, the New Minority? Non-Blacks and the Ever-Expanding Boundaries of Blackness." *Journal of Black Studies* 28: 200–218.

Waters, Mary C. 2002. "The Social Construction of Race and Ethnicity: Some Examples from Demography" in Stewart Tolnay and Nancy Denton (eds). *American Diversity: A Demographic Challenge for the Twenty-First Century*. Albany, NY: SUNY Press.

Waters, Mary C. 1999. *Black Identities: West Indian Immigrant Dreams and American Realities*. New York: Russell Sage Foundation and Cambridge, MA: Harvard University Press.

Welch, Michael, David Leege, and James Cavendish. 1995. "Attitudes toward Abortion among US Catholics: Another Case of Symbolic Politics?" *Social Science Quarterly* 76: 142–157.

Wenzel, James. 2006. "Acculturation Effects on Trust in National and Local Government among Mexican Americans." *Social Science Quarterly* 87: 1073–1087.

West, Cornell. 1994. *Race Matters*. New York: Vintage.
Whitten N. and A. Torres. 1998. *Blackness in Latin America and the Caribbean*. Bloomington: Indiana University Press.
Williams, David R., Risa Lavizzo-Mourney, and Rueben C. Warren. 1994. "The Concept of Race and Health Status in America." *Public Health Reports* 109: 26–42.
Wimmer, Andreas. 2008. "Elementary Strategies of Ethnic Boundary Making." *Ethnic and Racial Studies* 31: 1025–55.
Wimmer, Andreas. 2007. "How (Not) to Think about Ethnicity in Immigrant Societies." Oxford Centre on Migration, Policy and Society Working Paper Series 07-44:1–38.
Wolfinger, Raymond E. and Steven J. Rosenstone. 1980. *Who Votes?* New Haven: Yale University Press.
Wong, Janelle S. 2000. "The Effects of Age and Political Exposure on the Development of Party Identification among Asian American and Latino Immigrants in the United States." *Political Behavior* 22: 341–371.
Wrinkle, Robert D., Joseph Stewart, Jr., J. L. Polinard, Kenneth J. Meier and John R. Arvizu. 1996. "Ethnicity and Nonelectoral Participation." *Hispanic Journal of Behavioral Sciences* 18: 142–151.
Yancey, George. 2003. *Who is White? Latinos, Asians, and the New Black/Non-Black Divide*. Boulder: Lynne Rienner.
Yinger, J. 1991. "Housing Discrimination Study: Incidence of Discrimination and Variations in Discriminatory Behavior." Washington, DC: Office of Policy Development and Research, U.S. Department of Housing and Urban Development.
Zweigenhaft, Richard and G. William Domhoff. 1998. *Diversity in the Power Elite*. New Haven, CT: Yale University Press.

Index

A
Aberbach, J. D., 50, 51, 60
Abortion, 102, 105, 106, 112t, 114
Abrajano, M. A., 50, 52, 55, 56, 60, 66
Abramson, P. R., 50, 60, 66
Acculturation, and race, factors predicting, 39t, 41, 42, 43t; foreign- or American-born and identity, 47t; racial construction, 4; racial identity, 34, 37; political orientation, 56, 58t; political orientation predictions and immigrants, 65t; political participation, 89–90; political partisanship, 70, 78t, 97t; political partisanship predictions, 75t, 76, 92t, 93; political partisanship preferences, 74; public opinion, 101, 102, 106, 109t, 111; public opinion and immigrants, 116t
Activism, local, 31
Affigne, T., 122
Affirmative action, 107
Affordable Care Act, 107. *See also* Health care reform; Public opinion
African Americans, 6, 7, 9, 36, 40, 42, 45, 50, 60, 61, 69, 74, 76, 79, 84, 94, 100, 101, 102, 110, 111, 114, 122, 123
Age, immigration policy, 101–102; Latino racial identity, 35; focus group, 11 12, 13; LNS questionnaire, A126; political orientation predictions, 61; political participation, 89; political participation of immigrants, 96t; political participation predictions, 91t, 93; political partisanship preferences, 73; predicted political orientation of immigrants, 63, 64t; public opinion, 106, 108t, 110, 115t. *See also* Demographic characteristics
Agius Vallejo, J., 33
Akresh, I. R., 3, 4
Alba, R., 17, 22, 30, 37
Albert, N. G., 2
Aldrich, J. H., 45, 50, 66
Alesina, A., 56
Almond, G., 50, 66, 84
Alvarez, R. M., 15, 50, 52, 55, 56, 60, 66, 67, 68, 69, 70, 71, 73, 74, 76, 100
American politics, 1, 48
American racial stratification system, 24–25
American society, public opinion, 100
Anderson, M., 22
Antunes, G., 31
Aparicio, A., 23, 122
Appealing to Latino voters, 70. *See also* Partisanship
Arce, C., 32
Arel, D., 3, 26
Arizona immigration law, 104. *See also* Immigration
Arvizu, J. R., 83, 85, 87
Assimilation, model and predicting racial identity, 41, 42; political orientation, 56, 58t; political orientation by immigrants, 65t; political participation, 89–90; political participation by immigrants, 97t; political participation predictions, 92t,

93; political partisanship by immigrants, 78t; political partisanship predictions, 75t; political partisanship preferences, 74; public opinion, 106, 109t; public opinion and immigrants, 116t; racial construction, 4
Astone, N. M., 21
Attachment, 6
Attitude, 11, 59

B
Bailey, B., 48
Baldassare, M., 52
Baluja, K. F., 34
Barker, L. J., 121
Barreto, M. A., 2, 70, 73, 83, 84, 90, 123
Bashi, V., 18
Basler, C., 7
Bates N. A., 4
Bean, F. D., 8, 30
Beauty, as human capital, 48
Beck, P., 68
Beliefs, 11
Berelson, B. R., 67, 83
Big interests, 59, 60f, 61
Bilingualism, 101
Binder, N. E., 101, 102, 106
Bishin, B. G., 83
Blackness, 49, 90, 122
Black Latinos, opinion on abortion, 105; opinion on health care reform, 103, 104; opinion on standardized testing, 105; party preference and race, 71, 72; political participation, 86, 88, 95; political orientation predictions, 59, 59f, 60f, 61, 62; political participation predictions, 90; political partisanship by immigrants, 79; political partisanship predictions, 74, 75t, 76, 80t; political trust, 54–55; public opinion, 110; rejection, 32, 122; racial identity, 37
Bobo, L., 60, 100
Bohara, A. K., 32
Bolks, S. E., 102, 106
Bonvilla-Silva, E., 4, 8, 9, 17, 18, 30, 31, 37
Brady, H., 50, 83, 84, 94, 99
Branton, R., 33, 73, 101, 102, 105, 106, 107, 111

Brown, J. S., 17, 28, 119
Browning, R. P., 85
Brubaker, R., 28
Burch, T., 89
Burns, N., 51
Burris, A. L., 83, 84, 85, 135n4

C
Cabrera, Fernando, 69
Cain, B. E., 68, 69, 70, 73, 101
Calvo, M. A., 1
Campbell, A., 67, 68, 73, 74
Campbell, A. G., 83, 84, 87
Campbell, A. L., 50, 51, 66, 107
Campbell, C. E., 32, 33
Campbell, M. E., 17, 21, 119
Candidate-focused approach, 70. See also Partisanship
Candidates, 68, 123–124. See also Partisanship
Caribbean Latinos, 102
Cassidy, R. C., 2, 21
Categories, census, 19
Categorizations, 25, 26t, 119
Catholics, 102. See also Public opinion
Cavendish, J., 102
Census, 19–22, 120, 121
Central Americans, 69, 73, 102
Chicago, focus group, 11
Chicano movement, 23
Classification, Latinos, 28
Codina, G. E., 34
Coffin, M., 73
Cohn, D'Vera, 1
Collective identity, 121
Color line, 6, 14, 22, 30, 50, 120, 121, 122. See also Tri-racial color line model and White-Black color line
Combs, M., 100
Commonality, 5, 6; LNS commonality, A126–A127; political orientation, 56, 58t, 61; political orientation predictions, 63, 65t; political participation, 83, 89, 92t, 94; political participation by immigrants, 95; political partisanship direction, 78t; political partisanship predictions, 75t, 80t; political partisanship preferences, 73–74; public opinion, 106, 109t, 111, 114, 116t
Conover, P. J., 67, 101

Index 157

Contact with elected official, 90, 91t, 92t, 93, 94; political participation by immigrants, 95
Contemporary experience, United States and Latino racial identity, 31
Converse, P., 50, 51, 67, 68, 73, 74, 107
Conway, M. M., 15, 67, 84
Cook, E. A., 102
Cooper, F., 28
Cordero-Guzman, H., 4, 23, 31, 33
Cork, D. L., 136n1
Cornell, S., 3, 30
Costanzo, J. M., 34
Craig, S.C., 51
Crenshaw, K., 19
Cubans, alignment with Republican Party and partisanship, 69, 70, 73; foreign- or American-born and identity, 45; political orientation by immigrants, 63; political orientation predictions, 60; political participation predictions, 93; political partisanship predictions, 76; public opinion, 102, 110, 113, 115t; White identification, 34
Cue, L., 123
Cultural assimilation, 34, 37. *See also* Assimilation
Cultural factors, political participation, 85
Cultural heritage, 33, 34, 37
Cultural identifiers, 17

D

Dahl, 84
Dalton, R. J., 93
Daniel, G. R., 4
Darity, W., Jr., 4, 5, 21, 33, 40, 48, 119, 134n7
Davila, A., 32
Davis, C. J., 34
Dawson, M., 5, 7, 9, 33, 56, 73, 100, 106
de la Garza, R. O, 1, 6, 33, 52, 73, 83, 84, 85, 89, 90, 94, 101, 102, 106, 135n4
de la Puente, M., 4
De Maio, T. K., 4
Death penalty, 7, 101
DeFrancesco, V.M., 123
Delgado, R., 19

Democratic Party, alignment and partisanship, 68, 70; health care reform and party affiliation, 107; political partisanship by immigrants, 79; political partisanship predictions, 74, 76; public opinion, 112; public opinion by immigrants, 114; race and Latino preferences, 71–74
Demographic characteristics, factors predicting racial identity, 39t, 43t; foreign- or American-born and identity, 46t; political orientation, 55, 56, 57t; political orientation of immigrants, 64t; political participation, 88–89; political participation of immigrants, 96t; political participation predictions, 91t; political partisanship preferences, 73; public opinion, 105–106, 108t; public opinion and immigrants, 115t; strength of political partisanship predictions, 80t. *See also* Age; Gender; Income; Skin color; Time in United States
Denton, N.A., 20
DeSipio, L., 1, 6, 31, 83, 84, 85, 89, 90, 100, 102
Discrimination, direction of political partisanship by immigrants, 78t; factors predicting identity, 39t, 40–41, 43t, 44; foreign- or American-born and identity, 45, 47t; LNS questionnaire, A127–A128; opinion about salient issues, 103; party alignment and partisanship, 70; political orientation, 56; political orientation predictions, 58t, 61; political participation, 89; political participation of immigrants, 95, 97; political participation predictions, 92t, 94; political partisanship predictions, 75t, 76; political partisanship preferences, 73; political partisanship and strength of predictions, 80t; predicted political orientation of immigrants, 63, 65t; public opinion, 106, 109t, 111; public opinion and immigrants, 114,

116t; racial identity and perceptions, 33; racial identity of Mexicans and Puerto Ricans, 31; racial self-identification, 4–5, 36–37
Disempowerment, 87
Domhoff, G. W., 32
Dominant racial hierarchy, 3
Dominicans, Black identification, 34; discrimination, 31; foreign- or American-born and identity, 45; political orientation predictions, 60, 61; political partisanship predictions, 76; political orientation prediction of immigrants, 63; public opinion of immigrants, 115t
Door-to-door mobilization, 85
Dore-Cabral, C., 1, 23, 31
Downs, A., 68
Duany, J., 9, 35, 90, 122
Du Bois, W. E. B., 121

E

Earnings, survey respondents, 10. *See also* Income; Socioeconomic status
Echevarria, S., 102
Economic advantage, 19
Economic status, 76. *See also* Income; Socioeconomic status
Economic support, 31. *See also* Cubans
Education, Black versus White Latinos, 7; focus group, 12, 13; foreign- or American-born and racial identity, 45; immigration policy, 101–102; Latino National Survey respondents, 10; LNS questionnaire, A126; political orientation, 55; political orientation of immigrants, 63, 64t; political orientation predictions, 61political participation, 83, 89; political participation of immigrants, 95; political participation predictions, 91t, 93; political partisanship direction by immigrants, 78t; political partisanship predictions, 76; political partisanship preferences, 73; public opinion, 108t, 110; public opinion and immigrant identity, 114, 115t; race identity and socioeconomic status, 106; racial identity, 32–33, 35, 48; racial identity predictions, 38; racialized concept of identity, 121; strength of political partisanship predictions, 80t
Efficacy, interest in politics of multiracial Latinos, 62; political behavior, 51; political orientations, 53–54; political orientation predictions, 61; political participation, 84
Elder, G. H., Jr., 17, 28, 119
Elected officials, contacting, 88
Elections, 84
Ellison, C. G., 74, 76, 102
Embrick, D. G., 9, 35
English-dominant Latinos, 56, 94, 102
English, State language, 101
English proficiency, factors predicting racial identity, 40; foreign- or American-born and identity, 45; influence on racial identity, 34; political orientation predictions, 61; political orientation of immigrants and predictions, 63, 65t; political participation, 89;political participation of immigrants, 97t, 98; political participation predictions, 92t; political partisanship predictions, 76; political partisanship preferences, 74; public opinion, 107, 109t, 111, 112, 114, 116t; racial identity, 37; strength of predictions of political partisanship, 80t
Ennis, S. R., 2
Entwistle, D. R., 21
Erikson, R. S., 68
Espino, R., 32
Ethnic identity, 18, 19, 120
Ethnic immigrant populations, 8
Evans, D., 102, 106

F

Falcon, A., 1, 6, 73, 83, 101, 102
Farley, R., 17, 22, 30
Feagin, J. R., 17
Feldman, S., 67
Females, 35. *See also* Gender
Feree, M., 100
Fergus, E., 23
Fergus, J. R., 32

Fiorina, M., 68
Focus Group Questionnaire, 131
Focus groups, Latino National Survey respondents, 11–13, 12f-13f; Latinos self-report on racial identity, 22–29; questionnaire, B131. *See also* Latino National Survey
Foreign-born Latinos, nativity and racial identity, 44–48; political participation, 85; public opinion, 106.
Forman, T., 9, 35, 135n4
Fraga, L. R., 81, 104
Frank, R., 3, 4, 31, 32
Franz, M. M., 32
Freese, J., 37
Fry, R., 1

G

Gaitz, C.M., 31
Gans, H. J., 8
Garcia Bedolla, L.G., 15, 23. 34, 37, 56, 67, 68, 69, 70, 71, 73, 74, 76, 83, 84, 85,100, 111
Garcia, C., 133n3
Garcia, F. C., 1, 6, 67, 68, 70, 73, 76, 83, 85, 101, 102, 105, 106
Garcia, J. A., 1, 6, 23, 60, 83, 89, 101, 102
Garcia, L., 83
Garcia, S., 89
Gaskill, S. P., 32, 89
Gaudet, H., 67
Gender, abortion and public opinion, 102; factors predicting racial identity, 38; focus group, 11, 12, 13; Latino racial identity, 35; LNS questionnaire, A125; political orientation, 55; political orientation predictions and immigrants, 63, 64t; political orientation predictions, 61; political participation, 89;political participation of immigrants, 95, 96t; political participation predictions, 93–94; political partisanship preferences, 73; public opinion, 106, 108t, 110, 113, 115t. *See also* Demographic characteristics
Generational status, first- versus later and political trust, 56; Latino racial identity, 34, 37; political orientation predictions, 61; political participation predictions, 92t; political partisanship predictions, 76; public opinion, 111, 112
Geographic diversity, 1
Geographic heritage, 30
Geron, K., 133n7
Gilliam, F. D., 60
Giorguli, S., 32
Glover, K.S., 18
Goar, C., 9, 35, 135n4
Golash-Boza, T., 4, 5, 21, 33, 40, 48, 119, 134n7
Gomez, C., 32, 34
Gordon, M., 34, 74
Government spending, 112, 114
Gray, M. M., 76
Grieco, E. M., 2, 21
Grievances, 31
Group goals, 85
Group consciousness, 33, 89, 94, 135
Group identity, 1, 83. *See also* Political participation
Group interest, 6
Group membership, 5, 6, 28, 47, 52, 120, 124
Group participation, 94. *See also* Political participation
Guidelines, census, 19
Gurin, G., 67
Gurin, P., 67
Guzman, B., 31, 134n2

H

Hacker, A., 18
Hajnal, Z.L., 52, 69, 70, 71, 72, 73, 135n1
Hakken, K., 32
Hall, E., 100
Hall, R. E., 31, 48
Hansen, J. M., 15, 67, 70, 83, 84
Haney-Lopez, I., 18, 19, 22, 121
Hardy-Fanta, C., 89
Hartmann, D., 3, 30
Hazuda, H., 32, 89
Health care reform, Black Latinos public opinion, 7; public opinion, 104, 110, 111, 112, 113, 114; public opinion predictions, 107. *See also* Public opinion
Henson, J.R., 31
Hernandez, R., 60
Hero, R. E., 83, 84, 87
Herrera, E., 4
Hertel, B., 102

Hetherington, M. J., 51
Highton, B., 83, 84, 85, 135n4
Hill, K. A., 123
Hirschman, C., 2, 17, 22, 30
Hispanic origin question, census, 2
Hispanic ethnic category, census, 20–21
History, unique and Latino racial identity, 31
Hitlin, S., 17, 28, 119
Hochschild, J., 14, 19, 20, 89
Hood, M. V., 101, 102, 106, 111
Hritzuk, N., 52, 84, 89, 90, 135n4
Hughes, M., 102
Humes, K., 20, 21
Hunt, L. L., 136n1
Hy, R. J., 135n4

I
Immigrants, direction of political partisanship, 77, 78t, 79; partisanship and party preference, 70; political orientation predictions, 62–66; political participation, 95; public opinion, 113–117, 115t, 116t
Immigration policy, public opinion, 104, 110, 111, 112; public opinion by immigrants, 113; public opinion research, 101; socioeconomic status, 106
Income, direction of political partisanship, 78t; focus group, 11, 12, 13; higher and racial identity, 32; LNS questionnaire, A126; political orientation predictions, 61; political participation of immigrants, 95, 96t; political participation predictions, 91t; public opinion, 108t, 110; public opinion and immigrants, 115t. *See also* Demographic characteristics
Independent Party, direction of political partisanship of immigrants, 79; political partisanship predictions, 74, 75t; public opinion, 112; race and preferences, 71–72; research on partisanship, 68, 70
Indeterminant group, 27
Interest, political orientation predictions, 61
Interminority alliance/political coalitions, 9, 122

Interviews, 11; LNS questionnaire, A128. *See also* English proficiency; Spanish-speaking skills
Issues, addressing, 88; *See also* Political participation
Itzigsohn, J., 1, 4, 23, 31, 32, 60, 122

J
Jackson, R. A., 50, 51, 55, 56
Jacoby, W. G., 67
Jelen, T. G., 102
Jennings, J.T., 31, 84
Jennings, M., 68
Jimenez, T. R., 33
Johnson, M., 98 2003
Jones, M. J., 121
Jones, N. A., 20, 21
Jones-Correa, M., 1, 35, 105, 135n4

K
Kam, C. D., 15, 67
Kao, G., 31, 34
Karnig, A. J., 9
Kaufmann, K. M., 9, 83
Kelly, J. M., 70, 73, 74
Kelly, N. J., 70, 73, 74
Kendal, P. I., 11
Kertzer, D. I., 3, 26
Kiewiet, D.R., 68, 69, 70, 73, 101
Kinder, D., 100
King, G., 41
Kissam, E., 4
Kluegal, J. R., 100
Korgen, K. O., 32

L
La Ferrara, E., 56
Landale, N. S., 5, 32, 33, 34
Lane, R.E., 51
Language, 25. *See also* Categorization
Language abilities, immigrants, 98
Language proficiency, 56. *See also* English proficiency; Political orientation
Latin America, race definition, 19
Latino National Survey (LNS), alignment with Democratic Party and research on partisanship, 68, 70; factors predicting racial identity, 40; processing of group membership, 120; residents, 9–10; political trust and Latinos, 54; questionnaire,

Index   161

125–129; state role in shaping racial identity, 22–29, 24t
Latino National Survey—New England (LNS—New England), 10
Latino politicians, trust, 54
Latino racial identity, foundations, factors predicting, 38–44; foundations, nativity, 44–48; foundations, research, 30–37. *See also* Racial identity
Latino rights, Hispanic origin question on 1970 census, 2
Latinos, constructing identity, 119; population and 1970 census, 20; rejection of American categorization of race, 26; religious affiliation and public opinion on abortion and vouchers, 102
Lavizzo-Mourney, R., 30
Lay, J. C., 110
Lazarsfeld, P. F., 67, 83
Leal, D. L., 1, 81, 83, 101, 102, 104, 105, 110, 117
Lee, J., 8, 30, 33, 52, 83, 84, 89, 94, 122, 135n4
Lee, T., 69, 70, 71, 72, 73, 135n1
Leege, D., 102
Leighley, A.V., 52, 84, 135n4
Length of residency, 70. *See also* Time in United States
Lewis, A. E., 9, 35, 135n4
Lewis-Beck, M. S., 67
Lien, P., 15, 67
Life chances, 6, 19
LNS. *See* Latino National Survey
LNS–New England. *See* Latino National Survey–New England
Logan, J. R., 2, 7, 9, 25, 28, 32, 34, 60, 76, 122, 136n2
Long, J. S., 37
Lopez, L., 104
Lopez, M.H., 68
Lu, B., 3, 4, 31, 32

M

Macdonald, S. E., 68
MALDEF. *See* Mexican Americans Legal Defense and Education Fund
Males, 35
Malone, N., 34
Manzano, S., 123
Marable, M., 27
Marginalization, 19

Markus, G. B., 68
Marquez, B., 31, 118
Marrow, H. B., 1, 4
Marshall, D. R., 83
Martin, E. A., 4
Martinez, 105
Martinez-Ebers, V., 104
Marx, A., 22, 25
Mason, P. L., 32, 89
Masouka, N., 26, 85, 99
Massey, D. S., 20, 31
Masuoka, N., 1, 74, 81, 122, 135n1
McClain, P. D., 9, 31, 84
McDaniel, A., 18
McDaniel, E., 74, 76
McKuen, M. B., 68
McLemore, S.D., 31
McPhee, W. N., 67, 83
Medeiros, J., 107
Meier, K. J., 9, 83, 87
Menchaca, M., 18
Merton, R. K., 11
Mexican Americans, census, 2
Mexican Americans Legal Defense and Education Fund (MALDEF), 21
Mexican immigration, 19–20
Mexicans, alignment with Democratic Party and partisanship, 69, 70, 73; discrimination against, 31; foreign- or American-born and racial identity, 45; governmental trust, 55; opinion about abortion, 102;, opinion and immigration policy, 102; political orientation predictions, 60; political participation predictions, 93; political orientation of immigrants and predictions, 63; public opinion, 113, 115t
Michael, J., 31, 32
Michelson, M. R., 50, 51, 52, 54, 55, 56, 61, 83, 85, 102, 105, 135n2
Miller, H., 67
Miller, L., 33, 101, 106
Miller, W., 50, 67, 68, 73, 74, 107
Mitchell, F., 5, 9
Mixed racial origins, 31
Mobilization, 84; *See also* Political participation
Moe, 102, 100
Montalvo, F. F., 34
Montoya, L., 89
Moreno, D. V., 123

Morgan, D. L., 11
Morris, I., 101, 102, 106, 111
Motivations, focus group, 11
Mulatto, 19, 31
Multinomial logistic regression models, 38
Multiracial identity, attitudes and behaviors, 122; contacting elected officials, 88; creating distance, 48; factors predicting racial identity, 41; interest in politics, 53–54, 55; opinion on abortion, 105; opinion on government-supported health care, 104; opinion on health care reform, 107; opinion on same-sex marriage, 110; opinion on standardized testing, 105; party alignment,72; political orientation predictions, 59, 59f, 60f; political participation, 86, 95; political partisanship predictions, 74; self-identification in LNS, 25, 26t
Munoz, J. A., 83, 84, 90
Murguia, E., 32
Muta, A. D., 27

N
Nagel, J. L., 3, 30
Nagler, J., 70, 73
Nakamoto, J. M., 4
NALEO. *See* National Association of Latino Elected and Appointed Officials
National Association of Latino Elected and Appointed Officials (NALEO), 21
National Council of La Raza (NCLR), 21
National origin, factors predicting racial identity, 38; focus group, 11, 12, 13; immigrants and public opinion, 113; Latino racial identity, 31; LNS questionnaire, A125; political participation, 83; political participation predictions, 93; political partisanship predictions, 76; question and Hispanics/Latinos, 21. *See also* Nationality
Nationality, focus group, 11, 12, 13; political orientation, 55; political partisanship preferences, 73; public opinion, 110; political

participation, 88–89; public opinion, 105–106. *See also* National origin
Native-born Latinos, 85, 106. *See also* Foreign-born Latinos
Nativity, length of time in United States and immigration policy, 101; political participation, 85; racial identity, 44–48
Naturalization, direction of political partisanship by immigrants, 78t; LNS questionnaire, A129; political orientation predictions, 63, 64t; political participation of immigrants, 98; public opinion, 114, 115t
NCLR. *See* National Council of La Raza
Nee, V., 37
Nelson, F. D., 45
Neuman, R. W., 51
New York, focus group, 11
Nicholson, S. P., 7, 25, 33, 51, 60, 107, 122
Nie, N., 56, 6, 83, 84, 87, 89, 100
Niemi, R.G., 51
Nobles, M., 2, 19, 20, 22, 26
Nonelectoral activities, 87, 90, 96t, 98, 123
Norpoth, H., 67
Nutini, H. G., 35
Nuyorican movement, 23

O
Oboler, S., 17, 23, 27, 37
Office of Management and Budget (OMB), 2, 20
OMB. *See* Office of Management and Budget
Omi, M., 3, 5, 17, 22, 30
Oropesa, R. S., 5, 32, 33, 34
Ortiz, A. M., 15, 67
Other race identity, 2010 census, 21; contacting elected officials, 88; factors predicting racial identity, 41, 42; foreign- or American-born and identity, 34, 45; immigrants and public opinion, 113; immigrants identifying with in United States, 31; opinion on abortion, 105; opinion on immigrant legalization and health care reform, 104, 107; opinion on same-sex marriage, 110; political participation, 95;

Index   163

political orientation predictions, 62, 62t; political participation predictions, 90, 94, 95t; political partisanship predictions, 77t; public opinion, 112, 112t, 113; self-identification and focus group, 24–25, 26, 27; skin color and factors predicting racial identity, 38; strength of political partisanship prediction, 80t; view on politics, 120; voter registration and political participation, 86

P
Pachon, H., 89
Padgett, T., 21
Padilla, F. M., 1, 27, 118
Panethnic identity, 8, 15, 25, 27, 28, 42, 49
Pantoja, A. D., 7, 25, 33, 50, 73, 85, 107
Park, D. K., 52, 84, 89, 90, 135n4
Parker Frisbie, W., 32
Parkin, M., 94
Partisanship, 112, 114
Partisanship politics, racial identity, immigrants, 77–79; LNS questionnaire, A128; overview, 67–68; prediction of direction, 74–77; prediction of strength, 79–81; preferences, 71–74; research, 68–71
Party labels, 68. See also Partisanship
Passel, J. S., 1, 4, 134n2, n3, n5
Patton, M. Q., 11
Pedraza, F. I., 70, 73
Perceptions, 5, 22, 24
Perez, A. D., 2
Pessimism, 56
Pew Hispanic Center, 1, 30, 60, 68
Phenotype, factors predicting identity, 38; LNS questionnaire, A125; political orientation, 55; political participation, 88–89; political participation predictions, 93; political partisanship predictions, 76; political partisanship preferences, 73; public opinion, 105–106, 110, 113; racial identity, 32, 34–35, 48
Polarization, 103
Policy issues, 70
Policy making, 85
Polinard, J., 33, 83, 87, 101, 102, 106

Political activism, 86
Political behavior, 5, 122
Political coalitions, 9
Political commonality, 35–36. See also Commonality
Political consequences, 3, 3f
Political engagement, 52
Political ideology, 70; LNS questionnaire, A128–A129. See also Partisanship
Political interest, 52, 84, 92t, 97t, A129
Political knowledge, 77, 78t, A129
Political orientation, Latinos, predictions, 56–62; race, 53–56, racial identity among immigrants, 62–66; research on interest, efficacy, and trust, 51–52
Political participation, impact of race, factors predicting, 90–95, 91t, 92t, 93f, 95t; immigrants, 95–98, 96t, 97t; race, 85–90; research, 84–85; racialization of Latinos, 119
Political party, 84, 94
Political perceptions, 7
Political power, 31, 85, 123
Political problems, 5
Political trust, 51, 52, 54, 56
Politicians, 54
Politics, 5, 7, 119, 123
Polls, 100
Portes, A., 1, 4, 5, 48, 56
Poverty, 7
Powell, B.M, 14, 19, 20
Predictions, factors and racial identity, 38; political participation, 90–95, 91t, 92t, 93f, 95t; political partisanship preferences, 74–77; public opinion, 107–113, 108t, 109t, 112t; strength of political partisanship, 79, 80t, 81
Privilege, White membership, 26
Problem solving, 93, 94, 95, 98
Pro-choice, 102. See also Abortion
Professional occupation, 55–56
Profile, LNS respondents, 10
Pro-life, 106
Public opinion, dynamics and Latinos, factors predicting, 107–113, 108t, 109t, 112t; race identity among Latino immigrants, 113–117, 115t, 116t; research, 101–103
Public policy, 71, 101, 119

Index

Puerto Ricans, 31, 69, 73, 102
Putnam, R. D., 123

R
Rabinowitz, G., 68
Race, categorization and shifting nature, 121; identity and the census, 19–22; measurement in 2000 and 2010 census, 20–22; overview of meaning and measurement, 17–18; party preferences, 71–74; political orientation, 52, 53–56; political participation, 85–90; public opinion, 103–107; self-reports and racial identity, 22–29; social construction, 18–19
Racial bias, 28
Racial categories, 17, 120
Racial choices, 3
Racial divide, 8, 100
Racial groups, 19
Racial hierarchy, 17
Racial identification, LNS questionnaire, A125
Racial identification choices, 4
Racial identification patterns, 8
Racial identity, choice and discrimination, 5; community and creation of social realities, 2, 3, 3f; connection to public opinion, 100; focus group, 11; negotiation between individual and society, 3; self-report, 22–29; shared by group members and political incorporation, 8; shift and society conceptualization, 25, 26t
Racial mixing, 4
Racialization, 28, 119
Ramirez, R. R., 20, 21, 73, 85
Rational choice theory, 68
Reclassification, 19
Redstone Akresh, I., 31, 32
Relethford, J. H., 32, 89
Religion, 70
Religious affiliation, 102
Reorganization, 19
Republican Party, affiliation by immigrants and public opinion, 114, 116t, 117; alignment and research on partisanship, 68, 70, 73; direction of political partisanship by immigrants, 78t, 79; political partisanship predictions, 74, 75t, 76; opinion toward health care reform and party affiliation, 107; public opinion, 112; race and preferences, 71–74
Rios-Vargas, M., 2
Rodriguez, C., 4, 5, 18, 19, 20, 21, 22, 23, 25, 31, 32, 35, 44, 117, 119, 120, 121, 134n4, 135n4
Rogalin, C. L., 17, 21, 32, 33, 119
Romo, R., 31
Rosenstone, S.J., 1, 15, 67, 70, 83, 89
Rumbaut, R. G., 1, 2, 5, 56

S
Same-sex marriage, public opinion, 105, 110, 111, 112, 112t; immigrants and public opinion, 113
Sanchez, G. R., 23, 33, 48, 73, 83, 89, 94, 98, 101, 102, 105, 106, 107, 133n3, 135n2, 135n4
Sanders, L., 100
Schildkraut, D.J., 55
Schlozman, K. L., 50, 83, 84, 94, 99, 100
Schuman, H., 100
Segmented assimilation, 4
Segura, G. M., 7, 25, 33, 50, 73, 83, 85, 107
Self-identification, 3, 4, 119, 85, 119
Settlement patterns, 1
Shamdasani, P., 11
Shared fate, direction of political partisanship by immigrants, 78t; factors predicting racial identity, 39t, 43t; foreign- or American-born and identity, 47t; immigrants and public opinion, 114, 116t; Latino racial identity, 36; LNS questionnaire, A127 perceptions and identity, 33; political orientation predictions, 58t, 61; political orientation, 56; political orientation predictions of immigrants, 63, 65t; political participation, 83, 89; political participation of immigrants, 95; political participation predictions, 92t, 94; political partisanship, 74; political partisanship preferences, 73–74 political partisanship predictions, 74, 75t; public opinion, 106, 109t, 111; strength of political partisanship predictions, 80t

Index 165

Shaw, D., 52, 83, 84, 94, 135n4
Shingles, R.D., 51
Shirkley, K., 101, 102, 106, 111
Sigelman, L., 100
Silver, G.E., 51
Skin color, discrimination, 37, 44; factors predicting racial identity, 38; foreign- or American-born and identity, 45; immigrant identity and public opinion, 115t, 117; Latino racial identity, 31–32; political orientation, 55; political orientation predictions, 64t; political participation, 89; political participation of immigrants, 95, 96t; political participation predictions, 91t, 93; political partisanship prediction, 76; public opinion, 105, 108t, 110; racial definition, 19. *See also* Demographic characteristics
Skrentny, J. D., 8
Smith, B., 102
Smith, E. R., 100
Social change, 52
Social construction of race, 18–19
Social exclusion, 19
Social group identity, 5, 6, 67
Social identity theory, 5, 6
Social meaning, 19
Social problems, 5
Social welfare, 106, 114
Social-psychological view, 68
Socioeconomic class, 32
Socioeconomic commonality, 35–36, 38, 40. *See also* Commonality
Socioeconomic status, direction of political partisanship by immigrants, 78t; factors predicting racial identity, 39t, 43t, 44; foreign- or American-born and racial identity, 46t; opinion and immigrants identity, 114, 115t; opinion and immigration policy, 101–102; party alignment and research on partisanship, 70; political orientation, 55–56; political orientation predictions, 57t; political orientation predictions of immigrants, 64t; political participation, 83, 89; political participation predictions, 93; political partisanship predictions, 75t; political partisanship preferences, 73; public opinion, 106, 108t, 110; strength of political partisanship predictions, 80t
Spanish-speaking skills, factors predicting racial identity, 41; foreign- or American-born and identity, 45; immigrants and public opinion, 114, 116t; LNS questionnaire, A128; political orientation prediction of immigrants, 63, 65t; political participation predictions, 92t, 94; political participation of immigrants, 97t, 98; political partisanship predictions, 76; political partisanship preferences, 74; predictions of strength of political partisanship, 80t; public opinion, 109t, 111; retaining and racial identity, 34, 37
Standardized testing, 105, 110, 111, 112. *See also* Public opinion
Steeh, C., 100
Stein, R.M., 98
Stern, M. P., 32, 89
Stevens, D. P., 83
Stewart, D. W., 11, 31, 84
Stewart, J., Jr., 9, 83, 87
Stimson, J. A., 68
Stokes, D. E., 1, 50, 66, 67, 73, 74, 83, 89, 94, 107, 135n2
Stokes-Brown, A. K., 7, 21, 25, 33, 48, 59, 85, 110, 111, 123
Suarez, R., 21
Suro, R., 4, 106

T
Tabb, D. H., 83
Tafoya, S. M., 27, 32, 34
Tajfel, H., 5, 33
Tate, K., 100, 106, 121
Taylor, P., 68
Telles, E. E., 32
Three-tier model, 9
Tienda, M., 5, 9
Timberlake, J.M., 31, 32
Time in United States, direction of political partisanship by immigrants, 79, 96t; immigrant identity and public opinion, 115t; political orientation predictions of immigrants, 63, 64t; political participation, 85; strength

of political partisanship prediction, 81
Tomz, M., 41
Torres, A., 35
Torres-Saillant, S., 3
Tri-racial color line model, 121
Trucios-Hayes, E., 27
Trust, political participation, 84; political orientation predictions, 59, 59f, 60, 60f, 61
Turner, J., 5
Turnout rate, 93f
Twine, F. W., 8

U
U.S. Census, 11
U.S. Census Bureau, 133
Uhlaner, C. J., 15, 33, 67, 68, 69, 70, 73, 76, 89, 90, 101, 105, 106
Undercount, census, 21
United States, 4, 19
United States-born children of immigrants, 34, 44–48

V
Valdez, Z., 48, 85, 89, 94, 99, 135n1
Vaquera, E., 31, 4
Vasquez, O., 32
Vaughan, D., 33
Vedlitz, A., 52, 84
Vega, A., 104
Verba, S., 50, 52, 56, 66, 83, 84, 85, 89, 100, 135n4
Voss, P. R., 136n1
Voter registration, political participation, 86; political participation predictions, 90, 91t, 92t, 93f; political participation predictions of immigrants, 95
Voting, 7, 86, 87, 90
Vouchers, immigrant identity and public opinion, 105, 114, 117; public opinions, 102, 105, 110, 111

W
Walker, J. L., 51, 60
Warren, J. W., 8
Warren, R. C., 30
Waters, M. C., 5, 8, 18, 32
Wattenberg, J., 41
Weaver, V., 89
Weisberg, H. F., 67
Welch, M., 102
Welch, S., 100

West, C., 16
Whiteness, 2, 7, 20, 26, 35, 41, 48
White-Black color line 50. *See also* Color line *and* Tri-racial color line model
White Latinos, Cuban immigrants identifying with in United States, 31; contacting elected officials and political participation, 88; direction of political partisanship by immigrants, 79; educational attainment, 33, 38; expansion to include Latinos and Asian Americans, 8; foreign- or American-born and racial identity, 45; opinion on abortion, 105; opinion on health care reform, 104; opinion on same-sex marriage, 110, 113; opinion on standardized testing, 105; party preference and race, 71, 72; political orientation predictions, 59, 59f, 60f, 61; political participation, 86, 95; political participation predictions, 90; political partisanship predictions, 74, 75t, 76; political trust, 54–55; racial identity, 37; spatial assimilation versus Black identity, 6–7; strength of political partisanship predictions, 80t
Whitening effect, 121–122
Whites, separation from Blacks in early census, 19
Whitten, N., 35
Wilcox, C., 102
Williams, D. R., 30
Wimmer, A., 3, 4
Winant, H., 3, 5, 17, 22, 30
Wolfinger, R. E., 83, 89
Wollscheid, J. R., 135n4
Wong, J. S., 33, 69, 70, 135n1
Woods, N. D., 73, 83, 123
Wrinkle, R. D., 33, 83, 87, 98, 101, 102, 106

Y
Yancey, G., 8, 34
Yinger, J., 32

Z
Zhou, M., 4
Zlotnick, F., 94
Zweigenhaft, R., 32